ALGORITHMS FOR ANALYSIS, INFERENCE, AND CONTROL OF BOOLEAN NETWORKS

ALGORITHMS FOR ANALYSIS, INFERENCE, AND CONTROL OF BOOLEAN NETWORKS

Tatsuya Akutsu

Kyoto University, Japan

World Scientific

NEW JERSEY · LONDON · SINGAPORE · BEIJING · SHANGHAI · HONG KONG · TAIPEI · CHENNAI · TOKYO

Published by

World Scientific Publishing Co. Pte. Ltd.

5 Toh Tuck Link, Singapore 596224

USA office: 27 Warren Street, Suite 401-402, Hackensack, NJ 07601

UK office: 57 Shelton Street, Covent Garden, London WC2H 9HE

British Library Cataloguing-in-Publication Data
A catalogue record for this book is available from the British Library.

ALGORITHMS FOR ANALYSIS, INFERENCE, AND CONTROL OF BOOLEAN NETWORKS

ISBN 978-981-3233-42-3

For any available supplementary material, please visit
http://www.worldscientific.com/worldscibooks/10.1142/10801#t=suppl

Printed in Singapore

Preface

Analysis of biological networks is an important topic in various fields including bioinformatics, computational biology, complex networks, and systems biology. In order to perform computational analysis, mathematical models of biological networks are required and thus various models have been proposed and utilized. Among them, many studies have been done on the Boolean network (BN). The BN is a discrete model of biological networks, in which each node takes either 0 (inactive) or 1 (active) at each time step and the states of nodes are synchronously updated according to regulation rules assigned to nodes, where each regulation rule is given as a Boolean function. BNs have been mainly used as a model of genetic networks in which node corresponds to a gene. Although the BN is a simple and old model that was proposed about 50 years ago by Stuart Kauffman, BNs exhibit complex behavior and thus extensive studies have been done in order to understand their behavior.

While BNs are deterministic, biological systems contain intrinsic stochasticity and observed data also include noise. Therefore, various probabilistic extensions of the BN model have been proposed. Among them, extensive studies have been done on the probabilistic Boolean network (PBN). Although one Boolean function is assigned to one node in a BN, multiple Boolean functions can be assigned to one node in a PBN and one of them is randomly selected at each time step according to the prescribed probability distribution.

As mentioned above, many studies have been done on BNs and PBNs and many algorithms have also been proposed. However, not so much attention was paid on the computational complexity of these algorithms although many of them are practically useful. Since we often need to handle genome-scale models nowadays, it is important to analyze the

v

computational complexity of algorithms and problems. Therefore, this book focuses on the computational complexity of algorithms and problems on BNs and PBNs. In particular, this book mainly considers three fundamental problems: (i) finding a steady state in a given network, (ii) inference of a network structure from sample data, and (iii) finding a control strategy to drive a network from a given initial state to a given target state. In addition to explanations of algorithmic aspects on BNs and PBNs, this book gives a brief introduction to the semi-tensor product approach that was proposed and developed by Daizhan Cheng and his colleagues because many studies have recently been done based on this approach.

The main target readers of this book are graduate students and researchers studying bioinformatics and computational biology. This book might also be useful for graduate students and researchers in computer science who are interested in systems biology. This book is basically self-contained. Necessary background information on computer scientific aspects is given in the first chapter and theoretical proofs are given for most algorithms. Furthermore, figures and/or examples are often given for illustrating algorithms and problems. It is to be noted that although this book presents algorithms with theoretical guarantees, these algorithms are not necessarily practically better than existing algorithms. The purpose of this book is to theoretically analyze algorithms and problems on BNs and PBNs.

Many of the algorithms explained in this book were developed by the author and collaborators. Therefore, I would like to thank all the collaborators who worked on BNs/PBNs. Chelsea Chin, Kim Tan, and their colleagues at World Scientific have been very helpful in completing this book, for which I thank them. I would also like to thank my parents, wife, and daughter for their continuous support.

Tatsuya Akutsu
November 2017

Contents

Chapter 1

Preliminaries

The *Boolean network* (BN) is a mathematical model of genetic networks and is based on *Boolean functions*. Boolean functions are functions on the Boolean domain that consists of Boolean values, 0 and 1. Boolean functions also give a foundation of computer science because signals in computers are represented by 0 and 1. Among various aspects of BNs, this book focuses on algorithms for BNs. Computational complexity is a very important factor of algorithms. And, in this book, we employ algorithms and techniques for the Boolean satisfiability problem, integer linear programming, and graphs. Therefore, in this chapter, we review definitions and fundamental properties on Boolean functions, computational complexity, the Boolean satisfiability problem, integer linear programming, and graphs. Readers familiar with these topics can skip this chapter.

1.1 Boolean Functions

Boolean values are integers 0 and 1, which are sometimes called bits. Boolean functions have close relationships with propositional logic in which 1 and 0 correspond to *true* and *false*, respectively. In this book, we use an italic symbol such as x_i to denote a variable representing a Boolean value and a bold symbol such as $\mathbf{x}$ to denote a vector of Boolean variables. We also use an italic symbol such as a_i to denote a Boolean value and a bold symbol such as $\mathbf{a}$ to denote a vector of Boolean values. In this book, a vector $\mathbf{x}$ with n Boolean variables is represented as

$$\mathbf{x} = [x_1, x_2, \ldots, x_n]$$

unless otherwise stated. A *Boolean function* $f(x_1, \ldots, x_n)$ of n variables is a mapping from $\{0, 1\}^n$ to $\{0, 1\}$. We also use $f(\mathbf{x})$ to denote $f(x_1, \ldots, x_n)$ where $\mathbf{x} = [x_1, \ldots, x_n]$.

1

A Boolean function $f(x_1, \ldots, x_n)$ need not depend on all its variables. We say that f depends on the ith variable x_i if there exist Boolean values $a_1, \ldots, a_{i-1}, a_{i+1}, \ldots, a_n$ such that

$$f(a_1, \ldots, a_{i-1}, 0, a_{i+1}, \ldots, a_n) \neq f(a_1, \ldots, a_{i-1}, 1, a_{i+1}, \ldots, a_n).$$

If f depends on the $i_1, \ldots, i_k$th variables, it is called that f has *degree* k and $x_{i_1}, \ldots, x_{i_k}$ are called the *relevant variables* of f. Furthermore, such f is also represented as

$$f(x_{i_1}, \ldots, x_{i_k})$$

if there is no confusion. For $\mathbf{a} \in \{0,1\}^n$, $\mathbf{a}[i]$ denotes the 0-1 value of the ith element, and $\mathbf{a}_{(i)}$ denotes the n-dimensional 0-1 vector obtained by flipping 0-1 values of the ith element. For example, for $\mathbf{a} = [0, 1, 1, 0, 1]$, $\mathbf{a}[1] = 0$, $\mathbf{a}[2] = 1$, $\mathbf{a}_{(1)} = [1, 1, 1, 0, 1]$, and $\mathbf{a}_{(2)} = [0, 0, 1, 0, 1]$. Therefore, an input variable x_i is relevant if and only if there exists $\mathbf{a} \in \{0,1\}^n$ such that $f(\mathbf{a}_{(i)}) \neq f(\mathbf{a})$.

The followings are the fundamental Boolean functions.

> **Constant functions:** $f = 0$ and $f = 1$,
> **Identity function:** $f(x) = x$,
> **NOT (negation):** $f(x) = \overline{x}$,
> **AND (conjunction):** $f(x, y) = x \wedge y$,
> **OR (disjunction):** $f(x, y) = x \vee y$,
> **XOR (exclusive OR):** $f(x, y) = x \oplus y$,
> **Implication:** $f(x, y) = x \to y = \overline{x} \vee y$.

The meanings of these functions (except constant functions) are explained in the truth tables shown in Tab. 1.1, where a *truth table* is a table describing all input-output relations.

Table 1.1   Truth table of fundamental Boolean functions.

x	y	0	1	x	$\overline{x}$	$x \wedge y$	$x \vee y$	$x \oplus y$	$x \to y$
0	0	0	1	0	1	0	0	0	1
0	1	0	1	0	1	0	1	1	1
1	0	0	1	1	0	0	1	1	0
1	1	0	1	1	0	1	1	0	1

AND, OR. XOR functions satisfy the commutative law:

$$x \wedge y = y \wedge x, \quad x \vee y = y \vee x, \quad x \oplus y = y \oplus x.$$

These functions also satisfy the associative law:

$$(x \wedge y) \wedge z = x \wedge (y \wedge z), \quad (x \vee y) \vee z = x \vee (y \vee z), \quad (x \oplus y) \oplus z = x \oplus (y \oplus z).$$

Therefore, we often omit parentheses and write as

$$x_1 \wedge x_2 \wedge \cdots \wedge x_n, \quad x_1 \vee x_2 \vee \cdots \vee x_n, \quad x_1 \oplus x_2 \oplus \cdots \oplus x_n.$$

AND and OR functions satisfy the distributive law:

$$x \wedge (y \vee z) = (x \wedge y) \vee (x \wedge z), \quad x \vee (y \wedge z) = (x \vee y) \wedge (x \vee z),$$

NOT, AND, and OR satisfy the De Morgan's laws:

$$\overline{x \vee y} = \overline{x} \wedge \overline{y}, \quad \overline{x \wedge y} = \overline{x} \vee \overline{y}.$$

As mentioned above, input-output behaviors of a Boolean function are described by a truth table. For a Boolean functions with n variables, there are 2^n rows in the truth table. Since there are two possibilities, 0 and 1, of the output value for each row, there are 2^{2^n} different Boolean functions with n variables, where all variables are not necessarily relevant.

A *literal* is a Boolean variable or its negation. A *clause* is an OR of literals, and a *term* is an AND of literals. A Boolean function is called in *disjunctive normal form* (DNF) if it is represented as an OR of terms, and is called in *conjunctive normal form* (CNF) if it is represented as an AND of clauses. That is, DNF and CNF formulas $D(\mathbf{x})$ and $C(\mathbf{x})$ are represented by

$$D(\mathbf{x}) = \bigvee_i \bigwedge_j \ell_{i,j}, \quad C(\mathbf{x}) = \bigwedge_i \bigvee_j \ell_{i,j},$$

respectively, where $\ell_{i,j}$ denotes the jth literal in the ith clause or term. For example, $x \oplus y \oplus z$ is represented in DNF and CNF as follows:

$$(x \wedge y \wedge \overline{z}) \vee (x \wedge \overline{y} \wedge z) \vee (\overline{x} \wedge y \wedge z) \vee (\overline{x} \wedge \overline{y} \wedge \overline{z}),$$
$$(x \vee y \vee z) \wedge (x \vee \overline{y} \vee \overline{z}) \wedge (\overline{x} \vee y \vee \overline{z}) \wedge (\overline{x} \vee \overline{y} \vee z).$$

The following is a well-known fact.

Proposition 1.1. *Every Boolean function has both DNF and CNF representations.*

Proof. From a given Boolean function $f(\mathbf{x})$ on $\{x_1, \ldots, x_n\}$, we can construct a DNF formula $D(\mathbf{x})$ as follows. For each $\mathbf{a} = [a_1, \ldots, a_n]$ such that $f(\mathbf{a}) = 1$, we create a term $\ell_1 \wedge \cdots \wedge \ell_n$ such that $\ell_i = x_i$ if $a_i = 1$, otherwise $\ell_i = \overline{x_i}$. Then, we construct an OR of all terms. It is clear that $D(\mathbf{a}) = f(\mathbf{a})$ holds for all $\mathbf{a} \in \{0, 1\}^n$.

We can also construct a CNF formula $C(\mathbf{x})$ as follows. For each $\mathbf{a} = [a_1, \ldots, a_n]$ such that $f(\mathbf{a}) = 0$, we create a clause $\ell_1 \vee \cdots \vee \ell_n$ such that $\ell_i = \overline{x_i}$ if $a_i = 1$, otherwise $\ell_i = x_i$. Then, we construct an AND of all clauses. It is clear that $C(\mathbf{a}) = f(\mathbf{a})$ holds for all $\mathbf{a} \in \{0, 1\}^n$. $\qquad \square$

Some Boolean functions require DNFs and/or CNFs of exponential size even if they have compact forms. For example, consider $f(\mathbf{x}) = x_1 \oplus x_2 \oplus \cdots \oplus x_n$ and its DNF representation $D(\mathbf{x})$. Then, each term must has n literals because flipping 1 bit in the input vector always changes the output value of f. Here, we note that $f(\mathbf{a}) = 1$ holds for 2^{n-1} as because we can uniquely determine the nth bit for any $n-1$ bit vector so that $f(\mathbf{a}) = 1$ is satisfied. Since each term can satisfy $f(\mathbf{a}) = 1$ only for one $\mathbf{a}$, we need 2^{n-1} terms. Analogously, it is seen that the CNF representation has 2^{n-1} clauses for this f.

Among various types of Boolean functions, canalyzing functions and nested canalyzing functions are known as biologically relevant functions [Harris *et al.* (2002); Jarrah *et al.* (2007); Kauffman (2004); Layne *et al.* (2012); Li *et al.* (2013)]. A Boolean function f is *canalyzing* if there exists a variable x_i such that $f(\mathbf{x}) = c$ holds for all $\mathbf{x}$ such that $x_i = b$, where b and c are constant Boolean values (i.e., (b, c) is one of $(0, 0)$, $(0, 1)$, $(1, 0)$, and (1.1)). For example, $f(\mathbf{x}) = x_1 \wedge (x_2 \oplus x_3)$ is a canalyzing function because $x_1 = 0$ always makes $f(\mathbf{x}) = 0$. A Boolean function is *nested canalyzing* if it can be represented as

$$f(\mathbf{x}) = \ell_1 \vee \cdots \vee \ell_{k_1-1} \vee (\ell_{k_1} \wedge \cdots \wedge \ell_{k_2-1} \wedge (\ell_{k_2} \vee \cdots \vee \ell_{k_3-1} \vee (\cdots))),$$

where $\ell_i \in \{x_1, \overline{x_1}, \ldots, x_n, \overline{x_n}\}$ and $1 \leq k_1 < k_2 < \cdots$. We can assume without loss of generality (w.l.o.g) that each variable appears at most once (in positively or negatively) in f. For example, suppose that f has the following form:

$$f(\mathbf{x}) = x_1 \vee (\cdots \wedge (x_i \vee x_j \vee (x_1 \wedge (\cdots))) \cdots).$$

Then, $x_1 = 1$ always makes $f(\mathbf{x}) = 1$ and $x_1 = 0$ always makes $(x_1 \wedge (\cdots)) = 0$. Therefore, f can be re-defined as

$$f(\mathbf{x}) = x_1 \vee (\cdots \wedge (x_i \vee x_j) \cdots).$$

Another interesting class of Boolean functions is that of threshold functions. Let $w_1, \ldots, w_n$ and θ be real numbers. Then, a Boolean function f is a (Boolean) *threshold function* if f is represented as

$$f(\mathbf{x}) = \begin{cases} 1 \text{ if } w_1 x_1 + w_2 x_2 + \cdots + w_n x_n \geq \theta, \\ 0 \text{ otherwise,} \end{cases}$$

Many Boolean functions are threshold functions. For example, $x \wedge y$ can be represented as $x + y \geq 2$, $x \wedge \overline{y}$ can be represented as $x - y \geq 1$, $x \vee y$ can be represented as $x + y \geq 1$, and $x \vee \overline{y}$ can be represented as $x - y \geq 0$, In fact, it is known that every nested canalyzing function can be represented as a threshold function. For example, $x \vee (\overline{y} \wedge z)$ can be represented as $2x - y + z \geq 1$. Since the class of nested canalyzing functions includes AND and OR of literals, AND and OR of literals can also be represented as threshold functions. Threshold functions having the following form are called *majority functions*:

$$f(\mathbf{x}) = \begin{cases} 1 \text{ if } x_1 + x_2 + \cdots + x_n \geq \frac{n}{2}, \\ 0 \text{ otherwise.} \end{cases}$$

It is known that the class of nested canalyzing functions (resp., the class of canalyzing functions) does not include the class of majority functions. On the other hand, there are much more Boolean functions that are not threshold ones. For example, it is known that $x \oplus y$ is not a threshold function. Boolean threshold functions have been widely used as a discrete model of neural networks [Anthony (2001)].

1.2 Computational Complexity

1.2.1 *Big O Notation*

In many cases, the efficiency of an algorithm is measured via the time complexity. In order to evaluate the time complexity, we usually use Big O notation.

Let $f(n)$ be a function from the set of non-negative integers to the set of non-negative integers. f is said to be $O(g(n))$ if the following holds:

$$(\exists k > 0)(\exists n_0)(\forall n > n_0)(f(n) \leq k \cdot g(n)),$$

which means that f is asymptotically bounded above by g. f is said to be $\Omega(g(n))$ if the following holds:

$$(\exists k > 0)(\exists n_0)(\forall n > n_0)(f(n) \geq k \cdot g(n)),$$

which means that f is asymptotically bounded below by g. If f is both $O(g(n))$ and $\Omega(g(n))$, f is said to be $\Theta(g(n))$. f is said to be $o(g(n))$ if the following holds:

$$(\forall k > 0)(\exists n_0)(\forall n > n_0)(f(n) \leq k \cdot g(n)),$$

which means that f's order is smaller than that of $g(n)$.

Suppose that an algorithm A uses at most $f(n)$ steps for every input of size n. Then, we say that the time complexity of A is $O(f(n))$. Note that since we consider all inputs of size n, this complexity means the *worst case* time complexity. Of course, the number of time steps depends on types of computers. However, by using big O notation, we need not mind about constant factor differences among computers.

Usually, we assume the *random access machine* (RAM) as a model of computers, in which basic operations (e.g., addition, subtraction, multiplication, comparison, table look up) on $O(\log n)$ bit integers (i.e., $O(\log n)$ bit words) can be done in one step. Note that $\log n$ means $\log_2 n$ in this book. If the size of input is not too large, this model well approximates the behavior of most CPUs.

An algorithm is said to be of *polynomial time* if its time complexity is $O(n^k)$ for some constant k. An algorithm is said to be of *polynomial space* if it uses $O(n^k)$ memory space for some constant k. An algorithm is said to be of *exponential time* if its time complexity is $O(2^{n^k})$ for some constant k. If there exists an $O(f(n))$ time algorithm for solving a problem X, we say that X is solved in $O(f(n))$ time. For example, selection of the maximum number among n integers can be done trivially in $O(n)$ time, and it is well-known that sorting of n integer numbers can be done in $O(n \log n)$ time, assuming that each integer can be stored in one word. It is well-known that the class of problems that can be solved in polynomial time by RAM is the same as that by the Turing machine. Therefore, if we discuss the polynomial time solvability, we need not mind about types of computers (except parallel computers).

In some cases, we consider algorithms having exponential time complexities [Fomin and Kratsch (2010)]. In such a case, the time complexity would have the form of $O(f(n)poly(n))$, where $f(n)$ is an exponential function of n and $poly(n)$ is a polynomial of n. For simplicity, we may use $O^*(f(n))$ to represent such a term, where a polynomial factor can also depend on other parameters. We sometimes round the base of the exponent up to the third digit after the decimal point. For example, instead $O((\sqrt{2})^n poly(n))$ or $O^*((\sqrt{2})^n)$, we may use $O(1.415^n)$ because $(\sqrt{2})^n n^k < 1.415^n$ holds for sufficiently large n for any constant k.

1.2.2 *Complexity Classes*

In some parts of this book, we discuss computational hardness of problems. In order to discuss hardness, we need to define some complexity classes. Complexity classes are basically defined for decision problems: whether input data x satisfies the target property. For example, consider the problem of finding a singleton attractor (i.e., a stable state) of a given BN. Then, the decision version of the problem is to ask whether or not there exists a singleton attractor for a given BN. Then, P is the class of problems that can be solved in polynomial time by deterministic Turing machines. Another important class, NP, is the class of problems that can be solved in polynomial time by non-deterministic Turing machines. Note that NP does not denote non-polynomial but denotes non-deterministic polynomial. Instead of introducing non-deterministic Turing machines, we review another characterization of NP.

Since we are considering decision problems, we can discuss whether or not an input data x belongs to a set of data X each of which satisfies the target property (i.e., whether or not $x \in X$). It also means that a problem is represented by a set of data X. We also consider an algorithm A that takes two inputs x and y and outputs 1 or 0. Then, NP is the set of decision problems each of which has a polynomial time algorithm A such that

$$x \in X \iff (\exists y)(A(x,y) = 1).$$

In the above, y is a bit vector whose size is a polynomial of the size of x, where the polynomial depends on X. y corresponds to a sequence of non-deterministic choices of a non-deterministic Turing machine. Similarly, we have the following classes.

coNP: $x \in X \iff (\forall y)(A(x,y) = 1)$,
$\sum_2^P$: $x \in X \iff (\exists y)(\forall z)(A(x,y,z) = 1)$,
$\prod_2^P$: $x \in X \iff (\forall y)(\exists z)(A(x,y,z) = 1)$,

where z is a bit vector whose size is a polynomial of the size of x, P, NP, and coNP are also denoted as $\sum_0^P = \prod_0^P$, $\sum_1^P$, and $\prod_1^P$, respectively. In addition, the following classes are often considered.

PSPACE: whether $x \in X$ can be determined by a polynomial space algorithm,
EXPTIME: whether $x \in X$ can be determined by an exponential time algorithm.

1.2.3 *Completeness*

In order to compare the hardness of problems, reductions are often used. A *polynomial-time reduction* from problem X to problem Y is a polynomial-time algorithm for transforming an input x to problem X to an input y to problem Y such that $x \in X$ if and only if $y \in Y$.

A problem X in NP is called *NP-complete* if for every problem Y in NP, there exists a polynomial-time reduction from Y to X. A problem X not necessarily in NP is called *NP-hard* if for every problem Y in NP, there exists a polynomial-time reduction from Y to X, where X need not

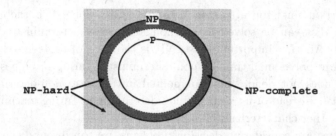

Fig. 1.1   Relationships among P, NP, and NP-complete classes.

be a decision problem if there is an efficient way to decide $y \in Y$ from a solution x of X. Intuitively, an NP-complete problem is a hardest problem in NP, and an NP-hard problem is a problem that is at least as hard as NP-complete problems (see also Fig. 1.1). From the definitions, every NP-complete problem is also NP-hard. Many NP-complete problems are known [Garey and Johnson (1979)]. For each of $coNP$, $\sum_2^P$, $\prod_2^P$, PSPACE, and EXPTIME, completeness and hardness are defined too.

From the definitions, $P \subseteq NP$ holds. It is widely believed that $P \neq NP$ although it is still unknown. If $P \neq NP$, any NP-hard problem cannot be solved in polynomial time. Therefore, once a problem X is shown to be NP-hard, it suggests that there is no polynomial-time algorithm for X. Although NP-hardness suggests that there is no theoretically efficient algorithm, it does not necessarily mean that there is no practical algorithm for the problem. Actually, practically efficient algorithms have been developed for such NP-hard problems as the satisfiability and integer linear programming problems.

The following relations are also known (see also Fig. 1.2):

- $(NP \cup coNP) \subseteq \sum_2^P$,
- $(NP \cup coNP) \subseteq \prod_2^P$,
- $\sum_2^P \cup \prod_2^P \subseteq PSPACE$,
- $PSPACE \subseteq EXPTIME$,

where it is still unknown whether each inclusion is strict. Only one non-equivalence relationship known about these classes is $P \neq EXPTIME$. Showing $\sum_2^P$-hardness or $\prod_2^P$-hardness of a problem X suggests that even efficient solvers for some NP-complete problems are not applicable to efficiently solving X. Actually, we will show in this book that some control problems on BNs are $\sum_2^P$-hard.

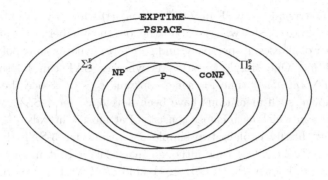

Fig. 1.2 Relationships among several complexity classes.

1.3 Satisfiability Problem

The *Boolean satisfiability problem* (SAT) is the problem of determining if, for a given Boolean formula f, there exists a 0-1 vector $\mathbf{a}$ such that $f(\mathbf{a}) = 1$. In general, setting a 0-1 vector $\mathbf{a}$ to a vector of variables is called an *assignment*, and $\mathbf{a}$ itself is also called an assignment. When $f(\mathbf{a}) = 1$, we say that f is *satisfied* (by an assignment $\mathbf{a}$). If there exists $\mathbf{a}$ such that $f(\mathbf{a}) = 1$, f is called *satisfiable*. Therefore, SAT is the problem of asking whether or not a given f is satisfiable. It is usually assumed in SAT that a Boolean formula f is given in CNF:

$$C(\mathbf{x}) = \bigwedge_i \bigvee_j \ell_{i,j}.$$

In this book, we follow this tradition.

Here we give simple examples for SAT. Suppose that f_1 is given as

$$f_1(\mathbf{x}) = (x_1 \vee x_2) \wedge (x_1 \vee \overline{x_2}) \wedge (\overline{x_1} \vee x_2).$$

Then, f_1 is satisfied by an assignment $[x_1, x_2] = [1, 1]$, Next, suppose that f_2 is given as

$$f_2(\mathbf{x}) = (x_1 \vee x_2) \wedge (x_1 \vee \overline{x_2}) \wedge (\overline{x_1} \vee x_2) \wedge (\overline{x_1} \vee \overline{x_2}).$$

Then, there is no assignment that satisfies f_2 and thus f_2 is not satisfiable.

SAT is known to be NP-complete. Furthermore, SAT remains NP-complete even if each clause consists of at most three literals, whereas SAT can be solved in polynomial time if each clause consists of at most two literals. SAT has close relationships with various combinatorial problems. Since a BN is a kind of collection of Boolean functions, there is also a close relationship between SAT and BN.

SAT is trivially solved in $O(2^n poly(m, n))$ time by examining all assignments $\mathbf{a} \in \{0, 1\}^n$, where n and m denote the number of variables and the number of clauses, respectively, and $poly(x, y)$ denotes some polynomial of x and y. One simple question is whether SAT can be solved in $O((2 - \epsilon)^n poly(m, n))$ time for some constant $\epsilon > 0$. Since the answer is still known, such algorithms have been developed for k-SAT, a special case of SAT in which each clause consists of at most k literals.

Here we briefly explain two simple algorithms for 3-SAT that work in $O((2 - \epsilon)^n poly(m, n))$ time although much faster (but more complex) algorithms are known [Hertli (2014); Makino *et al.* (2013)]. Suppose that f has the following form:

$$f(\mathbf{x}) = (x_1 \vee x_2 \vee \overline{x_3}) \wedge (x_3 \vee x_4 \vee x_5) \wedge (x_2 \vee x_4 \vee \overline{x_5}) \wedge \cdots .$$

Consider the three variables appearing in the first clause, x_1, x_2, and x_3. If we examine all assignments on all variables, we need to examine $2^3 = 8$ assignments on these three variables. However, we need not examine $[x_1, x_2, x_3] = [0, 0, 1]$ because this does not satisfy $x_1 \vee x_2 \vee \overline{x_3}$. Therefore, it is enough to examine 7 assignments on x_1, x_2, and x_3. We can continue this procedure by repeatedly finding a clause with three literals and examining 7 assignments. If no literal has three clauses, we can solve the remaining subproblem in polynomial time because it corresponds to 2-SAT. Therefore, the total time complexity of this algorithm is $O(7^{n/3} poly(m, n))$, which is in $O(1.913^n poly(m, n))$.

In the above, we considered assignments on three variables. Here we present a recursive procedure that repeatedly examines assignments on one variable (see Fig. 1.3). Consider the same f as in the above. Suppose that $x_1 = 1$ is assigned. Then, the first clause is satisfied and the SAT formula is simplified into

$$(x_3 \vee x_4 \vee x_5) \wedge (x_2 \vee x_4 \vee \overline{x_5}) \wedge \cdots .$$

Consequently, the number of variables decreases from n to $n - 1$.

Next, suppose that $x_1 = 0$ is assigned. Then, the SAT formula is simplified into

$$(x_2 \vee \overline{x_3}) \wedge (x_3 \vee x_4 \vee x_5) \wedge (x_2 \vee x_4 \vee \overline{x_5}) \wedge \cdots .$$

In this case, there remain $n - 1$ variables as in the above. However, the first clause still remains in this case. Thus, we consider assignments on the remaining variables in the first clause. Suppose that $x_2 = 1$ is assigned. Then, $(x_2 \vee \overline{x_3})$ is satisfied and the SAT formula is simplified into

$$(x_3 \vee x_4 \vee x_5) \wedge \cdots ,$$

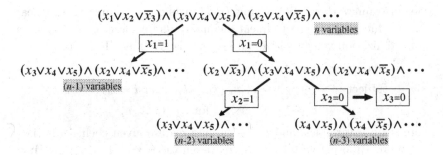

Fig. 1.3   Illustration of a recursive procedure for 3-SAT.

which contains $n - 2$ variables. Conversely, suppose that $x_2 = 0$ is assigned. Then. $x_3 = 0$ must hold because $(x_2 \vee \overline{x_3})$ must be satisfied. Therefore, the SAT formula is simplified to

$$(x_4 \vee x_5) \wedge (x_4 \vee \overline{x_5}) \wedge \cdots ,$$

which contains $n - 3$ variables. Therefore, the original instance with n variables is divided into three SAT instances with $n - 1$ variables, with $n - 2$ variables, and with $n - 3$ variables, respectively.

Let $T(n)$ denote the maximum number of this recursive steps. Clearly, we have

$$T(n) \leq T(n - 1) + T(n - 2) + T(n - 3),$$

where $T(n) = 1$ for $n \leq 3$. Suppose that $T(n) = c_1 a^n$, Since our purpose is to estimate the order of $T(n)$, by replacing '$\leq$' with '$=$', we have the following equation:

$$c_1 a^n = c_1 a^{n-1} + c_1 a^{n-2} + c_1 a^{n-3}.$$

Dividing both sides by $c_1 a^{n-3}$, we have

$$a^3 = a^2 + a + 1.$$

Solving this equation, we have $a \approx 1.840$ and thus $T(n)$ is $O(1.840^n)$. Since each recursive step can be clearly done in $O(poly(m, n))$ time, the total time complexity of this algorithm is $O(1.840^n poly(m, n))$.

1.4   Integer Linear Programming

Integer linear programming (ILP) is a useful tool to practically solve NP-hard problems. ILP is based on *linear programming* (LP). LP is a problem/framework for optimizing (minimizing or maximizing) a linear objective function subject to linear inequality and equality constraints. In the maximization version of LP, an instance is given as a linear program:

$$\text{maximize} \quad c_1 x_1 + \cdots + c_n x_n,$$
$$\text{subject to} \quad a_{i,1} x_1 + \cdots + a_{i,n} x_n \leq b_i, \quad \text{for } i = 1, \ldots, m,$$
$$x_i \geq 1, \qquad \text{for } i = 1, \ldots, n,$$

where x_is are variables, and $a_{i,j}$s, b_is, and c_is are given coefficients (i.e., constants). By using vector/matrix representations $\mathbf{x} = [x_1, \ldots, x_n]^\top$, $\mathbf{b} = [b_1, \ldots, b_m]^\top$, $\mathbf{c} = [c_1, \ldots, c_n]^\top$, and $A_{i,j} = a_{i,j}$ where $(\cdots)^\top$ denotes the matrix transpose, this can be written as:

$$\text{maximize} \quad \mathbf{c}^\top \mathbf{x},$$
$$\text{subject to} \quad A\mathbf{x} \leq \mathbf{b},$$
$$\mathbf{x} \geq \mathbf{0}.$$

Each $\mathbf{x}$ satisfying all constraints is called a *feasible solution*. If a feasible solution attains the optimum objective value, it is called an *optimal solution*.

In ILP, *integral constraints* are added to the set of constraints, which state that all variables must take integer values. Accordingly, optimal solutions may differ between LP and ILP.

It is known that LP can be solved in polynomial time with respect to the size (the number of bits) of a given instance, whereas the decision problem version of ILP is NP-complete. However, several practically efficient solvers have been developed for ILP, which can solve large size instances to some extent.

Example 1.1. Consider the following linear program (see Fig. 1.4):

$$\text{maximize} \quad x_1 + x_2,$$
$$\text{subject to} \quad -x_1 + 2x_2 \leq 6,$$
$$2x_1 + 5x_2 \leq 27,$$
$$2x_1 - x_2 \leq 6,$$
$$x_1 \geq 0,$$
$$x_2 \geq 0.$$

Then, the objective function takes the optimal value of $\frac{33}{4}$ at $[x_1, x_2] = [\frac{19}{4}, \frac{7}{2}]$. On the other hand, in integer linear programming, the objective function takes the optimal value of 7 at $[x_1, x_2] = [3, 4]$ or $[x_1, x_2] = [4, 3]$.

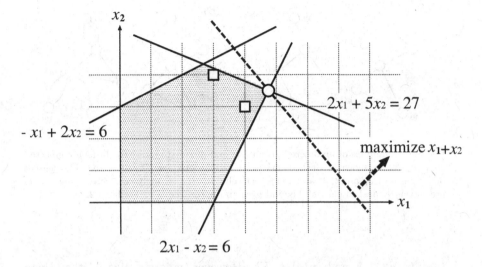

Fig. 1.4 Illustration of linear programming (LP) and integer linear programming (ILP). The set of feasible solutions in LP is shown by gray area. Optimal solutions in LP and ILP are shown by white circle and white boxes, respectively.

1.5 Graphs

Graphs are the basic subject in computer science and discrete mathematics. A *graph* is a structure consisting of a set of *vertices* and a set of *edges*. A vertex corresponds to some object and an edge represents a related pair of vertices. Vertices are also called *nodes*. In this book, we use nodes to denote vertices in BNs.

Each graph is denoted as $G(V, E)$ where V and E denote the set of vertices and the set of edges in the graph, respectively. There are two major kinds of graphs: *directed graphs* and *undirected graphs* (see Fig. 1.5). Each edge has a direction in directed graphs, whereas no edge has a direction in undirected graphs. Accordingly, an edge in a directed graph is represented as an ordered pair of vertices (u, v), which means that the edge is directed from vertex u to vertex v. An edge in an undirected graph is represented as a set of two vertices $\{u, v\}$, which means that u and v are directly connected. In this book, we mainly consider directed graphs because BNs have directed graph structures. When considering directed graphs, self loops are allowed where a *self loop* is an edge from and to the same vertex (i.e., an edge from v to v). It is also allowed that there exist edges with the opposite directions

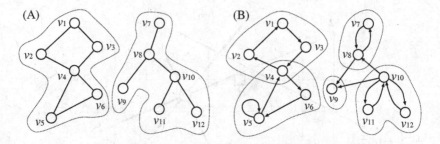

Fig. 1.5 Examples of undirected graph (A) and directed graph (B). In (A), connected components are shown by dashed curves, where one component forms a tree. The degrees of v_1, v_4, and v_7 are 2, 4, and 1, respectively. In (B), strongly connected components are shown by dashed curves. The indegree and outdegree of v_4 are both 2.

(i.e., $(u, v) \in E$ and $(v, u) \in E$). However, it is not allowed that there exist multiple self loops for the same vertex or there exist two identical edges (i.e., two (u, v)s) since E denotes a set of edges. We often consider undirected graphs obtained from directed graphs by ignoring directions of edges. In such a case, we delete self loops and consider at most one edge per pair of vertices (i.e., multiple edges are not allowed in undirected graphs). Therefore, in both undirected graphs and directed graphs, E is not a multi-set but a set (i.e., we do not consider multigraphs). In an undirected graph, the number of edges connecting to a vertex is called the *degree* of the vertex. In a directed graph, the number of incoming edges and the number of outgoing edges for a vertex are called the *indegree* and *outdegree*, respectively.

A graph $G'(V', E')$ is called a *subgraph* of a graph $G(V, E)$ if $V' \subseteq V$ and $E' \subseteq E$ hold. In an undirected graph (resp., a directed graph), A graph $G'(V', E')$ is called an *induced subgraph* of a graph $G(V, E)$ if $V' \subseteq V$ and $E' = \{\{u, v\} \in E | \ u, v \in V'\}$ (resp., $E' = \{(u, v) \in E | \ u, v \in V'\}$) hold. In this case, it is also called that $G'(V', E')$ is a subgraph induced by V' from $G(V, E)$. In an undirected graph (resp., in a directed graph) $G(V, E)$, a finite sequence of vertices $(v_{i_0}, v_{i_1}, \ldots, v_{i_k})$ $(k > 0)$ is called a *path* of length k if $\{v_{i_j}, v_{i_{j+1}}\} \in E$ (resp., $(v_{i_j}, v_{i_{j+1}}) \in E$) holds for all $j = 0, \ldots, k - 1$. A path is called *simple* if the same vertex does not appear more than once. If $v_{i_0} = v_{i_k}$, a path if called a *cycle*. If $v_{i_j} \neq v_{i_h}$ holds for all j, h such that $0 \leq j < h < k$, a cycle is called *simple*. An undirected graph is called *connected* if for each pair of distinct vertices $\{v_{i_0}, v_{i_k}\}$, there exists

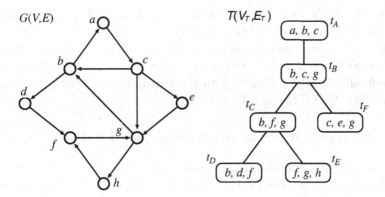

Fig. 1.6   Example of tree decomposition with treewidth 2.

a path $(v_{i_0}, v_{i_1}, \ldots, v_{i_k})$. A *connected component* of an undirected graph is a maximal induced subgraph that is connected. A directed graph is called *strongly connected* if for each pair of distinct vertices (v_{i_0}, v_{i_k}), there exists a path $(v_{i_0}, v_{i_1}, \ldots, v_{i_k})$. A *strongly connected component* of a directed graph is a maximal induced subgraph that is strongly connected. Note that a single vertex can be a connected component or a strongly connected component. An undirected graph is called a *tree* if it is connected and does not have a cycle. A directed graph is called a *rooted tree* if there exists one specially designated vertex called the *root* and there is a unique path from the root to each vertex (except the root). If $(v, u) \in E$ in a rooted tree $G(V, E)$, u is called a *child* of v, and v is called a *parent* of u. A vertex with outdegree 0 is called a *leaf*.

The *treewidth* is an integer number measuring how a graph looks like a tree. It is known that many NP-hard problems can be solved in polynomial time using dynamic programming if a graph has a fixed treewidth [Flum and Grohe (2006)]. To define treewidth, we need the notion of tree decomposition. A *tree decomposition* of a graph $G = (V, E)$ is a pair $\langle \mathcal{T}(\mathcal{V}_\mathcal{T}, \mathcal{E}_\mathcal{T}), (B_t)_{t \in \mathcal{V}_\mathcal{T}} \rangle$, where $\mathcal{T}(\mathcal{V}_\mathcal{T}, \mathcal{E}_\mathcal{T})$ is a rooted tree and $(B_t)_{t \in \mathcal{V}_\mathcal{T}}$ is a family of subsets of $V = \{v_1, \ldots, v_n\}$ such that (see also Fig. 1.6)

- for every $v_i \in V$, $B^{-1}(v_i) = \{t \in \mathcal{V}_\mathcal{T} | v_i \in B_t\}$ is nonempty and connected in $\mathcal{T}$, and
- for every edge $\{v_i, v_j\} \in E$ (resp., $(v_i, v_j) \in E$), there exists $t \in \mathcal{V}_\mathcal{T}$ such that $v_i, v_j \in B_t$.

Intuitively, $\mathcal{T}(\mathcal{V}_\mathcal{T}, \mathcal{E}_\mathcal{T})$ represents a tree structure of $G(V, E)$ by regarding a small subset of vertices in G as a node in the tree.

The *width* of a decomposition is defined as $\max_{t \in \mathcal{V}_\mathcal{T}} (|B_t| - 1)$ and the *treewidth of G* is the minimum of the widths among all the tree decompositions of G. Graphs with treewidth at most k are also known as *partial k-trees* [Flum and Grohe (2006)].

1.6 Additional Remarks and Bibliographical Notes

Details of Boolean functions can be found in many textbooks. For example, see [Crama and Hammer (2011); Kunz and Stoffel (1997)]. For advanced topics, see [O'Donnell (2014)]. Details of computational complexity can also be found in many textbooks. For example, see [Garey and Johnson (1979); Sipser (2012)]. Details on the treewidth and its algorithmic issues can be found in several textbooks. For example, see [Flum and Grohe (2006); Fomin and Kratsch (2010)]. Extensive studies have been done on the Boolean satisfiability problem. For example, see [Balyo *et al.* (2017); Vizel *et al.* (2015)] for practical solvers and [Hertli (2014); Makino *et al.* (2013)] for some recent theoretical developments. Extensive studies have also been done on Integer Linear Programming and related optimization problems. For example, see [Newman and Weiss (2013); Vielma (2015)].

Chapter 2

Boolean Networks

The Boolean network (BN) is a mathematical model of genetic networks. It has a long history beginning from studies by Kauffman in 1960s [Kauffman (1969a,b)] and extensive studies have been done. In this chapter, we review the definition of the BN, important concepts, and some of their basic mathematical properties.

2.1 Definition of Boolean Network

In this section, we give the definition of the synchronous Boolean network. Among various variants of the BN, it is the most fundamental model and thus a BN refers to this synchronous model in this book unless otherwise stated.

A BN $N(V, F)$ consists of a set $V = \{x_1, \ldots, x_n\}$ of *nodes* and a list $F = (f_1, \ldots, f_n)$ of *Boolean functions*. Each node corresponds to a gene and takes either 1 or 0 at each discrete time step t, where 1 and 0 correspond to that the gene is expressed and is not expressed, respectively, The state of node x_i at time t is denoted by $x_i(t)$, where the states on nodes change synchronously according to given regulation rules. A Boolean function $f_i(x_{i_1}, \ldots, x_{i_k})$ with inputs from specified nodes $x_{i_1}, \ldots, x_{i_k}$ is assigned to each node, where it represents a regulation rule for node x_i. We use $IN(x_i)$ to denote the set of input nodes $x_{i_1}, \ldots, x_{i_k}$ to x_i. We also use $IN(f_i)$ to denote the set of relevant variables of Boolean function f_i. Then, the state of node x_i at time $t+1$ is determined the states of nodes in $IN(x_i)$ by

$$x_i(t+1) = f_i(x_{i_1}(t), \ldots, x_{i_{k_i}}(t)).$$

Here we let

$$\mathbf{x}(t) = [x_1(t), \ldots, x_n(t)],$$

17

which is called a *Gene Activity Profile* (GAP) at time t, a global state of BN at time t, or simply a state of BN at time t. We also write

$$x_i(t+1) = f_i(\mathbf{x}(t))$$

or

$$x_i(t+1) = f_i(x_1(t), \ldots, x_n(t))$$

to denote the regulation rule for x_i if there is no confusion. Furthermore, we write

$$\mathbf{x}(t+1) = \mathbf{f}(\mathbf{x}(t))$$

to denote the regulation rule for the whole BN.

$N(V, F)$ defines the network structure of a BN, where the structure is represented as a directed graph. From F, we determined the set of edges E by

$$E = \{(x_{i_j}, x_i) | x_{i_j} \in IN(x_i)\}.$$

Then, $G(V, E)$ is the directed graph representing the network structure of a BN. In $G(V, E)$, an edge from x_{i_j} to x_i means that x_{i_j} directly affects the expression of x_i. The number of input nodes to x_i (i.e., $|IN(x_i)|$) is called the *indegree* of x_i. The *maximum indegree* of a BN is denoted by K. This K is an important parameter in analysis of both behaviors of BNs and computational complexity of various problems on BNs.

(A) $N(V,F)$ (B) $G(V,E)$

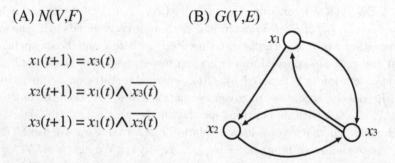

$$x_1(t+1) = x_3(t)$$

$$x_2(t+1) = x_1(t) \wedge \overline{x_3(t)}$$

$$x_3(t+1) = x_1(t) \wedge \overline{x_2(t)}$$

Fig. 2.1   Example of (A) BN $N(V, F)$ and (B) the corresponding graph $G(V, E)$.

Example 2.1. An example of a BN is given in Fig. 2.1. In this example, there are three nodes x_1, x_2, and x_3. The state of node x_1 at time $t+1$ is determined by the state of node x_3 at time t. The state of node x_2 at time

$t + 1$ is determined by AND of the state of x_1 and NOT of the state of x_3 at time t. The state of node x_3 at time $t + 1$ is determined by AND of the state of node x_1 and NOT of the state of node x_2 at time t. For example, if the state of BN is $[1, 1, 0]$ at time t, the state of BN becomes $[0, 1, 0]$ at time $t + 1$. For another example, if the state of BN is $[1, 0, 0]$ at time t, the state of BN becomes $[0, 1, 1]$ at time $t + 1$. In this BN, $IN(v_1) = IN(f_1) = \{x_3\}$, $IN(v_2) = IN(f_2) = \{x_1, x_3\}$, $IN(v_3) = IN(f_2) = \{x_1, x_2\}$, the indegree of v_1, f_1 is 1, the indegree of v_2, v_3, f_2, f_3 is 2, and $K = 2$.

The dynamics of a BN can be well-described by a *state transition table* and a *state transition diagram*. A state transition table is a table in which each row represents a state of BN $\mathbf{a} \in \{0, 1\}^n$ at time t and the corresponding state of BN $\mathbf{f}(\mathbf{a})$ at time $t + 1$. A state transition diagram is a directed graph in which each node corresponds to a state of BN $\mathbf{a} \in \{0, 1\}^n$ and there exists a directed edge from $v_{\mathbf{a}}$ to $v_{\mathbf{a}'}$ if only only if $\mathbf{a}' = \mathbf{f}(\mathbf{a})$ holds, where $v_{\mathbf{a}}$ (resp., $v_{\mathbf{a}'}$) is the node corresponding to the state $\mathbf{a}$ (resp., $\mathbf{a}'$). Although these two representations have very different looks, they have the same information. It is to be noted that a state transition table has 2^n rows and a state transition diagram has 2^n nodes.

Example 2.2. Tab. 2.1 and Fig. 2.2 give the state transition table and the state transition diagram for the BN in Example 2.1, respectively. In Tab. 2.1, the first row means that if the state is $[0, 0, 0]$ at time t, the state remains $[0, 0, 0]$ at time $t + 1$, the second row means that if the state is $[0, 0, 1]$ at time t, the state becomes $[1, 0, 0]$ at time $t + 1$, and so on. In Fig. 2.2, the edge from $[0, 0, 0]$ to $[0, 0, 0]$ means that if the state is $[0, 0, 0]$ at time t, the state remains $[0, 0, 0]$ at time $t + 1$, the edge from $[0, 0, 1]$ to $[1, 0, 0]$ means that if the state is $[0, 0, 1]$ at time t, the state becomes $[1, 0, 0]$ at time $t + 1$, and so on.

Table 2.1 State transition table for BN in Example 2.1.

$x_1(t)$	$x_2(t)$	$x_3(t)$	$x_1(t+1)$	$x_2(t+1)$	$x_3(t+1)$
0	0	0	0	0	0
0	0	1	1	0	0
0	1	0	0	0	0
0	1	1	1	0	0
1	0	0	0	1	1
1	0	1	1	0	1
1	1	0	0	1	0
1	1	1	1	0	0

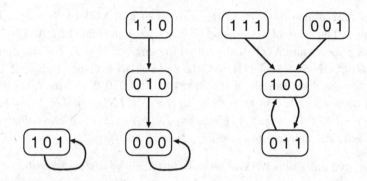

Fig. 2.2   State transition diagram for BN in Example 2.1.

One important property of the state transition diagram is that each node in the diagram has exactly one outgoing edge since the next state of BN is uniquely determined from the current state of BN. It is seen from this property that a state transition diagram is a collection of tree-like structures, each of which consists of a tree and a cycle, where a tree and/or a cycle can consist of a single node and a self-loop.   In each of these tree-like structures, edges are directed from the leaves to the root and the cycle corresponds to the root of the tree.

2.2   Attractors

Consider a BN with n nodes. Since the next state of the BN is uniquely determined from the current state, beginning from any state, the BN will eventually reach a previously visited state, and then stay in a cycle of states. This cycle of the state is called an *attractor*. An attractor is represented by a set of states $\{a_0, a_1, \ldots, a_{p-1}\}$, where $a_{i+1} = f(a_i)$ $(i = 0, \ldots, p-2)$ and $a_0 = f(a_{p-1})$ hold. If $p = 1$, an attractor is called a *singleton attractor*. If $p > 1$, an attractor is called a *periodic attractor*. In both cases, p is called the *period* of an attractor. Note that singleton attractors are attractors of period 1. Note also that a periodic attractor is essentially a sequence of states. However, the sequence is uniquely determined once a set of states is specified under the target BN. Therefore, we use a set to represent a periodic attractor unless otherwise stated. Singleton and periodic attractors are sometimes called as *point attractors* and *cyclic attractors*, respectively. The set of states that will evolve to the same attractor is called the *basin of attraction*. Different basins of attraction correspond to different connected components in the state transition diagram (if the diagram is regarded as an undirected graph by ignoring the directions of edges), and each connected component contains exactly one directed cycle.

Example 2.3. Consider the BN given in Example 2.1 (see also Fig. 2.2). This BN has three attractors, $A_1 = \{[0,0,0]\}$, $A_2 = \{[1,0,1]\}$, and $A_3 = \{[0,1,1],[1,0,0]\}$, where A_1 and A_2 are singleton attractors and A_3 is a periodic attractor with period 2. Then, $\{[0,0,0],[0,1,0],[1,1,0]\}$, $\{[1,0,1]\}$, and $\{[0,0,1],[0,1,1],[1,0,0],[1,1,1]\}$ are the basins of attraction for A_1, A_2, and A_3, respectively.

Attractors are often regarded as cell types: different attractors correspond to different cell types [Kauffman (1993)]. From this interpretation, extensive studies have been done on the distribution and length of attractors. In particular, existing studies focus on the *NK model* of BN. In this model, a BN contains N nodes and each node has randomly selected K input nodes and is associated with a Boolean function randomly selected from all possible 2^{2^K} functions. Although we use the term of the NK model, in this book, the number of nodes in a BN is denoted by n, instead of N. About the number of singleton attractors in this NK model, the following simple but interesting result is well-known [Harvey and Bossomaier (2007); Mochizuki (2005)].

Proposition 2.1. *The expected number of singleton attractors in the NK model is 1 for every $K > 0$ and $n \geq K$.*

Proof. Suppose that $\mathbf{x}(0) = [0,0,\ldots,0]$. Then, for each node x_i, the probability that $x_i(1) = 0$ is $\frac{1}{2}$ because a randomly selected Boolean function is assigned to x_i and thus the output value of the function is 0 with probability $\frac{1}{2}$ regardless of input node values. Since Boolean functions are selected independently to all nodes, the probability that $\mathbf{x}(1) = [0,0,\ldots,0]$ is $\frac{1}{2^n}$. From the same reason, for any $\mathbf{x}(0) = \mathbf{a}$ ($\mathbf{a} \in \{0,1\}^n$), the probability that $\mathbf{x}(1) = \mathbf{a}$ is $\frac{1}{2^n}$. Therefore, from the linearity of expectation, the expected number of singleton attractors is given by

$$\sum_{\mathbf{a} \in \{0,1\}^n} Prob(\mathbf{x}(1) = \mathbf{a} | \mathbf{x}(0) = \mathbf{a}) = 2^n \cdot \frac{1}{2^n} = 1.$$

$\square$

Readers may think that this argument can be extended for obtaining the expected number of periodic attractors of a fixed period (e.g., period 2). However, in such a case, we cannot repeatedly use the assumption that a random Boolean function is assigned to each node because the same Boolean function is used for each node at all time steps. This causes the difficulty of mathematically rigorous analysis of the distribution of attractors. Nevertheless, deep theoretical studies have been done on the length and distribution of periodic attractors [Drossel *et al.* (2005); Samuelsson and Troein (2003)].

2.3 Robustness against Perturbation

One of the well-studied research topics on BN is robustness against perturbation. As in the previous section, we consider the NK model of random BNs: each node has K different input nodes randomly selected from n nodes and a Boolean function randomly selected from a specified set Boolean functions. In a simplest case, we consider the set of all 2^{2^K} possible Boolean functions with K input variables. Note that some input nodes may not be relevant because all input variables are not necessarily relevant in 2^{2^K} Boolean functions.

For two n-bit vectors $\mathbf{x} = [x_1, \ldots, x_n]$ and $\mathbf{y} = [y_1, \ldots, y_n]$, the Hamming distance $d_H(\mathbf{x}, \mathbf{y})$ is defined to be the number of different bits (i.e., $d_H(\mathbf{x}, \mathbf{y}) = |\{i | x_i \neq y_i\}|$). We consider the following problem. Suppose that two different initial states $\mathbf{x}(0)$ and $\mathbf{y}(0)$ such that $d_H(\mathbf{x}(0), \mathbf{y}(0)) = d_0$ are given. Then, how $d_H(\mathbf{x}(t), \mathbf{y}(t))$ grows on the average as t grows? That is, we are interested in estimating the influences of change of d_0 bits. In the following, we present an intuitive and simple (but not rigorous) method for estimating this measure (see also Fig. 2.3).

Suppose that $d_H(\mathbf{x}(t), \mathbf{y}(t)) = d$ at time t. Let $\{i_1, \ldots, i_d\}$ be the set of bits such that $x_{i_k}(t) \neq y_{i_k}(t)$. Since we are considering the NK model, each node has K outgoing edges on the average. Then, the number of nodes having different input values between $\mathbf{x}(t)$ and $\mathbf{y}(t)$ is estimated to be dK, assuming that each of such nodes has an exactly one input node from those corresponding to $i_1, \ldots, i_d$. Let U be the set of these dK nodes and $V - U$ be the set of the remaining nodes.

Here, we consider a set of Boolean functions (*biased Boolean functions*) such that a function outputs 1 with probability p and 0 with probability $1 - p$ on the average. Then, each node in $V - U$ has the same value between $\mathbf{x}(t + 1)$ and $\mathbf{y}(t + 1)$ because all input values for this node are the same between $\mathbf{x}(t)$ and $\mathbf{y}(t)$. The probability that each node in U has different values between $\mathbf{x}(t + 1)$ and $\mathbf{y}(t + 1)$ is estimated as $2p(1 - p)$ because there are two such cases each of which occurs with probability $p(1 - p)$:

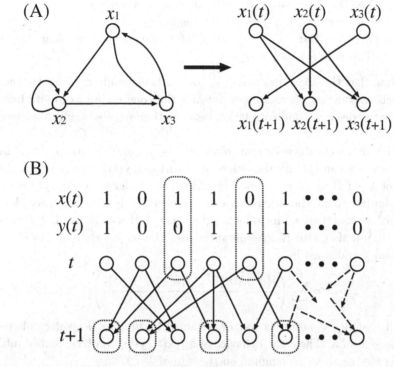

Fig. 2.3   Illustration for analysis of growth of the Hamming distance. (A) We consider a time-expanded network obtained from the original BN. (B) In this example, $x_3(t) \neq y_3(t)$ and $x_5(t) \neq y_5(t)$ and thus $d_H(\mathbf{x}(t), \mathbf{y}(t)) = 2$. For each node x_i in $U = \{x_1, x_2, x_4, x_6\}$ (shown by small dotted boxes). $x_i(t+1) \neq y_i(t+1)$ holds with probability $2p(1-p)$. Nodes shown by long dotted boxes correspond to W in analysis of overlap.

$(x_{i_k}(t+1), y_{i_k}(t+1)) = (1,0)$ and $(x_{i_k}(t+1), y_{i_k}(t+1)) = (0,1)$. Therefore, $d_H(\mathbf{x}(t+1), \mathbf{y}(t+1))$ is estimated as

$$d_H(\mathbf{x}(t+1), \mathbf{y}(t+1)) \approx 2p(1-p)dK \qquad (2.1)$$
$$= 2p(1-p)Kd_H(\mathbf{x}(t), \mathbf{y}(t)).$$

By letting $\lambda = 2Kp(1-p)$, we have

$$d_H(\mathbf{x}(t), \mathbf{y}(t)) \approx \lambda^t d_0. \qquad (2.2)$$

Consider the set of all 2^{2^K} possible Boolean functions with K input variables. Then, $p = \frac{1}{2}$ and thus $\lambda = \frac{K}{2}$. Behaviors of $d_H(\mathbf{x}(t), \mathbf{y}(t))$ are largely classified into the following three cases

$K > 2$ **(i.e., $\lambda > 1$))**: $d_H(\mathbf{x}(t), \mathbf{y}(t))$ grows exponentially.

The perturbation propagates quickly.

$K < 2$ **(i.e., $\lambda < 1$)):** $d_H(\mathbf{x}(t), \mathbf{y}(t))$ decreases exponentially.
The perturbation does not propagate.

$K = 2$ **(i.e., $\lambda = 1$)):**   Behavior of $d_H(\mathbf{x}(t), \mathbf{y}(t))$ is not very clear.
This case is called *critical*.

Note that the above discussion is not mathematically rigorous because of such reasons as: there are possibilities that one node has inputs from different nodes in U, and correlation between time steps was not taken into account.

The above classification can obviously be generalized for $p \neq \frac{1}{2}$. In this case, we can classify the behavior of $d_H(\mathbf{x}(t), \mathbf{y}(t))$ depending on the sign of $\lambda - 1$ (i.e., $2Kp(1-p) - 1$). Although we have considered biased Boolean functions, the discussion can be generalized to an arbitrary class of Boolean functions by introducing the concept of sensitivity. Let f be a Boolean function with K relevant variables. The *sensitivity* λ of a Boolean function f is defined by

$$\lambda = \sum_{i=1}^{K} \left(\frac{|\{\mathbf{a} \in \{0,1\}^K | \ f(\mathbf{a}_{(i)}) \neq f(\mathbf{a})\}|}{2^K} \right).$$

Recall that $\mathbf{a}_{(i)}$ denotes the vector obtained by flipping 0-1 values of the ith element of $\mathbf{a}$. Then, the behavior of $d_H(\mathbf{x}(t), \mathbf{y}(t))$ can be classified into three cases as above, depending on the sign of $\lambda - 1$.

In the above, we have considered how the Hamming distance grows. However, if t is not small, $d_H(\mathbf{x}(t), \mathbf{y}(t))$ in Eq. (2.2) may exceed n, which is not possible in practice. Therefore, we also consider another measure, overlap between $\mathbf{x}$ and $\mathbf{y}$. This *overlap* measure $ov(\mathbf{x}, \mathbf{y})$ is defined by

$$ov(\mathbf{x}, \mathbf{y}) = 1 - \frac{d_H(\mathbf{x}, \mathbf{y})}{n},$$

which means the fraction of nodes whose values are the same between $\mathbf{x}$ and $\mathbf{y}$. Suppose that $\alpha = ov(\mathbf{x}(t), \mathbf{y}(t))$. As before, let W be the set of nodes whose values are different between $\mathbf{x}$ and $\mathbf{y}$ at time t and $V - W$ be the set of the remaining nodes. Since each node has K inputs, the probability that a node has inputs only from $V - W$ is estimated to be α^K. Therefore, the expected number of nodes that has at least one input from W is estimated to be

$$(1 - \alpha^K)n.$$

For each of these nodes, the probability that it takes different values in $\mathbf{x}(t+1)$ and $\mathbf{y}(t+1)$ is $2p(1-p)$ as mentioned before. Thus, the expected number of nodes whose values are different between $\mathbf{x}(t+1)$ and $\mathbf{y}(t+1)$ is estimated to be

$$2p(1-p)(1-\alpha^K)n.$$

Therefore, we have

$$ov(\mathbf{x}(t+1), \mathbf{y}(t+1)) \approx 1 - 2p(1-p)\left[1 - ov(\mathbf{x}(t), \mathbf{y}(t))^K\right]. \quad (2.3)$$

For the case of $p = \frac{1}{2}$, the overlap given above converges to 1 as t grows if $K \leq 2$, otherwise it converges to some constant value depending on K (see Fig. 2.4).

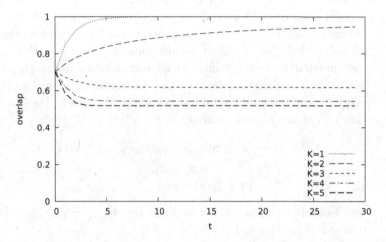

Fig. 2.4 Graph showing how overlap changes according to Eq. (2.3), where $ov(\mathbf{x}(0), \mathbf{y}(0)) = 0.7$ and $p = 0.5$.

Here, note that $d_H(\mathbf{x}, \mathbf{y}) = n(1 - ov(\mathbf{x}, \mathbf{y}))$ holds. Let $\delta(\mathbf{x}, \mathbf{y}) = \frac{d_H(\mathbf{x}, \mathbf{y})}{n}$. Then, the above relation can be rewritten as

$$\begin{aligned}
\delta(\mathbf{x}(t+1), \mathbf{y}(t+1)) &\approx 2p(1-p)\left[1 - (1 - \delta(\mathbf{x}(t), \mathbf{y}(t)))^K\right] \\
&\approx 2p(1-p)\left[1 - (1 - K\delta(\mathbf{x}(t), \mathbf{y}(t)))\right] \\
&= 2p(1-p)K\delta(\mathbf{x}(t), \mathbf{y}(t)).
\end{aligned}$$

This relation is essentially the same as Eq. (2.1).

2.4 Asynchronous Boolean Networks

This book focuses on the synchronous BN model in which the states of all nodes are updated simultaneously because it is simple and thus extensive studies have been done. However, there exists variety of time scales associated with different types of processes in biological systems. In order to take this fact into account, *asynchronous BN* models have been proposed in which different nodes are updated based on different time scales. However, since the actual durations of specific biological scales are not clear in many cases, the random updating scheme has widely been employed. Although there exist various asynchronous BN models based on the random updating scheme, we briefly review three major asynchronous BNs [Saadatpour *et al.* (2010)].

- Random Order Asynchronous (ROA) model.

    Each node in a BN is updated exactly once during each round, where a random order of nodes is generated at the beginning of each round. Precisely, a random permutation $[\pi_1, \ldots, \pi_n]$ of $[1, \ldots, n]$ is generated at the beginning of each round, which means that the ith node is updated at the π_ith step in the round. Suppose that $\mathbf{x}(t)$ is the state of the BN at the beginning of round t. Then, state $\mathbf{x}(t+1)$ of the BN after round t is given by

$$t_i(t+1) = f_i(x_1(\tau_{1,t}), \ldots, x_n(\tau_{n,t})), \quad i = 1, \ldots, n,$$

$$\tau_{j,t} = \begin{cases} t, & \text{if } \pi_j \geq \pi_i, \\ t+1, & \text{otherwise.} \end{cases}$$

    For example, suppose that $n = 3$ and $[\pi_1, \pi_2, \pi_3] = [3, 1, 2]$. Then the states are updated as

$$x_2(t+1) = f_2(x_1(t), x_2(t), x_3(t)),$$
$$x_3(t+1) = f_3(x_1(t), x_2(t+1), x_3(t)),$$
$$x_1(t+1) = f_1(x_1(t), x_2(t+1), x_3(t+1)).$$

- General Asynchronous (GA) model.

    Only one randomly selected node is updated at each time step. Suppose that x_i is selected among n nodes at step t. Then the states are updated as

$$x_i(t+1) = f_i(x_1(t), \ldots, x_n(t)),$$
$$x_j(t+1) = x_j(t), \quad \text{for } j \neq i.$$

    Therefore, it is possible that the same node is selected at both t and $t+1$. One time step in the GA model corresponds to $\frac{1}{n}$ of one round in the ROA model.

- Deterministic Asynchronous (DA) model.

  Each node x_i is associated with a specified time unit γ_i and the state of x_i is updated at time steps $t = k\gamma_i$ for any positive integer k. That is, states of nodes are updated by

$$x_i(t+1) = \begin{cases} f_i(x_1(t), \ldots, x_n(t)), & \text{if } t+1 = k\gamma_i, \quad k = 1, 2, \ldots. \\ x_i(t), & \text{otherwise.} \end{cases}$$

  Precisely, it is not a random model but a deterministic model.

Example 2.4. Consider the GA model of the BN in Example 2.1. Suppose that $\mathbf{x}(t) = [0, 0, 0]$. Then, $\mathbf{x}(t + 1) = [0, 0, 0]$ even if any of x_1, x_2, x_3 is selected and updated. Next, suppose that $\mathbf{x}(t) = [0, 0, 1]$. In this case, there are three possibilities:

- if x_1 is updated, $\mathbf{x}(t+1) = [1, 0, 1]$,
- if x_2 is updated, $\mathbf{x}(t+1) = [0, 0, 1]$,
- if x_3 is updated, $\mathbf{x}(t+1) = [0, 0, 0]$,

and thus node $[0, 0, 1]$ has three outgoing edges in the state transition diagram corresponding to the GA model. Fig. 2.5 shows the state transition diagram for the GA model. It is seen that this diagram is very different from the diagram for the synchronous BN (Fig. 2.2).

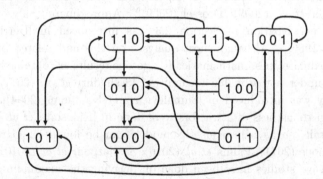

Fig. 2.5 State transition diagram for asynchronous (GA) model for the BN in Example 2.1.

It is seen from Fig. 2.5 that cycles in the state transition diagram of the synchronous model of a BN are not necessarily cycles in the state transition diagram of the corresponding asynchronous (GA) model of the BN. Furthermore, some cycles for the GA model have outgoing edges. Therefore, it is needed to change the definition of attractors. One reasonable definition is to define an attractor as a strongly connected component without outgoing edges. Recall that a strongly connected component is a maximal subset of nodes such that there exists a path from any node to any other node in the subset. In the diagram of Fig. 2.5, there are 8 strongly connected components: $\{[0,0,0]\}$, $\{[0,0,1]\}$, $\{[0,1,0]\}$, $\{[0,1,1]\}$, $\{[1,0,0]\}$, $\{[1,0,1]\}$, $\{[1,1,0]\}$, and $\{[1,1,1]\}$. Since each of components $\{[0,0,1]\}$, $\{[0,1,0]\}$, $\{[0,1,1]\}$, $\{[1,0,0]\}$, $\{[1,1,0]\}$, and $\{[1,1,1]\}$ has outgoing edge(s), only $\{[0,0,0]\}$ and $\{[1,0,1]\}$ correspond to attractors. It is interesting to note that these are also singleton attractors in the synchronous BN model. Furthermore, it can be shown that the synchronous model and the GA model have the same set of singleton attractors.

2.5   Additional Remarks and Bibliographical Notes

The Boolean network (BN) was introduced by Kauffman [Kauffman (1969a,b, 1993)]. The BN and its variants have been used for modeling of various biological systems [Abdallah (2017); Albert and Thakar (2014); Bornholdt (2008); DasGupta and Liang (2011); Flöttmann *et al.* (2013); Rother *et al.* (2013); Thomas (1973); Thomas *et al.* (1995)]. More detailed reviews on contents of Section 2.2 and Section 2.3 are given in [Aldana *et al.* (2003); Drossel (2009)]. Approximate analysis of the effect of perturbation in Section 2.3 was introduced in [Derrida and Pomeau (1986)]. Although most analyses on this and related problems are approximate ones, mathematically rigorous results are obtained for this problem under a reasonable assumption [Seshadhri *et al.* (2011)]. The sensitivity was introduced in [Shmulevich and Kauffman (2004)]. Some studies on robustness of attractors were done in [Kinoshita *et al.* (2009)]. Some details on asynchronous BN models can be found in [Garg *et al.* (2008); Inoue (2011); Palma *et al.* (2016); Saadatpour *et al.* (2010)].

Extensive studies have been done on deriving the maximum number of singleton and periodic attractors, in particular, for special classes of AND/OR BNs [Aracena *et al.* (2004b, 2014, 2017); Jarrah *et al.* (2010); Veliz-Cuba and Laubenbacher (2012)], where an AND/OR BN is an BN in which each function assigned to a node is an AND or OR of literals.

Chapter 3

Detection of Attractors

In this chapter and the following two chapters, we consider the problem of detection of attractors. As discussed in Chapter 2, extensive studies have been done on the length and distribution of attractors in the NK model, motivated by a possible correspondence between attractors and cell types. Since Boolean models of various biological systems have been constructed, it is also important to detect and/or enumerate attractors in a given BN.

Attractors can be enumerated once we have a state transition diagram. To this end, it is enough to enumerate cycles in the diagram since attractors correspond to cycles. For example, three cycles in Fig. 2.2 correspond to attractors. Enumeration of cycles can be done by identifying strongly connected components, which can be done in time linear to the size of the diagram by using the technique called depth first search, assuming that each elementary operation on n-bit words can be done in a constant time (which may not be appropriate in this case). However, the state transition diagram consists of 2^n nodes and 2^n edges. Therefore, this approach would require $\Omega(2^n)$ time. If n is not large (e.g., $n < 30$), it may be possible to apply this direct approach to enumerate all attractors. However, if n is large, it is impossible to store and analyze the state transition diagram. Therefore, we need more efficient methods.

In this chapter, we focus on BNs with maximum indegree K and present algorithms for detection of a singleton attractor and enumeration of singleton and periodic attractors with short periods.

3.1 Problem Definitions

We begin with a formal definition of Singleton Attractor Detection, which is given as follows.

Definition 3.1.   [Singleton Attractor Detection]
Instance: a BN $N(V, F)$ with n nodes,
Problem: decide whether or not there exists a singleton attractor $\mathbf{x}$ in $N(V, F)$, and output one if it exists.

Since $x_i(t + 1) = x_i(t)$ must holds for all $i = 1, \ldots, n$ for any singleton attractor $\mathbf{x}$, we omit t and we identify a node x_i with a Boolean value (or Boolean variable) in an attractor if there is no confusion.

If we consider a general BN, exponential space may be required to represent a BN with n nodes because there exist 2^{2^n} Boolean functions and thus 2^n bits are required to specify a Boolean function. Therefore, we need some constraints on Boolean functions. In this chapter, we only consider BNs with maximum indegree K where K is a constant larger than 1. Since the number of Boolean functions with K input variables is 2^{2^K}, each Boolean function can be specified using constant space and computation of the value of a Boolean function can be done in constant time,

The above definition can be generalized for including periodic attractors.

Definition 3.2.   [Attractor Detection]
Instance: a BN $N(V, F)$ with n nodes, and a positive integer p,
Problem: decide whether or not there exists an attractor $\mathbf{x}$ of period p in $N(V, F)$, and output one if it exists.

Note that the case of $p = 1$ corresponds to Singleton Attractor Detection. Attractor Detection for $p > 1$ is also referred to as Periodic Attractor Detection.

3.2   NP-hardness of Singleton Attractor Detection

Since a BN consists of Boolean functions, there are close relationships between BNs and the Boolean satisfiability problem (SAT).

First, we show that Singleton Attractor Detection is NP-hard by using a reduction from 3-SAT.

Theorem 3.1. *Singleton Attractor Detection is NP-hard.*

Proof. We use a polynomial-time reduction from 3-SAT. Let $z_1, \ldots, z_N$ be Boolean variables. Let $c_1, \ldots, c_L$ be a set of clauses over $z_1, \ldots, z_N$. Recall that a clause is a disjunction (OR) of literals, and a literal is a variable or its negation (i.e., NOT of a variable). Recall also that the satisfiability problem is to ask whether or not there exists an assignment of 0-1 values to $z_1, \ldots, z_N$ that satisfies all the clauses (i.e., the values of all clauses are 1). 3-SAT is a special case of the satisfiability problem in which each clause is a disjunction of at most three literals.

From an instance of 3-SAT, we construct a BN $N(V, F)$ as follows (see Fig. 3.1). We let $V = \{x_1, \ldots, x_{N+L}\}$, where each x_i with $i = 1, \ldots, N$ corresponds to z_i, and each x_{N+j} with $j = 1, \ldots, L$ corresponds to c_j. For each x_i with $i \le N$, we assign the following Boolean function:

$$x_i(t + 1) = x_i(t).$$

We can assume without loss of generality that c_i has the form of $c_i = \ell_{i_1} \vee \ell_{i_2} \vee \ell_{i_3}$ where ℓ_j is either x_j or $\overline{x_j}$. Then, for x_{N+i} $(i = 1, \ldots, L)$, we assign the following function:

$$x_{N+i}(t + 1) = w_{i_1}(t) \vee w_{i_2}(t) \vee w_{i_3}(t) \vee \overline{x_{N+i}(t)}, \tag{3.1}$$

where $w_j(t) = x_j(t)$ if $\ell_j = z_j$, and $w_j(t) = \overline{x_j(t)}$ otherwise.

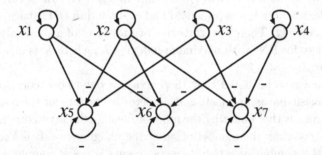

Fig. 3.1 Example of a reduction from 3-SAT to Singleton Attractor Detection. This BN is constructed from 3-SAT instance: $(z_1 \vee \overline{z_2} \vee z_3) \wedge (\overline{z_1} \vee z_2 \vee \overline{z_4}) \wedge (z_2 \vee \overline{z_3} \vee \overline{z_4})$. Arrows with '-' correspond to negative inputs.

Now we show the correctness of the reduction. Suppose that there exists an assignment of Boolean values $b_1, \ldots, b_N$ to $z_1, \ldots, z_N$ which satisfies all clauses $c_1, \ldots, c_L$. Then, we define $\mathbf{x}$ by

$$x_i = \begin{cases} b_i & \text{for } i = 1, \ldots, N, \\ 1 & \text{for } i = N + 1, \ldots, N + L. \end{cases}$$

We can see that $w_{i_1} \vee w_{i_2} \vee w_{i_3}$ takes value 1 because $\ell_{i_1} \vee \ell_{i_2} \vee \ell_{i_3}$ is satisfied. Therefore, $x_i(t + 1) = x_i(t) = x_i$ holds for all $i = 1, \ldots, N + L$ and thus $\mathbf{x}$ is a singleton attractor of $N(V, F)$.

Conversely, suppose that there exists a singleton attractor $\mathbf{x}$. We can see from the form of Eq. (3.1) that $x_{N+i} = 1$ $(i = 1, \ldots, L)$ must hold in any singleton attractor $\mathbf{x}$. Furthermore, $w_{i_1} \vee w_{i_2} \vee w_{i_3}$ must take value 1. Therefore, we can see that all clauses are satisfied by assigning the value x_i to z_i for $i = 1, \ldots, N$.

Since the reduction can clearly be done in polynomial time, the theorem holds. $\qquad\qquad\qquad\qquad\qquad\qquad\qquad\qquad\qquad\qquad\qquad\qquad\square$

In the above proof, the constructed BN has maximum indegree 4. However, we can modify the construction so that the maximum indegree is 2 [Tamura and Akutsu (2009)]. It is interesting because 2-SAT is known to be solvable in polynomial time whereas Singleton Attractor Detection remains NP-hard for the case of $K = 2$.

Readers may think that testing the existence of a singleton attractor is NP-complete. However, as mentioned in Section 3.1, exponential space may be needed to represent a BN without any restrictions. Therefore, it is difficult to discuss the time complexity for a general BN. However, if we only consider BNs with maximum indegree K for a constant K, each Boolean function is represented and evaluated in $O(1)$ space and $O(1)$ time, respectively. Therefore, the existence problem of a single attractor is NP-complete for BNs with maximum indegree K, where K is any constant larger than 1.

It should also be noted that there exists a one-to-one correspondence between satisfiable assignments and singleton attractors for the constructed BN. This means that counting the number of singleton attractors is at least as hard as counting the number of satisfying assignments. It is known that counting the number of satisfying assignments is a #P-complete problem (recall that it is believed that class #P is much wider.than class NP) even for 2-SAT [Valiant (1979)]. Since the reduction in the proof of Theorem 3.1 preserves the number of solutions, the following corollary holds [Akutsu *et al.* (1998)].

Corollary 3.1. *Counting the number of singleton attractors in a given BN is #P-hard.*

3.3   Reduction to SAT

We have used SAT to prove NP-hardness of Singleton Attractor Detection. Conversely, SAT can be used to solve Singleton Attractor Detection. Although SAT is NP-hard, many practical solvers have been developed, which can solve large-scale SAT instances [Balyo *et al.* (2017)]. Therefore, it is reasonable to try to apply existing algorithms for SAT to solve Singleton Attractor Detection.

As discussed in Section 3.3, representing a general BN requires exponential space, Therefore, we focus on BNs with maximum indegree K. Then, Singleton Attractor Detection for these restricted BNs can be transformed into $(K + 1)$-SAT with n variables in a simple manner. Here, we only show a reduction procedure for the case of $K = 2$, where the extension to general K is straightforward.

Let $\mathbf{x}$ be a state of a BN $N(V, F)$. Recall that $\mathbf{x}$ is a singleton attractor if $x_i = f_i(\mathbf{x})$ holds for all $i = 1, \ldots, n$. As in Section 3.2, we use x_i to denote the state of x_i. In the following, ℓ_i denotes either x_i or $\overline{x_i}$. We begin with the empty set. For $i = 1$ to n, we add clause(s) to the set according to the following rules (we omit the cases of constant and unary functions).

$$x_i = \ell_j \vee \ell_k \iff (\overline{x_i} \vee \ell_j \vee \ell_k) \wedge (x_i \vee \overline{\ell_j \vee \ell_k})$$
$$\iff (\overline{x_i} \vee \ell_j \vee \ell_k) \wedge (x_i \vee (\overline{\ell_j} \wedge \overline{\ell_k}))$$
$$\iff (\overline{x_i} \vee \ell_j \vee \ell_k) \wedge (x_i \vee \overline{\ell_j}) \wedge (x_i \vee \overline{\ell_k}),$$
$$x_i = \ell_j \wedge \ell_k \iff (\overline{x_i} \vee (\ell_j \wedge \ell_k)) \wedge (x_i \vee (\overline{\ell_j \wedge \ell_k}))$$
$$\iff (\overline{x_i} \vee \ell_j) \wedge (\overline{x_i} \vee \ell_k) \wedge (x_i \vee \overline{\ell_j} \vee \overline{\ell_k}),$$
$$x_i = \ell_j \oplus \ell_k \iff (\overline{x_i} \vee ((\ell_j \vee \ell_k) \wedge (\overline{\ell_j} \vee \overline{\ell_k}))) \wedge (x_i \vee \overline{(\ell_j \vee \ell_k) \wedge (\overline{\ell_j} \vee \overline{\ell_k})})$$
$$\iff (\overline{x_i} \vee \ell_j \vee \ell_k) \wedge (\overline{x_i} \vee \overline{\ell_j} \vee \overline{\ell_k}) \wedge (x_i \vee (\overline{\ell_j \vee \ell_k}) \vee (\overline{\overline{\ell_j} \vee \overline{\ell_k}}))$$
$$\iff (\overline{x_i} \vee \ell_j \vee \ell_k) \wedge (\overline{x_i} \vee \overline{\ell_j} \vee \overline{\ell_k}) \wedge (x_i \vee \overline{\ell_j} \vee \ell_k) \wedge (x_i \vee \ell_j \vee \overline{\ell_k}).$$

Then, we can see that a regulation rule for each node is transformed into at most four clauses in 3-SAT. Therefore, Singleton Attractor Detection for a BN with n nodes can be reduced to 3-SAT with n variables and at most $4n$ clauses. This reduction can be generalized to arbitrarily fixed K [Tamura and Akutsu (2009)].

Proposition 3.1. *Any instance of Singleton Attractor Detection for a BN of maximum indegree K with n nodes can be reduced in polynomial time to an instance of $(K + 1)$-SAT with at most $2^{K+1} \cdot n$ clauses and n variables.*

Extensive studies have been done on k-SAT and $O((2 - \delta)^n)$ time algorithms have been developed for small k. For example, an $O(1.3303^n)$ time (deterministic) algorithm has been developed for 3-SAT [Makino *et al.* (2013)]. Suppose that k-SAT can be solved in $O((\alpha_k)^n)$ time. Then, this proposition implies that Singleton Attractor Detection for BNs with maximum indegree K can be solved in $O^*((\alpha_{K+1})^n)$ time.

3.4   Reduction to Integer Linear Programming

In the above, we have presented a reduction from Singleton Attractor Detection to SAT. As mentioned in Chapter 1, there exists another NP-hard problem for which practical solvers have been developed: *Integer Linear Programming* (ILP). Recall that ILP is an optimization problem in which a linear objective function is maximized (or, minimized) under linear constraints (i.e., linear equalities and linear inequalities) and the condition that all variables must take integer values. In this section, we describe a reduction from Singleton Attractor Detection to ILP. In the following, each variable in ILP takes either 0 or 1 and we identify integer values with Boolean values. In particular, we use x_i to denote a 0-1 variable corresponding to node x_i.

We define $\sigma_b(x)$ by

$$\sigma_b(x) = \begin{cases} x, \text{ if } b = 1, \\ \overline{x}, \text{ otherwise.} \end{cases}$$

Note that $\sigma_b(x) = 1$ if and only if $x = b$. Thus, any Boolean function with k inputs can be represented as

$$f_i(x_{i_1}, \ldots, x_{i_k}) =$$
$$\bigvee_{[b_{i_1}, \ldots, b_{i_k}] \in \{0,1\}^k} (f_i(b_{i_1}, \ldots, b_{i_k}) \wedge \sigma_{b_1}(x_{i_1}) \wedge \cdots \wedge \sigma_{b_k}(x_{i_k})).$$

In order to represent this formula by ILP, we introduce $\tau_b(x)$ defined by

$$\tau_b(x) = \begin{cases} x, & \text{if } b = 1, \\ 1 - x, & \text{otherwise.} \end{cases}$$

If $f_i(b_{i_1}, \ldots, b_{i_k}) = 1$, we add constraints

$$x_{i,b_{i_1} \ldots b_{i_k}} \geq \left(\sum_{j=1}^{k} \tau_{b_{i_j}}(x_{i_j}) \right) - (k - 1),$$

$$x_{i,b_{i_1} \ldots b_{i_k}} \leq \frac{1}{k} \sum_{j=1}^{k} \tau_{b_{i_j}}(x_{i_j}),$$

where the first constraint forces $x_{i,b_{i_1} \ldots b_{i_k}}$ to be 1 if $\sigma_{b_1}(x_{i_1}) \wedge \cdots \wedge \sigma_{b_k}(x_{i_k})$ is satisfied, and the latter forces $x_{i,b_{i_1} \ldots b_{i_k}}$ to be 0 if it is not satisfied. If $f_i(b_{i_1}, \ldots, b_{i_k}) = 0$, we simply add a constraint $x_{i,b_{i_1} \ldots b_{i_k}} = 0$. These constraints ensure that $x_{i,b_{i_1} \ldots b_{i_k}} = 1$ if and only if $f_i(b_{i_1}, \ldots, b_{i_k}) \wedge$

$\sigma_{b_1}(x_{i_1}) \wedge \cdots \wedge \sigma_{b_k}(x_{i_k}) = 1$. Finally, for each x_i, we add constraints

$$x_i \leq \sum_{[b_{i_1},\ldots,b_{i_k}] \in \{0,1\}^k} x_{i,b_{i_1}\ldots b_{i_k}},$$

$$x_i \geq \frac{1}{2^k} \sum_{[b_{i_1},\ldots,b_{i_k}] \in \{0,1\}^k} x_{i,b_{i_1}\ldots b_{i_k}}.$$

These constraints ensure that $x_i = f_i(x_{i_1}, \ldots, x_{i_k})$ holds for every x_i, which means that any obtained feasible solution corresponds to a singleton attractor.

Example 3.1. Suppose that x_3 is determined by $x_3 = f_3(x_1, x_2) = x_1 \oplus x_2$. Then, $f_3(x_1, x_2)$ can be represented as

$$f_3(x_1, x_2) = (f_3(0,0) \wedge \overline{x_1} \wedge \overline{x_2}) \vee (f_3(0,1) \wedge \overline{x_1} \wedge x_2)$$
$$\vee (f_3(1,0) \wedge x_1 \wedge \overline{x_2}) \vee (f_3(1,1) \wedge x_1 \wedge x_2)$$
$$= (\overline{x_1} \wedge x_2) \vee (x_1 \wedge \overline{x_2}).$$

Then, this Boolean formula is transformed into the following inequalities.

$$x_{3,00} = 0,$$
$$x_{3,01} \geq (1 - x_1) + x_2 - 1 = x_2 - x_1,$$
$$x_{3,01} \leq \frac{1}{2}(1 - x_1 + x_2),$$
$$x_{3,10} \geq x_1 + (1 - x_2) - 1 = x_1 - x_2,$$
$$x_{3,10} \leq \frac{1}{2}(x_1 + 1 - x_2),$$
$$x_{3,11} = 0,$$
$$x_3 \leq x_{3,00} + x_{3,01} + x_{3,10} + x_{3,11},$$
$$x_3 \geq \frac{1}{4}(x_{3,00} + x_{3,01} + x_{3,10} + x_{3,11}).$$

By putting together all the constraints, the singleton attractor detection problem can be transformed into the following ILP.

Maximize x_1,
Subject to
$$x_{i,b_{i_1}\ldots b_{i_k}} \geq \left(\sum_{j=1}^k \tau_{b_{i_j}}(x_{i_j}) \right) - (k - 1),$$
$$x_{i,b_{i_1}\ldots b_{i_k}} \leq \frac{1}{k} \sum_{j=1}^k \tau_{b_{i_j}}(x_{i_j}),$$
$$\text{for all } i \in \{1, \ldots, n\} \text{ and } [b_{i_1}, \ldots, b_{i_k}] \in \{0,1\}^k$$
$$\text{such that } f_i(b_{i_1}, \ldots, b_{i_k}) = 1,$$
$$x_{i,b_{i_1}\ldots b_{i_k}} = 0,$$

for all $i \in \{1, \ldots, n\}$ and $[b_{i_1}, \ldots, b_{i_k}] \in \{0, 1\}^k$
such that $f_i(b_{i_1}, \ldots, b_{i_k}) = 0$,

$$x_i \leq \sum_{[b_{i_1}, \ldots, b_{i_k}] \in \{0,1\}^k} x_{i, b_{i_1} \ldots b_{i_k}},$$

$$x_i \geq \frac{1}{2^k} \sum_{[b_{i_1}, \ldots, b_{i_k}] \in \{0,1\}^k} x_{i, b_{i_1} \ldots b_{i_k}},$$

$$x_i \in \{0, 1\},$$

for all $i \in \{1, \ldots, n\}$,

$$x_{i, b_{i_1} \ldots b_{i_k}} \in \{0, 1\},$$

for all $i \in \{1, \ldots, n\}$ and $[b_{i_1}, \ldots, b_{i_k}] \in \{0, 1\}^k$.

It is to be noted that we do not need an objective function since Singleton Attractor Detection is not an optimization problem but a decision problem. Since some objective function is required in order to use ILP, we simply used 'maximize x_1' in the above.

3.5   Utilization of Feedback Vertex Sets

The *feedback vertex set* (FVS) is a well-known concept in graph theory. For a directed graph $G(V, E)$, a subset $U \subseteq V$ is called a *feedback vertex set* if removal of vertices in U and edges connecting to U makes the graph acyclic. The minimum feedback vertex set is the feedback vertex set with the minimum number of vertices. Some examples of FVSs are given in Fig. 3.2. Although computation of the minimum FVS is known to be NP-hard, some practical algorithms have been developed [Levy and Low (1988)]. Therefore, such algorithms may be used for obtaining an FVS of the minimum or near minimum size.

Since there is no cycle after removing nodes in an FVS, the state of every node is determined based on the states of nodes in FVS. Furthermore, the longest path from FVS nodes to each node is at most $n - 1$. Therefore, we have:

Proposition 3.2. *If we fix the states of nodes in an FVS, a BN falls into a stable state after at most $n - 1$ time steps.*

However, a stable state does not necessarily correspond to a singleton attractor because the fixed states of nodes in FVS may not be consistent with the states of FVS nodes determined from the states of their input nodes. Therefore, examining all possible states on nodes in FVS and testing their consistencies, we can enumerate all singleton attractors. Since there

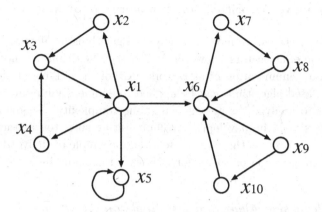

Fig. 3.2 Example of a BN for illustration of FVS. There are two minimum FVSs: $\{x_1, x_5, x_6\}$ and $\{x_3, x_5, x_6\}$. $\{x_3, x_5, x_8, x_9\}$ is an FVS but is not the minimum one.

are $2^{|U|}$ possible states on an FVS U, we have the following.

Theorem 3.2. *Let $N(V, F)$ be a BN such that each Boolean function can be evaluated in polynomial time, and let U be an FVS of the corresponding directed graph $G(V, E)$. Then, all singleton attractors for $N(V, F)$ can be enumerated in $O^*(2^{|U|})$ time.*

Example 3.2. Suppose that all nodes are OR nodes and all edges denote positive literals in Fig. 3.2. There exist $2^3 = 8$ possible 0-1 assignments on an FVS $\{x_1, x_5, x_6\}$, whereas there exist 5 singleton attractors. For example, $[x_1, x_5, x_6] = [1, 0, 0]$ is not consistent because x_5 and x_6 should take state 1 from the state of x_1 but their states are 0. Similarly, $[x_1, x_5, x_6] = [1, 0, 1]$ or $[x_1, x_5, x_6] = [1, 1, 0]$ is not consistent. Since the other assignments are consistent, there exist 5 singleton attractors.

This result can be extended to enumeration of periodic attractors of a given period p. In this case, we examine p combinations of 0-1 assignments on each node in an FVS. For example, the BN in Fig. 3.2 has an attractor of period 3 in which $[x_1, x_5, x_6]$ repeats the following states: $[1, 1, 0], [0, 1, 1], [0, 1, 0]$. It is seen that the whole BN falls into periodic states after at most $p + n - 1$ time steps. Therefore, we have:

Corollary 3.2. *Let $N(V, F)$ is a BN such that each Boolean function can be evaluated in polynomial time, and let U be an FVS of the corresponding directed graph $G(V, E)$. Then, all attractors of period p for $N(V, F)$ can be enumerated in $O^*(2^{p|U|})$ time.*

3.6 Recursive Algorithms for Enumeration of Attractors

In previous sections, we have seen several algorithms for detection and/or enumeration of attractors. However, ILP-based algorithms are not directly applicable to enumeration of attractors. Although SAT-based algorithms and FVS-based algorithms can be applied to enumeration of attractors, it is difficult to analyze the average case time complexity. Therefore, other algorithms should be developed for enumerating singleton attractors and periodic attractors. In this section, we describe simple recursive algorithms for these enumeration problems for BNs with maximum indegree K.

3.6.1 *Recursive Algorithm for Singleton Attractors*

The number of singleton attractors in a BN depends on the regulatory rules of the BN. If the rules are $x_i(t+1) = x_i(t)$ for all i, the number of singleton attractors is 2^n. Therefore, it would take at least $O(2^n)$ time in the worst case if we need to enumerate all the singleton attractors. On the other hand, as seen in Section 2.2, the average number of singleton attractors for the NK model is 1 regardless of n and K. Based on this fact, we design a simple recursive algorithm for enumeration of singleton attractors, which examines a much smaller number of global states than 2^n on the average.

In the algorithm, a partial global state (i.e., $[x_1, \ldots, x_m]$ for $m < n$) is extended one by one towards a complete global state (i.e., singleton attractor), according to a given ordering of nodes (i.e., a random ordering). As soon as it is found that a partial global state cannot be extended to a singleton attractor, the next partial global state is examined. In order to represent a partial global state, we use $\mathbf{x} = [x_1, \ldots, x_n]$ that is an n-dimensional vector each of whose elements is either 0, 1, or ϵ, where ϵ means that 0-1 value of this element is not yet determined. The pseudocode of the algorithm is given below, where it is invoked with $m = 1$ and $\mathbf{x} = [\epsilon, \ldots, \epsilon]$.

Procedure RecursiveEnumSatt($\mathbf{x}, m$)
if $m = n + 1$ **then** output $\mathbf{x}$; **return**;
for $b = 0$ **to** 1 **do**
$\quad x_m \leftarrow b$;
$\quad$ **if** it is found that $f_i(\mathbf{x}) \neq x_i$ for some $i \leq m$ **then continue**
$\quad$ **else RecursiveEnumSatt($\mathbf{x}, m + 1$)**;
return.

This algorithm extends a partial state one by one in a recursive manner. At the mth recursive step, the states of the first $m-1$ nodes (i.e., a partial state) are already determined. Then, the algorithm extends the partial state by letting $x_m = 0$. If $f_i(\mathbf{x}) = x_i$ holds or the value of x_i is not determined for each $i = 1, \cdots, m$, then there is a possibility that the current partial state can be extended to a singleton attractor and thus the algorithm proceeds to the next recursive step. Otherwise, it modifies the partial state by letting $x_m = 1$ and executes a similar procedure. After examining $x_m = 0$ and $x_m = 1$, the algorithm returns to the previous recursive step. Since the number of singleton attractors is small in most cases, it is expected that the algorithm does not examine many partial global states with large m in the average case.

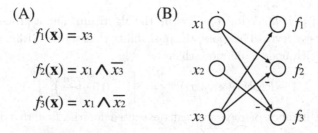

(A)

$f_1(\mathbf{x}) = x_3$

$f_2(\mathbf{x}) = x_1 \wedge \overline{x_3}$

$f_3(\mathbf{x}) = x_1 \wedge \overline{x_2}$

(B)

x_1 f_1

x_2 f_2

x_3 f_3

Fig. 3.3 Illustration for explaining **RecursiveEnumSatt**. (A) Boolean functions corresponding to BN in Example 2.1. (B) Graphical representation of f_is where arrows with '-' correspond to negative inputs.

Example 3.3. Consider the BN given in Example 2.1, where relevant information is shown in Fig. 3.3. **RecursiveEnumSatt** first examines $[0, \epsilon, \epsilon]$. Since no contradiction (i.e., $f_i(\mathbf{x}) \neq x_i$) is found, it proceeds to $[0, 0, \epsilon]$, Since no contradiction is found, it proceeds to $[0, 0, 0]$, Since no contradiction is found, it outputs $[0, 0, 0]$ as a singleton attractor and then it examines $[0, 0, 1]$. Since $f_1(\mathbf{x}) \neq x_1$ holds, it returns to a lower recursive level. Then, it examines $[0, 1, \epsilon]$. Since no contradiction is found, it proceeds to $[0, 1, 0]$, Since $f_2(\mathbf{x}) \neq x_2$ holds, it examines $[0, 1, 1]$. Since $f_1(\mathbf{x}) \neq x_1$ holds, it returns to a lower recursive level. Then, it returns to the first recursive level and examines $[1, \epsilon, \epsilon]$. We omit the remaining steps.

Since the correctness of **RecursiveEnumSatt** is obvious, we analyze the average case time complexity. Assume that we have tested the first m

Table 3.1   Exponential factors of time complexities of **RecursiveEnumSatt**.

K	2	3	4	5	6	7	8	9	10
	1.35^n	1.43^n	1.49^n	1.53^n	1.57^n	1.60^n	1.62^n	1.65^n	1.67^n

nodes, where $m \geq K$. For all $i \leq m$, $f_i(\mathbf{x}) \neq x_i$ holds with probability

$$Prob(f_i(\mathbf{x}) \neq x_i) = 0.5 \cdot \frac{\binom{m}{k_i}}{\binom{n}{k_i}} \approx 0.5 \cdot \left(\frac{m}{n}\right)^{|IN(v_i)|} \geq 0.5 \cdot \left(\frac{m}{n}\right)^K,$$

where the factor of 0.5 comes from a fact that Boolean functions of $k_i = |IN(x_i)|$ inputs are selected at uniformly random. Note that if $x_j \in IN(x_i)$ holds for some $j > m$, we cannot determine the value of $f_i(\mathbf{x})$ and thus cannot check $f_i(\mathbf{x}) \neq x_i$.

If $f_i(\mathbf{x}) \neq x_i$ holds for some $i \leq m$, the algorithm cannot proceed to the next recursive level. Therefore, the probability that the algorithm examines the $(m+1)$th node is no more than

$$[1 - Prob(f_i(\mathbf{x}) \neq x_i)]^m = \left[1 - 0.5 \cdot \left(\frac{m}{n}\right)^K\right]^m.$$

Thus, the number of recursive calls executed for the first m nodes is at most

$$h(m) = 2^m \cdot \left[1 - 0.5 \cdot \left(\frac{m}{n}\right)^K\right]^m.$$

Letting $s = \frac{m}{n}$, $h(m)$ can be represented as

$$h(m) = H(s) = [2^s \cdot (1 - 0.5 \cdot s^K)^s]^n = [(2 - s^K)^s]^n.$$

Then, the average case time complexity of the algorithm is estimated as $O^*((\max_s(g(s)))^n)$ for fixed K, where $g(s) = (2 - s^K)^s$. By means of numerical calculation for $\max_s(g)$, exponential factors (i.e., $\max_s(g(s))$) of the average case time complexities for $K = 2, \ldots, 10$ are estimated as in Tab. 3.1, where rounded down values are shown for the bases. It should be noted that the naive exhaustive search-based algorithm takes at least $O(2^n)$ time. Therefore, **RecursiveEnumSatt** is much faster than the naive algorithm for small K.

3.6.2   *Recursive Algorithm for Periodic Attractors*

RecursiveEnumSatt can be extended to enumerate periodic attractors of a fixed period p. The extension is very simple and the basic idea is to replace "$f_i(\mathbf{x}) \neq x_i$" with "$\mathbf{f}^p(\mathbf{x})[i] \neq x_i$", where $\mathbf{f}^p(\mathbf{x})$ denotes the vector obtained by applying $\mathbf{f}$ to $\mathbf{x}$ p times, and $\mathbf{f}^p(\mathbf{x})[i]$ denotes the ith element of a vector $\mathbf{f}^p(\mathbf{x})$. The following is a pseudocode of the extended algorithm.

Procedure RecursiveEnumPatt($\mathbf{x}, m, p$)
if $m = n + 1$ **then**
    if $\mathbf{f}^k(\mathbf{x}) \neq \mathbf{x}$ for all $k = 1, \ldots, p - 1$ **then** output $\mathbf{x}$;
    return;
for $b = 0$ **to** 1 **do**
    $x_m \leftarrow b$;
    if it is found that $\mathbf{f}^p(\mathbf{x})[i] \neq x_i$ for some $i \leq m$ **then continue**
    else RecursiveEnumPatt($\mathbf{x}, m + 1, p$);
return.

Since the correctness of this algorithm is obvious, we analyze the average case time complexity. The probability that $\mathbf{f}^p(\mathbf{x})[i] \neq x_i$ holds for each $i \leq m$ is approximated as

$$Prob(\mathbf{f}^p(\mathbf{x})[i] \neq x_i) \approx 0.5 \cdot \left(\frac{m}{n}\right)^K \cdot \left(\frac{m}{n}\right)^{K^2} \cdots \left(\frac{m}{n}\right)^{K^p},$$

where $(m/n)^K$ means that the K input nodes to node x_i at time $p - 1$ are among the first m nodes, $(m/n)^{K^2}$ means that the K input nodes to node x_i at time $p - 2$ are also among the first m nodes, and so on. Note that we assume here that selection of input nodes at each time step is independent, which is not necessarily true.

Then, the probability that **RecursiveEnumPatt** examines some specific assignment on m nodes is approximately given by

$$[1 - Prob(\mathbf{f}^p(\mathbf{x})[i] \neq x_i)]^m = \left[1 - 0.5 \cdot \left(\frac{m}{n}\right)^K \cdot \left(\frac{m}{n}\right)^{K^2} \cdots \left(\frac{m}{n}\right)^{K^p}\right]^m.$$

Therefore, the number of recursive calls executed for these m nodes is estimated as

$$h(m) = 2^m \cdot [1 - Prob(\mathbf{f}^p(\mathbf{x})[i] \neq x_i)]^m$$
$$= 2^m \cdot \left[1 - 0.5 \cdot \left(\frac{m}{n}\right)^K \cdot \left(\frac{m}{n}\right)^{K^2} \cdots \left(\frac{m}{n}\right)^{K^p}\right]^m.$$

As in Section 3.6.1, exponential factors of the average case time complexities can be obtained by numerical calculation, some of which are shown in Tab. 3.2, where rounded down values are shown for the bases. The result shown in this table suggests that **RecursiveEnumPatt** is much faster than the naive enumeration method if both K and p are small.

Table 3.2   Exponential factors of time complexities of **RecursiveEnumPatt**.

K	2	3	4	5	6	7	8	9	10
$p = 2$	1.57^n	1.70^n	1.78^n	1.83^n	1.87^n	1.89^n	1.91^n	1.92^n	1.93^n
$p = 3$	1.72^n	1.86^n	1.92^n	1.95^n	1.97^n	1.97^n	1.98^n	1.99^n	1.99^n
$p = 4$	1.83^n	1.94^n	1.97^n	1.99^n	1.99^n	1.99^n	1.99^n	1.99^n	1.99^n
$p = 5$	1.90^n	1.97^n	1.99^n	1.99^n	1.99^n	1.99^n	1.99^n	1.99^n	1.99^n

3.7   Additional Remarks and Bibliographical Notes

NP-hardness of Singleton Attractor Detection was proven in [Akutsu *et al.* (1998)], where another proof was given in [Aracena *et al.* (2004a)]. Use of SAT for Singleton Attractor Detection was proposed in [Leone *et al.* (2006)], in which a belief-propagation type algorithm was also proposed. Efficient and practical SAT-based algorithms were proposed in [de Jong and Page (2008); Dubrova and Teslenko (2011)]. From a theoretical viewpoint, an algorithm faster than a naive SAT-based algorithm for Singleton Attractor Detection for $K = 2$ is shown in [Akutsu and Tamura (2009)]. As another practical approach for detection and enumeration of attractors, algorithms using Binary Decision Diagrams (BDDs) were proposed [Dubrova *et al.* (2005); Garg *et al.* (2008)].

An ILP-based method described in this chapter was proposed in [Akutsu *et al.* (2012c)]. To be discussed later, the ILP-based approach was applied to other problems for analysis and control of BNs and PBNs.

An FVS-based algorithm for enumeration of singleton attractors was first proposed in [Akutsu *et al.* (1998)]. The FVS-based approach was further extended for more general non-linear models of biological networks [Mochizuki *et al.* (2013)]. Relations between the expected number of singleton attractors and feedback arc sets were studied in [Mori and Mochizuki (2017)]. **RecursiveEnumSatt** and **RecursiveEnumPatt** were proposed in [Zhang *et al.* (2007a)].

Various practical algorithms were developed for detection/enumeration of singleton/periodic attractors combining network reduction, network decomposition, and/or other techniques [Choo and Cho (2016); Veliz-Cuba *et al.* (2014); Zañudo *et al.* (2013)]. Constraint programming has also been applied to detection/enumeration of singleton attractors [Devloo *et al.* (2003)].

Chapter 4

Detection of Singleton Attractors

In Chapter 3, we have seen several algorithms for detecting and/or enumerating singleton and periodic attractors. However, unless there is any constraint on the maximum indegree, the worst case time complexity is at least $O(2^n)$. Therefore, it is reasonable to ask whether it is possible to develop an $O((2 - \delta)^n)$ time algorithm when there is no constraint on the maximum indegree, where $\delta > 0$ is some constant. It seems quite difficult to develop such an algorithm. However, it is possible if there exist some constraint on types of Boolean functions or the network structure. This chapter presents such algorithms for detection of a singleton attractor.

4.1 Singleton Attractor Detection for AND/OR BNs

Here we consider the case where each Boolean function in a given BN is a conjunction (AND) or disjunction (OR) of literals. As mentioned in Section 2.5, such a BN is called an *AND/OR BN*. This section presents an $O(1.792^n)$ time algorithm for detection of a singleton attractor in an AND/OR BN, which is obtained by a combination of a recursive procedure and an existing algorithm for solving SAT whose time complexity is dominated by the number of clauses.

Before presenting the pseudocode, we explain the basic idea of the algorithm. Suppose that the following Boolean function is assigned to a node x_i:

$$x_i = x_1 \wedge x_2 \wedge \cdots \wedge x_h,$$

where we omit dependence on $t + 1$ or t because we only consider singleton attractors in this section. Among four possible partial assignments $[0, 0]$, $[0, 1]$, $[1, 0]$ and $[1, 1]$ for $[x_1, x_i]$, three are consistent with the condition of a singleton attractor whereas one (i.e., $[0, 1]$) does not because $x_i = 0$

must hold whenever $x_1 = 0$. Therefore, we need not examine the partial assignment $[0, 1]$ and thus we can eliminate two nodes by examining the other three partial assignments. If we could continue this procedure until there is no remaining node, the complexity of $O^*(3^{(n/2)}) \le O(1.733^n)$ would be achieved.

However, we cannot continue this procedure if there is no remaining edge and only singleton nodes (possibly including self loops) are left. Let U be the set of nodes whose 0-1 assignments are already determined by this procedure, and W be the set of the remaining nodes (i.e., $W = V \setminus U$). Note that $S_1 \setminus S_2$ denotes the set $\{x | x \in S_1, x \notin S_2\}$. In the following, we explain how to determine 0-1 values on W.

If the number of remaining nodes is small (precisely, $|W| < (1 - \alpha)n$ for some constant α), we examine all possible 0-1 assignments on W and check whether each resulting assignment on V is consistent. A *consistent assignment* is an assignment on all variables that satisfies all Boolean constrains (i.e., $x_i = f_i(\mathbf{x})$ holds for all x_i). Since we are considering AND/OR functions, the consistency of each function can be tested in $O(n)$ time and the consistency of all functions can be tested in $O(n^2)$ time.

Otherwise, we utilize an algorithm for solving SAT whose time complexity is dominated by the number of clauses. For examine, we can use an algorithm by (Yamamoto, 2005), which solves SAT with n variables and m clauses in $O^*(1.234^m)$ time. Before applying such an SAT algorithm, we determine the (partial) state of each $x_i \in W$. At this stage, the states of all incoming nodes to $x_i \in W$ are already determined because there is no edge among W. Then, there are four possibilities for each $x_i \in W$:

 (i) no consistent assignment,
 (ii) 0 must be assigned to x_i,
 (iii) 1 must be assigned to x_i,
 (iv) both 0 and 1 are possible.

In the following, a partial assignment is represented by a set of literal and 0-1 value pairs. For example, $A = \{(x_i, 1), (\overline{x_j}, 1), (x_k, 0)\}$ means that 1, 1, and 0 are assigned to variables x_i, $\overline{x_j}$, and x_k, respectively. Furthermore, A is equivalent to a partial assignment $\{(x_i, 1), (x_j, 0), (x_k, 0)\}$. When we consider a partial assignment on one variable, we may omit the set symbols (e.g., $(x_i, 0)$ denotes a partial assignment of value 0 to variable x_i). We may use "0/1" for case (iv).

The partial states are determined as follows. First, consider the case of $x_i = x_j \wedge x_k$. If $\{(x_j, 1), (x_k, 1)\}$ is assigned, $(x_i, 1)$ must be assigned.

Otherwise, $(x_i, 0)$ must be assigned. Next, consider the case of $x_i = x_i \wedge x_k$. If $(x_k, 0)$ is assigned, $(x_i, 0)$ must be assigned. Otherwise, either $(x_i, 0)$ or $(x_i, 1)$ can be assigned (i.e., case (iv)). Next, consider the case of $x_i = \overline{x_i} \wedge x_k$. If $(x_k, 0)$ is assigned, $(x_i, 0)$ must be assigned. Otherwise, there is no consistent assignment on x_i (i.e., case (i)) and thus we need not examine further. It is straightforward to extend these rules for AND nodes with indegree 1 or more than 2, and OR nodes. Note that if there is no node corresponding to (iv), it is enough to check the consistency of the resulting assignment and we need not examine further.

In order to determine 0-1 values for nodes corresponding to (iv), we handle a constraint on each $x_i \in U$. Suppose that $f_i(\mathbf{x}) = \ell_{i_1} \wedge \cdots \wedge \ell_{i_k}$ and $(x_i, 0)$ is assigned. Then, we create a clause of $\overline{\ell_{i_1}} \vee \cdots \vee \overline{\ell_{i_k}}$. If $(x_i, 1)$ is assigned, we assign $(\ell_{i_j}, 1)$ for all $j = 1, \ldots, k$. Of course, some assignment may have a conflict with the current assignment. Therefore, consistency of the assignment must be checked before applying the SAT algorithm. Finally, we apply the SAT algorithm for the set of resulting clauses, where some clauses might be simplified due to the current assignment. The following is a formal description of the algorithm, where it is invoked as **SattAND-OR**$(\emptyset, \emptyset)$.

Procedure SattAND-OR$(U, \mathcal{A})$
  if there exists an edge (x_i, x_j) with $x_i \neq x_j$ and $\{x_i, x_j\} \subseteq (V \setminus U)$ **then**
    for all possible three partial assignments $\{(x_i, b_i), (x_j, b_j)\}$ **do**
      if SattAND-OR$(U \cup \{x_i, x_j\}, \mathcal{A} \cup \{(x_i, b_i), (x_j, b_j)\})$=TRUE
      then return TRUE
  else if $|U| > \alpha n$ **then**
    for all 0-1 assignments $\mathcal{A}'$ on $V \setminus U$ **do**
    if $\mathcal{A} \cup \mathcal{A}'$ is a consistent assignment on V
    then return TRUE **else return** FALSE
  else
    for all $x_i \in V \setminus U$ **do**
    determine the value of x_i from $\{\epsilon, 0, 1, 0/1\}$;
    if ϵ is selected **then return** FALSE;
    for all $x_i \in U$ **do** construct a clause for x_i or add a partial assignment;
    if the resulting assignment is consistent **and**
        the set of clauses is satisfiable
    then return TRUE **else return** FALSE.

Although this algorithm returns either TRUE or FALSE, it can be modified in a straightforward manner so that a singleton attractor is outputted if the algorithm returns TRUE.

Example 4.1. . Suppose that the following BN is given (see also Fig. 4.1):

$$x_1 = x_5 \wedge x_9, x_2 = \overline{x_1}, x_3 = x_2, x_4 = \overline{x_1} \wedge x_3 \wedge x_8 \wedge \overline{x_9}, x_5 = x_2 \wedge x_3 \wedge x_5,$$
$$x_6 = x_3, x_7 = x_3 \wedge x_4 \wedge \overline{x_7}, x_8 = x_8, x_9 = x_9,$$

where t is omitted. Suppose that edges (x_1, x_2) and (x_3, x_4) are selected in the first and second recursive steps, respectively, and $\{(x_1, 0), (x_2, 1), (x_3, 1), (x_4, 0)\}$ is assigned. Then, $U = \{x_1, x_2, x_3, x_4\}$ and $W = \{x_5, x_6, x_7, x_8, x_9\}$. Note that there is no edge among W (excluding self loops). Suppose that "**else if**" line fails. Then, the partial assignment on W is determined as follows:

$$\{(x_6, 1), (x_7, 0)\}.$$

Note that no assignment is given to x_5, x_8, or x_9 (i.e., 0/1 is given to each of them). Next, we process a constraint on each node in U. Since $(x_1, 0)$ is assigned, the following clause is added:

$$\overline{x_5} \vee \overline{x_9}.$$

Since $\{(x_2, 1), (x_3, 1)\}$ is assigned, the following partial assignment is added:

$$\{(x_1, 0), (x_2, 1)\},$$

which are consistent with the current assignment. Since $(x_4, 0)$ is assigned, the following clause is added:

$$x_1 \vee \overline{x_3} \vee \overline{x_8} \vee x_9,$$

where it is further simplified to

$$\overline{x_8} \vee x_9,$$

because $\{(x_1, 0), (x_3, 1)\}$ has already been assigned. Finally, we solve the following instance of SAT:

$$(\overline{x_5} \vee \overline{x_9}) \wedge (\overline{x_8} \vee x_9).$$

For example, $\{(x_5, 1), (x_8, 0), (x_9, 0)\}$ is a solution for it, and thus $\{(x_1, 0), (x_2, 1), (x_3, 1), (x_4, 0), (x_5, 1), (x_6, 1), (x_7, 0), (x_8, 0), (x_9, 0)\}$ is a resulting singleton attractor.

Theorem 4.1. *Singleton Attractor Detection can be solved in* $O(1.792^n)$ *time for an AND/OR BN.*

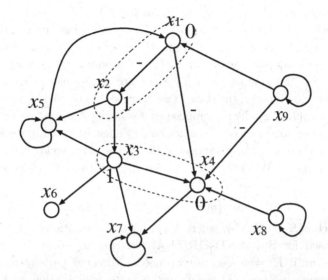

Fig. 4.1 BN used in Example 4.1. All nodes are AND nodes and arrows with '-' correspond to negative inputs.

Proof. Since the correctness of **SattAND-OR** is obvious from the above discussions, we only analyze the time complexity.

Let $K = |U|$ when there is no edge among $W = V \setminus U$ (excluding self loops). It means that the depth of the recursion is $K/2$. Since three assignments are examined at each recursive step, we have $3^{K/2}$ assignments in total, which is $O(1,733^K)$.

If all assignments on W are examined, the total computation time is

$$O^*(2^{n-K} \cdot 1.733^K).$$

Otherwise, the SAT algorithm is invoked. Since the number of generated clauses is at most K, the total computation time is

$$O^*(1.234^K \cdot 1.733^K).$$

By solving $1.234^K = 2^{n-K}$, we have $K = 0.767n$. Therefore, by letting $\alpha = 0.767$, the resulting time complexity is

$$O^*(1.234^{0.767n} \cdot 1.733^{0.767n}) \leq O(1.792^n).$$

$\square$

In the above, three assignments to a pair of nodes are examined at each recursive step. Let $g(K)$ be the number of assignments after K steps. Then,

$g(K)$ satisfies $g(K) \leq 3g(K-2)$, from which $g(K) \leq 3^{K/2}$ follows, where we assume $g(1) = 1$, and K is even. By applying another recursive procedure, the time complexity can be reduced. Here, we only present a basic idea using simple examples (see also Fig. 4.2). Suppose that $x_2 = x_1 \wedge x_4$ and $x_3 = x_2 \wedge x_5$. If 1 is assigned to x_2, the state of x_1 must be 1. Otherwise (i.e., 0 is assigned to x_2), the state of x_3 must be 0. This yields the recursion of $g(K) \leq 2g(K - 2)$. Next, suppose that $x_2 = x_1 \wedge x_4$ and $x_3 = \overline{x_2} \wedge x_5$. If 1 is assigned to x_2, the states of x_1 and x_3 must be 1 and 0, respectively. Otherwise, there is no propagation of the states. This yields the recursion of $g(K) \leq g(K - 3) + g(K - 1)$. By integrating these two inequality, we have:

$$g(K) \leq \max\{g(K - 3) + g(K - 1), 2g(K)\},$$

from which $g(K)$ is $O(\lambda^K)$, where $\lambda = 1.4656$, the solution to $\lambda^3 = \lambda^2 + 1$. As discussed for **SattAND-OR**$(U, \mathcal{A})$, we cannot repeat this recursive procedure until $K = n$ because we need a directed path of length two at each recursive step. Therefore, by using a combination with a SAT algorithm again, an $O(1.587^n)$ time algorithm was developed (Melkman *et al.*, 2010).

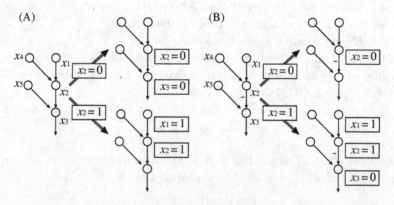

Fig. 4.2   Illustration of the basic idea for an $O(1.587^n)$ time algorithm for Singleton Attractor Detection. (A) and (B) correspond to cases of $x_3 = x_2 \wedge x_5$ and $x_3 = \overline{x_2} \wedge x_5$, respectively. Arrows with '-' correspond to negative inputs.

4.2   Singleton Attractor Detection for nc-BNs

As mentioned in Chapter 1, many biologically important functions are nested canalyzing ones. Therefore, it is reasonable to try to develop efficient algorithms for detection of a singleton attractor in a BN consisting of nested canalyzing functions. It might be possible to employ the same strategy as in Section 4.1: combination of a recursive procedure and a satisfiability algorithm. In order to emply this strategy, we need to develop an algorithm for deciding whether or not there exists a 0-1 assignment to variables that satisfies all given nested canalyzing functions. In this section, we present such a satisfiability algorithm for nested canalyzing functions and then combine it with a recursive procedure.

4.2.1 *Satisfiability for Nested Canalyzing Functions*

Before presenting the satisfiability algorithm, we need some definitions. Recall that a Boolean function is *nested canalyzing* over the variables $x_1, \ldots, x_k$ if it can be represented as

$$f_v = \ell_1 \vee \cdots \vee \ell_{k_1-1} \vee (\ell_{k_1} \wedge \cdots \wedge \ell_{k_2-1} \wedge (\ell_{k_2} \vee \cdots \vee \ell_{k_3-1} \vee (\cdots))),$$

where $\ell_i \in \{x_1, \overline{x_1}, x_2, \overline{x_2}, \ldots, \overline{x_n}\}$, and $1 \leq k_1 < k_2 < \cdots$. In the following, a nested canalyzing function is abbreviated as an *nc-function*, and a BN consisting of nc-functions is called an *nc-BN*. We will call the first clause in the above representation, $\ell_1 \vee \cdots \vee \ell_{k_1-1}$, the *initial clause* (IC) of the nc-function f. Note that if the initial clause is empty (i.e., $k_1 = 1$), all of $\ell_{k_1}, \ldots, \ell_{k_2-1}$ must take the value 1, which means that we can eliminate these literals. Therefore, we can assume w.l.o.g. that the initial clause is not empty. One of the characterizing properties of an nc-function is that its value is determined if any of the literals in the initial clause has value 1. Besides, recall that we can assume w.l.o.g. that an nc-function contains at most one appearance of any variable (see Section 1.1).

Definition 4.1. An *nc-SAT-formula* over the variables $x_1, \ldots, x_n$ is a collection F of m Boolean constraints f_i each of which is an nc-function. The *nc-SAT* problem is to determine whether there is an assignment to the variables that simultaneously satisfies all m nc-constraints, and if so to find one.

Example 4.2. The following is an instance of the nc-SAT problem.

$$f_1 = x \vee (y \wedge z \wedge u),$$
$$f_2 = \overline{x} \vee (\overline{y} \wedge (z \vee (u \wedge \overline{v}))),$$
$$f_3 = \overline{y} \vee z \vee (x \wedge (u \vee v)),$$
$$f_4 = \overline{u} \vee \overline{v} \vee (x \wedge y \wedge \overline{z}).$$

This instance can be satisfied by $x = 0, y = 1, z = 1, u = 1, v = 0$.

As described above, we recursively solve an instance of the nc-SAT problem with gradually constructing assignments. Recall that a partial assignment is represented by a set of literal and 0-1 value pairs. For example, $A = \{(x,1), (\overline{y},1), (\overline{z},0)\}$ means that 1, 0, and 1 are assigned to variables x, y, and z, respectively. We denote by $F[A]$ the formula resulting from the substitution of the partial assignment A in the formula F and its subsequent simplification.

The following is the pseudocode of the algorithm for the nc-SAT problem, which returns TRUE if the formula is satisfiable, and returns FALSE otherwise. It is straightforward to modify the algorithm so that one satisfying assignment is also returned if when the formula is satisfiable.

Procedure NC-SAT(F)
if F =TRUE **then return** TRUE
else if F =FALSE **then return** FALSE;
if there is $f_i = \ell_1 \vee (\ell_2 \wedge \cdots \wedge \ell_{k_2-1} \wedge (\ell_{k_2} \vee \cdots))$ and ℓ_1 appears negated in IC of another constraint **then (Case (1))**
  $A_0 = \{(\ell_1, 1)\}$; $A_1 = \{(\ell_1, 0), (\ell_2, 1), \ldots, (\ell_{k_2-1}, 1)\}$
else if there is a literal ℓ that appears in IC of at least two constraints, and that appears negated in IC of at least one constraint
then (Case (2)) $A_0 = \{(\ell, 0)\}$; $A_1 = \{(\ell, 1)\}$
else (Case (3)) return TRUE;
if NC-SAT$(F[A_0])$ =TRUE **then return** TRUE
else if NC-SAT$(F[A_1])$ =TRUE **then return** TRUE
else return FALSE.

In Case (3), it is guaranteed that there always exists a satisfying assignment, which can be found by procedure **NC-Bipartite**(F) shown below.

It is seen from the above procedure that when Case (3) is executed (i.e., when **NC-Bipartite**(F) is called), the initial clause of each constraint in F is of length 2 at least, and each variable that appears negated in one IC and non-negated in another IC appears in no other initial clause.

Procedure NC-Bipartite(F)
create a partial assignment A in which each literal that does not appear negated in any initial clause is set to 1;
let U and IC be the set of remaining unassigned variables and the set of remaining initial clauses;
construct a bipartite graph $G(U, IC, E)$ by letting

$E = \{(x, c) | x \text{ appears in } c\};$
find a maximum matching $M = \{(x_c, c) | c \in IC\}$ for $G(U, IC, E);$
for all $(x_c, c) \in M$ **do**
    if x_c appears non-negated in c **then** add $(x_c, 1)$ to A
    else add $(x_c, 0)$ to $A;$
assign 0 to the remaining variables;
return A.

Example 4.3. Consider an nc-SAT instance: $F = f_1 \wedge f_2 \wedge f_3 \wedge f_4 \wedge f_5$, with

$$f_1 = x \vee \overline{y} \vee (\overline{z} \wedge \overline{u}),$$
$$f_2 = y \vee \overline{z} \vee (\overline{x} \wedge (u \vee v)),$$
$$f_3 = x \vee w \vee (z \wedge (u \vee \overline{v})),$$
$$f_4 = u \vee v \vee (\overline{x} \wedge (y \vee z)),$$
$$f_5 = z \vee \overline{u} \vee \overline{v} \vee (x \wedge \overline{y}).$$

Since x does not appear negated in any initial clause, **NC-SAT**(F) first assigns $x = 1$. Next, it sets $IC = \{f_2, f_4, f_5\}$ and $U = \{y, z, u, v\}$, and constructs the bipartite graph. Then, a maximum matching for IC is obtained as shown in Fig. 4.3, which means that f_2, f_4, and f_5 are satisfied by $z = 0$, $u = 1$, and $v = 0$, respectively.

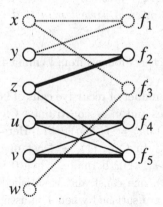

Fig. 4.3 Illustration of bipartite graph (normal and bold lines) and maximum matching (bold lines) for Example 4.3.

Here we show that **NC-Bipartite**(F) can always find a satisfying assignment when it is called by **NC-SAT**(F).

Lemma 4.1. *Suppose that the initial clause of each constraint in F is of length at least 2 and there is no literal that positively appears at least twice in the initial clauses and negatively appears at least once in the initial clauses of F. Then,* **NC-Bipartite**(F) *can always find a satisfying assignment in polynomial time.*

Proof. Note that creation of a partial assignment does not violate the condition of the lemma. Therefore, we only need to prove the correctness on the matching part.

It is obvious that if the matching of size $|IC|$ is found, F is satisfiable. To prove the existence of such a matching, we show that Hall's condition holds: for every $C' \subseteq IC$ the set of its neighbors $NB(C') = \{u|\ u$ is a neighbor of some $c \in C'\}$ has size no less than $|C'|$. By the assumption, each $c \in IC$ has length at least 2 and thus the total number of edges out of C' is no less than $2|C'|$. On the other hand, the total number of edges out of C' is at most $2|NB(C')|$ since each variable in $NB(C')$ appears in at most two initial clauses. Thus $|NB(C')| \geq |C'|$ holds for all $C' \subseteq IC$, which means that there exists a matching of size $|IC|$. Therefore, each initial clause is satisfied by a distinct variable. Since it is well-known that a maximum matching can be found in polynomial time, the lemma holds. □

Theorem 4.2. NC-SAT(F) *solves nc-SAT in $O^*(\min\{2^k, \mu^{k+m}, 2^m\})$ time, where k is the number of variables, m is the number of constraints, and $\mu = 1.325$.*

Proof. Since the correctness follows from Lemma 4.1. we analyze the time complexity.

Let $f(k, m)$ be the number of recursive calls of **NC-SAT** for an nc-SAT instance with k variables and m nc-constraints. Clearly, we have $f(k, 0) = f(k, 1) = f(k, 2) = f(1, m) = f(2, m) = 1$. Here we consider the three cases of the algorithm. In Case (1), at least one constraint is satisfied by assigning 0 or 1 to ℓ_1. Furthermore, when 0 is assigned, ℓ_2 must be assigned 1. In Case (2), one constraint is satisfied when 0 is assigned to ℓ, and two constraints are satisfied when 1 is assigned to ℓ. In Case (3), all constraints are handled in polynomial time. Therefore, we have the following recurrence inequalities for $f(k, m)$.

Case (1): $f(k, m) \leq f(k - 1, m - 1) + f(k - 2, m - 1)$, $k \geq 2$,
Case (2): $f(k, m) \leq f(k - 1, m - 1) + f(k - 1, m - 2)$, $m \geq 3$,
Case (3): $f(k, m) = 1$,

and thus we have

$$f(k, m) \leq \max\{f(k-1, m-2) + f(k-1, m-1), f(k-1, m-1) + f(k-2, m-1)\}.$$

From this inequality, we can see by induction that

$$f(k, m) \leq \min\{2^k, 2^m, \mu^{k+m}\}$$

holds for $\mu = 1.325$ because

$$f(k - 1, m - 2) + f(k - 1, m - 1) \leq \mu^{k+m}(\mu^{-3} + \mu^{-2})$$
$$\leq \mu^{k+m}$$

holds from $\mu^{-3} + \mu^{-2} \leq 1$, and similarly that

$$f(k - 1, m - 1) + f(k - 2, m - 1) \leq \mu^{k+m}$$

holds.

Since each recursive call need polynomial time, the theorem holds. $\quad\square$

4.2.2 *Singleton Attractor Detection for nc-BNs*

Here we present a recursive algorithm for attractor detection for nc-BNs.

First we introduce the concept of the canonical form of the nc-BN. An nc-BN is in *canonical form* if each nc-function contains at most one appearance of any variable, and has non-empty initial clause. It is to be noted that the first condition has already been justified in Section 1.1. The second condition is satisfied by replacing node x with a new node y and $f_x = \ell_1 \wedge \ldots \wedge \ell_k \wedge (\ell_{k+1} \vee \ldots)$ with $f_y = \overline{\ell_1} \vee \ldots \vee \overline{\ell_k} \vee (\overline{\ell_{k+1}} \wedge \ldots)$, and replacing all appearance of x with $\overline{y}$. Clearly, this can be done in polynomial time.

Suppose that u appears in the initial clause of f_v where $u \neq v$. Then, we consider the following two cases:

Case (1) 0 is assigned to u. Then, $\overline{f_u} = 1$ (i.e., $f_u = 0$) is added to the set of constraints and the incoming edges to u are deleted. If u appears negatively in f_v, 1 is assigned to v and the incoming edges to v are deleted.

Case (2) 1 is assigned to u. Then, $f_u = 1$ is added to the set of constraints and the incoming edges to u are deleted. If u appears positively in f_v, 1 is assigned to v and the incoming edges to v are deleted.

Otherwise, every node having incoming edge(s) must have a self loop. Let u be a node with a self loop and another incoming edge. Then, we consider the following two cases:

Case (3) u appears positively in the initial clause of f_u. We can assume $f_u = u \vee f'_u$, where f'_u does not include u. Then, $u \vee \overline{f'}_u$ is added to the set of constraints and the incoming edges to u are deleted.

Case (4) u appears negatively in the initial clause of f_u. Then, $f_u = 1$ is added to the set of constraints, the incoming edges to u are deleted, and 1 is assigned to u.

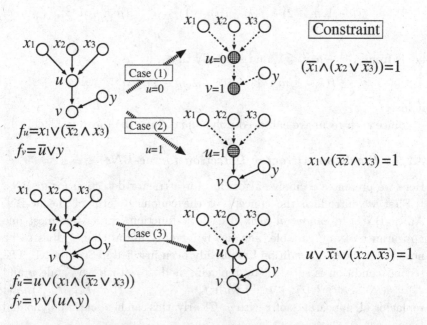

Fig. 4.4   Three cases for attractor detection for nc-BNs. Dotted arrows denote deleted edges, and gray circles mean that 0-1 values are assigned to these nodes.

The Cases (1)-(3) are illustrated in Fig. 4.4. The following presents the pseudo-code of the algorithm for detection of a singleton attractor for an nc-BN, where it is invoked as **SattNC**$(N(V,F), \emptyset)$ and Q is a parameter (depending on n) to be determined later.

Procedure SattNC(N, H)
if there is less than $n - Q$ variables **then**
    examine all 0-1 possible assignments to these variables;
    if there exists a singleton attractor **then return** TRUE
    else return FALSE;
if there is a node u appearing in the initial clause for another node v
then
    let $u = 0$; add $\overline{f_u} = 1$ to H; get the reduced network N_0;
    if SattNC(N_0, H) =TRUE **then return** TRUE;
    let $u = 1$; add $f_u = 1$ to H; get the reduced network N_1;
    if SattNC(N_1, H) =TRUE **then return** TRUE
else
    for all u with self loops **do**
        if u positively appears in the initial clause of f_u **then**
            add $u \vee f_u'$ to H
        else (i.e., u positively appears in the initial clause of f_u)
            let $u = 1$, add $f_u = 1$ to H;
if NC-SAT(H)=TRUE **then return** TRUE **else return** FALSE.

Since the correctness of the algorithm is almost obvious, we briefly analyze the time complexity. First note that if there exists a node u in the initial clause for another node v, two recursive calls are invoked: one with at most $n - 1$ variables and the other one with at most $n - 2$ variables. Let $G(q)$ be the number of recursive calls with q unassigned variables. Then, we have the following recurrence:

$$G(q) \leq G(q - 1) + G(q - 2).$$

From a well-known result on the Fibonnaci number, we have $G(q) < O(1.619^q)$. If the exhaustive search is executed at the first step, the time complexity is $O^*(2^{n-Q})$. If **NC-SAT**(H) is called where the number of the variables is R $(> n - Q)$, the time complexity is $O^*(\mu^{R+n})$ because Cases (3)-(4) add one constraint per variables. Suppose that all such calls are invoked when the number of the remaining variables is $n - Q$ (Assumption #1). Then, the total time complexity is bounded by

$$\min(O^*(2^{n-Q} \cdot 1.619^Q), O^*(\mu^{(n-Q)+n} \cdot 1.619^Q)).$$

By solving $2^{n-Q} = \mu^{2n-Q}$, we obtain $Q = 0.3172n$ and thus the time complexity is estimated as

$$O^*(2^{(1-0.3172)n} \cdot 1.619^{0.3172n}) \leq O(1.871^n).$$

However, Assumption #1 does not necessarily hold. By performing more details analysis [Melkman and Akutsu (2013)], we have the following.

Theorem 4.3. *Singleton Attractor Detection can be solved in $O(1.871^n)$ time for an nc-BN.*

4.3   Attractor Detection for nc-BNs with Bounded Treewidth

In the above, we have seen that Singleton Attractor Detection can be solved in $o(2^n)$ time for a BN consisting of nested canalyzing functions. Here, we show that the problem can be solved in polynomial time if a BN consists of nested canalyzing functions and it has a tree-like structure.

In Section 1.5, we reviewed the definition of treewidth. Recall that the *treewidth* is an integer number measuring how much a graph looks like a tree. It is known that many NP-hard problems can be solved in polynomial time by using dynamic programming if a graph has a fixed treewidth. In this section, we develop such a dynamic programming algorithm for Singleton Attractor Detection for an nc-BN with bounded treewidth.

The algorithm here is based on a simple but important observation on nc-functions. We explain it using an example. Let the nc-function associated with node x_5 be $f_5(\mathbf{x}) = x_1 \vee (x_2 \wedge \overline{x_3} \wedge (\overline{x_4} \vee x_5 \vee (x_6 \wedge (\overline{x_7} \vee x_8))))$. In order to satisfy $f_5(\mathbf{x}) = 1$, we need not consider 2^8 assignments. Instead, it is enough to consider the following partial assignments, where '*' means "don't care".

x_1	x_2	x_3	x_4	x_5	x_6	x_7	x_8
1	*	*	*	*	*	*	*
0	1	0	0	*	*	*	*
0	1	0	1	1	*	*	*
0	1	0	1	0	1	0	*
0	1	0	1	0	1	1	1

Observe that a singleton attractor satisfies the equation $f_5(\mathbf{x}) = x_5$, and that among the partial assignments satisfying $f_5(\mathbf{x}) = 1$ only the first three satisfy this equation. Similarly, in order to satisfy $f_5(\mathbf{x}) = 0$, it is enough to consider the following partial assignments.

x_1	x_2	x_3	x_4	x_5	x_6	x_7	x_8
0	0	*	*	*	*	*	*
0	1	1	*	*	*	*	*
0	1	0	0	1	0	*	*
0	1	0	0	1	1	1	0

To describe this result in general, we re-define a *partial assignment* as follows.

Definition.4.2. A *partial assignment* is any non-empty set $\phi = b_1 \times \cdots \times b_n$ such that $b_i \subseteq \{0,1\}$, where b_r, the rth component of ϕ is denoted by $(\phi)_r$. A complete assignment is a partial assignment ϕ in which b_i is a singleton for all i.

It should be noted that ϕ is an empty set if at least one b_i is an empty set. It is also noted that the intersection of two partial assignments ϕ, ψ is a partial assignment itself, unless it is empty (i.e., $((\phi)_r \cap (\psi)_r = \emptyset)$ in which case the partial assignments are said *disjoint*. Furthermore, we can see that the two assignments are disjoint if and only if there is a component $r \in \{1, \ldots, n\}$ such that $(\phi)_r \cap (\psi)_r = \emptyset$. If $(\phi)_r$ is a singleton set, $(\phi)_r$ may be identified with the Boolean value in the set. In order to relate partial assignments to singleton attractors, we introduce the concept of a *local fixed point* as below.

Definition 4.3. The partial assignment ϕ is a local fixed point at node x_i, with associated nc-function f_i, if the set $(\phi)_i$ is a singleton and $f_i(\mathbf{b}) = (\phi)_i$ holds for all $\mathbf{b} \in \phi$.

Then, a singleton attractor corresponds to a complete assignment that is a local fixed point at each node.

Example 4.4. Suppose that the following ϕ and ψ are given.

$$\phi = \{0,1\} \times \{1\} \times \{0,1\} = \{[0,1,0], [0,1,1], [1,1,0], [1,1,1]\},$$
$$\psi = \{1\} \times \{0,1\} \times \{0\} = \{[1,0,0], [1,1,0]\}.$$

Then, $(\phi)_1 = \{0,1\}$, $(\phi)_2 = \{1\}$, and $(\phi)_3 = \{0,1\}$ hold. Since $\phi \cap \psi = \{[1,1,0]\}$, ϕ and ψ are not disjoint. For $f_1 = x_2 \vee \overline{x_3}$, ψ is a local fixed point at x_1 with f_1, but ϕ is not.

Proposition 4.1. *Let f_i be an nc-function with m inputs. Then the set of all complete assignments that are local fixed points at node x_i can be* *partitioned into $m + 1 \leq n + 1$ disjoint partial assignments each of which is a local fixed point at node x_i.*

Proof. We prove it by induction on m. For the base case ($m = 1$), f_i is of the form x_k or $\overline{x_k}$. If $f_i = x_k$, the complete assignments that are a local fixed point at node x_i can be partitioned into two disjoint partial assignments: those with $x_i = x_k = 0$ and those with $x_i = x_k = 1$. Otherwise, the complete assignments can also be partitioned into two such assignments: those with $x_k = 1$ and $x_i = 0$ and those with $x_k = 0$ and $x_i = 1$.

For the induction step, we assume w.l.o.g. that f_i has one of the forms $x_1 \vee g$, $x_1 \wedge g$, $\overline{x_1} \vee g$, or $\overline{x_1} \wedge g$, where g is an nc-function with inputs $x_2, \ldots, x_m$. We only consider the case $f_i = x_1 \vee g$. Then in a complete assignment that is a local fixed point at node x_i either $x_1 = 1$, or $x_1 = 0$ and the assignment to the variables other than x_1 forms a local fixed point at node x_i of the function g. If $x_1 = 1$, only one partial assignment is needed. Otherwise (i.e., $x_1 = 0$), the number of partial assignments of $x_2, \ldots, x_m$ needed to cover all assignments to g is m by the induction hypothesis. Therefore, the the number of partial assignments of $x_1, \ldots, x_m$ needed to cover all assignments to f is $m + 1$. □

Hereafter, we will denote the partial assignments appearing in the statement of this proposition by $\phi_i^1, \ldots, \phi_i^{m_i+1}$.

Let $\mathcal{T}(\mathcal{V}_T, \mathcal{E}_T)$ be a tree decomposition with treewidth w for $G(V, E)$ associated with a given BN $N(V, F)$. As in many polynomial time algorithms for partial k-trees, we apply dynamic programming from the leaves to the root in $\mathcal{T}(\mathcal{V}_T, \mathcal{E}_T)$. The first step of the algorithm for finding a singleton attractor is to construct

$$\mathcal{A}_t^0 = \{ \bigcap_{x_i \in B_t} \phi_i^{j_i} \mid \bigcap_{x_i \in B_t} \phi_i^{j_i} \neq \emptyset \}$$

for each $t \in \mathcal{V}_T$. It is seen from Proposition 4.1 that $\mathcal{A}_t^0$ is a partition of the set of assignments that are local fixed points at all nodes in B_t. It is also seen that the size of $\mathcal{A}_t^0$ is at most $(m + 1)^{|B_t|}$. We will denote its elements by α_t^j, $j = 1, \ldots$. Note that $(\alpha_t^j)_i$ is a singleton for all $x_i \in B_y$, which is an important fact (Fact #1).

In order to describe a bottom-up process of the dynamic programming algorithm, we introduce the concepts of *compatible* and *refinement* as follows.

Definition 4.4. Two partial assignments ϕ and ψ are said to be *compatible* if $\phi \cap \psi \neq \emptyset$. A partial assignment ρ is a *refinement* of $\alpha \in \mathcal{A}_t^0$ if $\rho \subseteq \alpha$ and

ρ is a local fixed point at all nodes in B_s for all s in the subtree rooted at t.

In the bottom-up process, a set of disjoint partial assignments, $\mathcal{A}_t$, is computed for each node $t \in \mathcal{V_T}$. $\mathcal{A}_t$ is a set of local fixed points that are consistent with all nodes in $\cup_{t'} B_{t'}$, where t' is taken over t and all its descendants in $\mathcal{T}$. As we will see, this can be achieved by checking for each partial assignment in $\mathcal{A}_t^0$ that it is compatible with at least one partial assignment in $\mathcal{A}_{t_j}$, for all children t_j of t, and removing it if it does not pass this test. For a leaf node t, $\mathcal{A}_t = \mathcal{A}_t^0$ holds.

Example 4.5. Consider a BN defined by

$$f_1 = x_3, \quad f_2 = x_1 \vee x_5, \quad f_3 = \overline{x_2} \vee \overline{x_4}, \quad f_4 = \overline{x_3}, \quad f_5 = \overline{x_3},$$

and its tree decomposition shown in Fig. 4.5.

The following shows partitions of partial assignments that are local fixed points for each node:

$$\phi_1^1 = \langle \{1\}, \{0,1\}, \{1\}, \{0,1\}, \{0,1\} \rangle,$$
$$\phi_1^2 = \langle \{0\}, \{0,1\}, \{0\}, \{0,1\}, \{0,1\} \rangle,$$
$$\phi_2^1 = \langle \{1\}, \{1\}, \{0,1\}, \{0,1\}, \{0,1\} \rangle,$$
$$\phi_2^2 = \langle \{0\}, \{1\}, \{0,1\}, \{0,1\}, \{1\} \rangle,$$
$$\phi_2^3 = \langle \{0\}, \{0\}, \{0,1\}, \{0,1\}, \{0\} \rangle,$$
$$\phi_3^1 = \langle \{0,1\}, \{0\}, \{1\}, \{0,1\}, \{0,1\} \rangle,$$
$$\phi_3^2 = \langle \{0,1\}, \{1\}, \{1\}, \{0\}, \{0,1\} \rangle,$$
$$\phi_3^3 = \langle \{0,1\}, \{1\}, \{0\}, \{1\}, \{0,1\} \rangle,$$
$$\phi_4^1 = \langle \{0,1\}, \{0,1\}, \{0\}, \{1\}, \{0,1\} \rangle,$$
$$\phi_4^2 = \langle \{0,1\}, \{0,1\}, \{1\}, \{0\}, \{0,1\} \rangle.$$
$$\phi_5^1 = \langle \{0,1\}, \{0,1\}, \{0\}, \{0,1\}, \{1\} \rangle,$$
$$\phi_5^2 = \langle \{0,1\}, \{0,1\}, \{1\}, \{0,1\}, \{0\} \rangle.$$

Then, we have $\mathcal{A}_{t_A}^0 = \{\alpha_{t_A}^i | \ i = 1,2\}$, $\mathcal{A}_{t_B}^0 = \{\alpha_{t_B}^i | \ i = 1,2,3,4\}$, and $\mathcal{A}_{t_C}^0 = \{\alpha_{t_C}^i | \ i = 1,2,3\}$ with

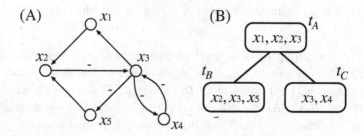

Fig. 4.5 (A) BN and (B) tree decomposition used in Example 4.5. Arrows with '-' correspond to negative inputs.

$$\alpha^1_{t_A} = \langle \{1\}, \{1\}, \{1\}, \{0\}, \{0,1\} \rangle,$$
$$\alpha^2_{t_A} = \langle \{0\}, \{1\}, \{0\}, \{1\}, \{1\} \rangle,$$
$$\alpha^1_{t_B} = \langle \{1\}, \{1\}, \{1\}, \{0\}, \{0\} \rangle,$$
$$\alpha^2_{t_B} = \langle \{0\}, \{1\}, \{0\}, \{1\}, \{1\} \rangle,$$
$$\alpha^3_{t_B} = \langle \{1\}, \{1\}, \{0\}, \{1\}, \{1\} \rangle,$$
$$\alpha^4_{t_B} = \langle \{0\}, \{0\}, \{1\}, \{0,1\}, \{0\} \rangle,$$
$$\alpha^1_{t_C} = \langle \{0,1\}, \{0\}, \{1\}, \{0\}, \{0,1\} \rangle,$$
$$\alpha^2_{t_C} = \langle \{0,1\}, \{1\}, \{1\}, \{0\}, \{0,1\} \rangle,$$
$$\alpha^3_{t_C} = \langle \{0,1\}, \{1\}, \{0\}, \{1\}, \{0,1\} \rangle.$$

Note that $\alpha^1_{t_A}$ is compatible only with $\alpha^1_{t_B}$ and $\alpha^2_{t_C}$, $\alpha^2_{t_A}$ is compatible only with $\alpha^2_{t_B}$ and $\alpha^3_{t_C}$. and $\alpha^1_{t_B}$ is a refinement of $\alpha^1_{t_A}$.

Procedure SattKtree$(N(V, F))$
let $\mathcal{T}(\mathcal{V}_\mathcal{T}, \mathcal{E}_\mathcal{T})$ be a tree decomposition of $G(V, E)$;
for all $t \in \mathcal{V}_\mathcal{T}$ **do** $\mathcal{A}^0_t \leftarrow \{ \bigcap_{x_i \in B_t} \phi^{j_i}_i \mid \bigcap_{x_i \in B_t} \phi^{j_i}_i \neq \emptyset \}$;
for all non-leaf nodes $t \in \mathcal{V}_\mathcal{T}$ **do** /* bottom-up manner */
    let $\mathcal{A}_t \leftarrow \{ \alpha^j_t \in \mathcal{A}^0_t \mid (\forall t_i \in \{t_1, \dots, t_d\}) \exists \alpha^k_{t_i} \in \mathcal{A}_{t_i})(\alpha^j_t \cap \alpha^k_{t_i} \neq \emptyset) \}$,
        where $t_1, t_2, \dots, t_d$ are the children of t;
if $\mathcal{A}_r \neq \emptyset$ for the root r of $\mathcal{T}$ **then return** TRUE
else return FALSE.

If it is found in the above procedure that $\alpha^j_t \in \mathcal{A}_t$ holds from $\alpha^j_t \cap \alpha^{j_i}_{t_i} \neq \emptyset, i = 1, \dots, d$, then a refinement, ρ^j_t, associated with α^j_t can be computed as $\rho_t^j = \alpha_t^j \cap \left(\cap_{i=1}^d \rho_{t_i}^{j_i} \right)$, where $\rho_{t_i}^{j_i}$ is the refinement associated with $\alpha_{t_i}^{j_i}$. Furthermore, it is seen from Fact #1 that $(\rho_t^j)_h$ be a singleton for any $x_h \in \bigcup_{t' \in \mathcal{T}_t} B_{t'}$, where $\mathcal{T}_t$ is the subtree of $\mathcal{T}$ induced by t and its descendants. Therefore, if the procedure returns TRUE, a singleton attractor can be obtained as ρ_r associated with any $\alpha_r \in \mathcal{A}_r$, by the traceback procedure.

Theorem 4.4. *Singleton Attractor Detection can be solved in $O^*(n^{2(w+1)})$ time for an nc-BN with bounded treewidth w.*

Proof. First we prove the correctness. Suppose that there exists a singleton attractor. Then, it is a refinement of some partial assignment in $\mathcal{A}_t^0$ for all $t \in \mathcal{V}_\mathcal{T}$, and it is clearly compatible with an assignment in every child of t. Therefore, $\mathcal{A}_r$ is not empty. Conversely, suppose that $\mathcal{A}_r$ is not empty. Then, a singleton attractor can be obtained as a refinement ρ_r associated with any $\alpha_r \in \mathcal{A}_r$. It is seen by the following facts: (i) for any $t \in \mathcal{T}$ and its children t_i and t_h such that $t_i \neq t_h$, $\alpha_{t_i}^k$ and $\alpha_{t_h}^l$ are compatible if α_t^j is compatible with both $\alpha_{t_i}^k$ and $\alpha_{t_h}^l$ because $(\alpha_{t_i}^k)_q$ is a singleton for any $x_q \in B_t$, and there is no edge in the network between a node in $B_{t_i} \cap (V - B_t)$ and a node in $B_{t_j} \cap (V - B_t)$, (ii) for any $t \in \mathcal{T}$ and its child t_i and its parent t_h, $\alpha_{t_i}^k$ and $\alpha_{t_h}^l$ are compatible if α_t^j is compatible with both $\alpha_{t_i}^k$ and $\alpha_{t_h}^l$ by the similar reason.

Next we analyze the time complexity. Since there exist at most $n+1$ partial assignments per node and each B_t consists of at most $w+1$ nodes, we need to check $O((n+1)^{w+1}) = O(n^{w+1})$ combinations of partial assignments per $t \in \mathcal{V}_\mathcal{T}$. Since the intersection of two partial assignments can be computed in $O(n)$ time, the consistency of each combination, $\cap_{i \in B_t} \phi_i^{j_i}$, can be tested in $O(wn)$ time. Therefore, for each leaf $t \in \mathcal{V}_\mathcal{T}$, it takes $O^*(n^{w+1})$ time to construct $\mathcal{A}_t^0$.

For each non-leaf node $t \in \mathcal{V}_\mathcal{T}$, we examine the compatibility for $O(n^{w+1} \times n^{w+1} \times h)$ pairs of partial assignments, where h is the number of children of t. Since the compatibility between two partial assignments can be tested in $O(wn)$ time and the total number of children is $O(n)$, $O^*(n^{2(w+1)})$ time is required to construct $\mathcal{A}_t$s for all non-leaf nodes. Since it is known that tree decomposition of a graph with n nodes can be computed in linear time for fixed w [Flum and Grohe (2006)], the total time complexity is $O^*(n^{2(w+1)})$. $\square$

4.4   Additional Remarks and Bibliographical Notes

Section 4.1 is based on [Tamura and Akutsu (2009)]. As briefly explained in that section, an improved $O(1.587^n)$ time algorithm was developed [Melkman *et al.* (2010)]. Section 4.2 is based on [Melkman and Akutsu (2013)]. Section 4.3 is based on [Akutsu *et al.* (2012a)], in which another algorithm using a reduction to a *constraint satisfaction problem* for graphs of bounded treewidth [Freuder (1990)] is shown for the same problem. **SattKtree** was improved for AND/OR BNs and a special case of nc-BNs [Chang *et al.* (2015)].

Chapter 5

Detection of Periodic Attractors

In Chapter 4, we have seen several algorithms for Singleton Attractor Detection with special classes of BNs. It is reasonable to try to extend the techniques in those algorithms to Periodic Attractor Detection. However, it is quite difficult to develop $o(2^n)$ time algorithms for Periodic Attractor Detection with long periods. Although we have not given a formal proof, it seems that (the decision problem version of) detection of a long periodic attractor is PSPACE-complete because the reachability problem on BNs is known to be PSPACE-complete [Barrett *et al.* (2006)]. Therefore, we focus on Periodic Attractor Detection with short periods in this chapter.

5.1 Reduction to Singleton Attractor Detection

A simple way to design an algorithm for Periodic Attractor Detection is to reduce it to Singleton Attractor Detection. In this section, we describe a simple transformation method, Although it does not give $o(2^n)$ time algorithms if it is simply combined with existing algorithms for Singleton Attractor Detection, it gives a foundation to design $o(2^n)$ time algorithms for special but non-trivial cases of Periodic Attractor Detection.

We construct from a given BN $N(V, F)$ a *p-multiplied network* $N^p(V^p, F^p)$ by

$$V^p = \{x_i(1), x_i(2), \cdots, x_i(p) \mid x_i \in V\},$$
$$F^p = \{f_{i(1)}(x_{i_1}(p), \ldots, x_{i_{k_i}}(p)),$$
$$f_{i(2)}(x_{i_1}(1), \ldots, x_{i_{k_i}}(1)), \cdots,$$
$$f_{i(p)}(x_{i_1}(p-1), \ldots, x_{i_k}(p-1))$$
$$\mid f_i(x_{i_1}, \ldots, x_{i_{k_i}}) \in F \text{ and } f_{i(t)} \cong f_i\},$$

where each $x_i(t)$ is regarded as a node (see also Fig. 5.1). Note that $f_{i(t)} \cong$

63

f_i means that $f_{i(t)}$ is the same Boolean functions as f_i except that input variables are different (i.e., $x_{i_j}(t)$s are used instead of x_{i_j}s). Note also that $t = 1, \ldots, p$ is used here for the simplicity of presentation although $t = 0, \ldots, p - 1$ was used in the definition of a periodic attractor. It is straightforward to see that a singleton attractor of $N^p(V^p, F^p)$ corresponds to an attractor of $N(V, F)$ with period q that divides p.

In order to guarantee that a singleton attractor of $N^p(V^p, F^p)$ corresponds to a periodic attractor of $N(V, F)$ with period p, the following constraint (Constraint (#)) must be satisfied:

for all $q = 2, \ldots, p$, $x_i(1) \neq x_i(q)$ holds for some $x_i \in V$.

It means that the state of $N(V, F)$ at time $t = 1$ must be different from the states of $N(V, F)$ at time $t = 2, \ldots, p$. It is to be noted that once Constraint (#) is satisfied, the state of $N(V, F)$ at time $t = q_1$ is different from the state of $N(V, F)$ at time $t = q_2$ for any (q_1, q_2) such that $1 \leq q_1 < q_2 \leq p$.

(A) $G(V,E)$ (B) $G^2(V^2,E^2)$

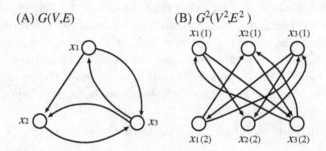

Fig. 5.1 Graphs corresponding to (A) $N(V, F)$ given in Example 2.1 and (B) $N^2(V^2, F^2)$.

Let $\phi(t)$ be a function from $\{2, \ldots, p\}$ to $\{1, \ldots, n\}$, and let $\psi(t)$ be a function from $\{2, \ldots, p\}$ to $\{0, 1\}$. Then, the existence of a singleton attractor of $N^p(V^p, F^p)$ satisfying Constraint (#) (i.e., the existence of an attractor of $N(V, F)$ with period p) can be decided by the following procedure.

Procedure SimplePeriodic$(N(V, F), p)$
for all functions ϕ from $\{2, \ldots, p\}$ to $\{1, \ldots, n\}$ **do**
   for all functions ψ from $\{2, \ldots, p\}$ to $\{0, 1\}$ **do**
      if there exists a singleton attractor of $N^p(V^p, F^p)$ such that
         $x_{\phi(t)}(1) = \psi(t)$ and $x_{\phi(t)}(t) = 1 - \psi(t)$ holds for all $t = 2, \ldots, p$
      then return TRUE;
return FALSE.

Since the number of possible ϕs is n^{p-1} and the number of possible ψs is 2^{p-1}, we need to execute singleton attractor detection for $(2n)^{p-1}$ times. Since it is still a polynomial of n for fixed p, we have the following.

Proposition 5.1. *The p-periodic attractor detection problem can be solved in $O^*((1 + \delta)^{pn})$ time if the singleton attractor detection problem with constraints can be solved in $O((1+\delta)^n)$ time where p and δ are constants.*

Note that most singleton attractor detection algorithms can cope with constraints given in **SimplePeriodic**. As mentioned in Chapter 4, the fastest known algorithm for singleton attractor detection for an AND/OR BN is $O(1.587^n)$ time one, which can cope with the above mentioned constraints. If Proposition 5.1 with $p = 2$ were applied to this algorithm, an $O^*(1.587^{2n})$ time algorithm would be obtained. However, it is not an $o(2^n)$ algorithm because $1.587^2 \approx 2.519$.

Example 5.1. Consider the BN given in Example 2.1, which is defined as below (see also Fig. 5.1(A)).

$$x_1(t+1) = x_3(t),$$
$$x_2(t+1) = x_1(t) \wedge \overline{x_3(t)},$$
$$x_3(t+1) = x_1(t) \wedge \overline{x_2(t)}.$$

Then, $N^2(V^2, F^2)$ is defined by $V^2 = \{x_1(1), x_2(1), x_3(1), x_1(2), x_2(2), x_3(2)\}$ and F^2 that is a set of following Boolean functions (see also Fig. 5.1(B)):

$$x_1(1) = x_3(2),$$
$$x_2(1) = x_1(2) \wedge \overline{x_3(2)},$$
$$x_3(1) = x_1(2) \wedge \overline{x_2(2)}.$$
$$x_1(2) = x_3(1),$$
$$x_2(2) = x_1(1) \wedge \overline{x_3(1)},$$
$$x_3(2) = x_1(1) \wedge \overline{x_2(1)}.$$

Note that we only consider singleton attractors in $N^2(V^2, F^2)$ and thus time steps are not taken into account. This $N^2(V^2, F^2)$ has the following set of singleton attractors

$$\{[0,0,0,0,0,0], [1,0,1,1,0,1], [0,1,1,1,0,0], [1,0,0,0,1,1]\}.$$

The first and second elements correspond to singleton attractors $[0,0,0]$ and $[1,0,1]$ of $N(V,F)$, respectively, whereas each of $[0,1,1,1,0,0]$ and

$[1, 0, 0, 0, 1, 1]$ corresponds to a periodic attractor $\{[0, 1, 1], [1, 0, 0]\}$ of $N(V, F)$. Note that each of the third and forth elements satisfies Constraint (#) (e.g., $x_1(1) \neq x_1(2)$). Therefore, there exists an attractor of period 2 in $V(N, F)$.

5.2   2-Periodic Attractor Detection for AND/OR BNs

In this section, we describe an $O(1.985^n)$ time algorithm for detection of a 2-periodic attractor in an AND/OR BN. The basic strategy is to find a singleton attractor in $N^2(V^2, F^2)$ with $2n$ nodes.

First we see a simple property on $N^2(V^2, F^2)$. From the construction, there exist directed edges only from $x_i(1)$ to $x_j(2)$ and from $x_i(2)$ to $x_j(1)$. Therefore, $N^2(V^2, F^2)$ is a bipartite graph without self-loops (even if $N(V, F)$ has self-loops). Furthermore, a set of nodes in $N^2(V^2, F^2)$ is partitioned into V_1^2 and V_2^2, where V_1^2 and V_2^2 are the sets of nodes corresponding to $t = 1$ and $t = 2$, respectively.

Next we show that singleton attractor detection for an AND/OR BN can be transformed into singleton attractor detection for an OR BN. Let $N(V, F)$ be an AND/OR BN. Let x_i be an AND node with a function:

$$x_i(t + 1) = \ell_{i_1} \wedge \cdots \wedge \ell_{i_k}.$$

Then, we replace it to

$$x_i(t + 1) = \overline{\ell_{i_1}} \vee \cdots \vee \overline{\ell_{i_k}}$$

and negate all occurrences of $x_i(t + 1)$ in f_j for all $x_j \in V$. We apply this transformation procedure to all AND nodes. Then, it is obvious that there is one-to-one correspondence between singleton attractors in $N(V, F)$ and those in the transformed network by negating 0-1 assignment to all AND nodes.

Therefore, we assume w.l.o.g. until the end of this section that $N^2(V^2, F^2)$ is an OR BN. Accordingly, each edge in $N^2(V^2, F^2)$ is given a sign $+/-$ depending on whether the corresponding input variable appears positively/negatively.

The basic strategy for detection of a singleton attractor in $N^2(V^2, F^2)$ is similar to that of the $O(1.587^n)$ time algorithm shown in Chapter 4: we recursively examine 0-1 assignments on nodes and finally apply a SAT algorithm. However, we make use of special properties on $N^2(V^2, F^2)$. Let $U(x)$ denote the number of unassigned neighboring nodes of x. The following is a high-level description of the algorithm, where H is a parameter to be determined later.

Procedure P2attAND-OR($N(V, F)$)

(1) Construct $N^2(V^2, F^2)$. Let all nodes be unassigned.
(2) Recursively examine 0-1 assignments on unassigned nodes x with $U(x) \geq 3$ until there does not exist such a node or the number of assigned nodes is more than H.
(3) Let A be the set of assigned nodes. Let $A_1 = A \cap V_1^2$ and $A_2 = A \cap V_2^2$. (We assume w.l.o.g. that $|A_1| \geq |A_2|$.)
(4) If $|A| > H$, then examine all possible assignments on $V_1 \setminus A_1$.
(5) Otherwise, recursively examine assignments on paths and cycles and then solve SAT.

In this procedure, we propagate the assignment whenever a new assignment to a node is given, where "propagate" means that we assign Boolean values to a set of nodes to which an assignment is determined uniquely from the current partial assignment.

We explain the details of each step. We begin with STEP 2 since STEP 1 is trivial. Consider a node x shown in Fig. 5.2 (A). If we assign 0 to x, in order to have a singleton attractor, assignments on two input nodes are uniquely determined and two additional constraints will be generated. Otherwise (i.e., we assign 1 to x), one assignment is given and one additional constraint will be generated. As in the algorithm in Section 4.1, these constraints are given as clauses. Next, consider a node x shown in Fig. 5.2 (B). If we assign 0 to x, assignments on all three neighboring nodes are uniquely determined and two additional constraints will be generated. Otherwise, no additional assignment is given but one additional constraint will be generated. The algorithm keeps all generated clauses until the final stage (STEP 4 or STEP 5).

By considering all cases on $U(x) \geq 3$, we can see that either one of the following holds:

- At least three nodes are assigned in one case and at least two nodes are assigned in the other case,
- At least four nodes are assigned in one case and at least one node is assigned in the other case.

We can also see that the number of newly generated constraints is at most k if k nodes are newly assigned.

Let $f(k)$ denote the maximum number of cases generated by recursive execution of STEP 2 under a condition that at most k nodes are assigned

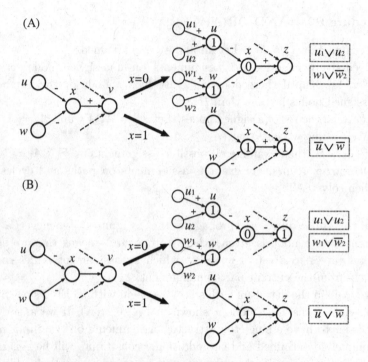

Fig. 5.2 Two cases of elimination of an unassigned node with three unassigned neighbors. Dotted boxes represent generated constraints. Arrows with '+' and '-' correspond to positive and negative inputs, respectively.

(per case). Then, we have

$$f(k) \leq \max \begin{cases} f(k-2) + f(k-3), \\ f(k-1) + f(k-4). \end{cases}$$

As in Section 4.2, by solving the equations of $x^3 = x+1$ and $x^4 = x^3 + 1$ and taking the larger solution, we have $f(k) = O(1.381^k)$. Since the number of assigned nodes until STEP 4 is bounded by H, we can bound the number of executions of STEP 4 and STEP 5.

Proposition 5.2. *The number of times that STEP 4 (resp., STEP 5) is executed is* $O(1.381^H)$.

In STEP 4, it is enough to examine all possible assignments to non-assigned nodes and check whether all constraints are satisfied. Since the number of such assignments is $O(2^{n-(H/2)})$ and testing all constraints can trivially be done in polynomial time, we have

Proposition 5.3. *STEP 4 works in* $O^*(2^{n-(H/2)})$ *time per execution.*

If STEP 5 is executed, there does not exist a node x with $U(x) \geq 3$. Furthermore, there does not exist a node with indegree 0.

Proposition 5.4. *Before STEP 5 is executed, the graph induced by non-assigned nodes is a set of paths and cycles (with bidirectional edges) in which every node has indegree greater than 0.*

Here we describe the procedure to eliminate paths and cycles by dividing it into several subcases, where the complexity is summarized in Tab. 5.1.

Table 5.1 Complexity for Subcases of **P2attAND-OR**.

type of path	#assignments	#clauses	complexity
(a1)	2	0	$f(k-2) + f(k-3)$
(a2)	1	1	$1.234 \cdot f(k-1)$
(b1)	0	0	$f(k-2)$
(b2)	2	0	$2 \cdot f(k-3)$
(b3)	2	0	$2 \cdot f(k-4)$
(b4)	2	1	$1.234 \cdot f(k-3)$ $+ f(k-4)$
(c1)	2	0	$2 \cdot f(k-4)$
(c2)	5	0	$5 \cdot f(k-6)$
(c3)	4	0	$f(k-3) + f(k-5)$ $+2 \cdot f(k-6)$
(d1)	2	0	$f(k-2) + f(k-3)$
(d2)	2	0	$f(k-2) + f(k-3)$

#clauses denotes the maximum number of added clauses.

First, we consider the following two cases (Fig. 5.3).

(a1) there is a bidirectional edge (u, v) whose signs are $(+,+)$ and there is a unidirectional edge from w to v.

It is enough to examine $u = v = 0$ and $u = v = 1$ because other assignments do not lead to a singleton attractor. Furthermore, w is uniquely determined when $u = v = 0$.

(a2) there is a bidirectional edge (u, v) whose signs are $(+, -)$.

$v = 1$ must hold because otherwise u becomes 1 which makes $v = 1$. In addition, one clause is generated as a constraint. For example, if (w, v) is $(+,+)$, $u = 1$ or $w = 1$ must hold in order to satisfy $v = 1$, and thus a clause $u \lor w$ is generated.

Let $f(k)$ be the exponential factor of the time complexity for k nodes. Then, we have the following recurrence on $f(k)$

$$f(k) \leq \max \begin{cases} f(k-2) + f(k-3), \\ 1.234 \cdot f(k-1), \end{cases}$$

where the factor of 1.234 comes from the fact that SAT with k clauses can be solved in $O^*(1.234^k)$ time [Yamamoto (2005)]. Then, $f(k) = O^*(1.234^k)$ follows from this recurrence.

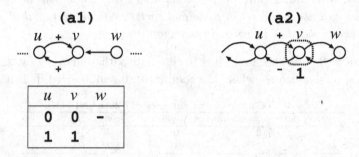

Fig. 5.3   Two types of basic elimination. Each bidirectional edge is represented by two directed edges. '-' in the table for (a1) means that the value of w is uniquely determined.

Suppose that there is no edge of type (a1) or (a2). Then, all bidirectional edges in any connected component have type $(-, -)$ except a path of length one. For elimination of paths, we consider the following four cases (Fig. 5.4).

(b1) path of length 1.

This path must be a bidirectional edge because every node has indegree more than 0. Then, the edge must have type $(+, +)$ or $(-, -)$ in order to have a stable state. In the case of $(+, +)$, $u = v$ must hold. Otherwise, $u = \overline{v}$ must hold. In both cases u can be substituted by v or $\overline{v}$, and v becomes a free variable.

(b2) path of length 2.

There exist at most 2 possible assignments on three nodes, and no constraint is generated. The states of u and w are uniquely determined from that of v, which means that 3 nodes are eliminated.

(b3) path of length 3.

There exist at most 2 possible assignments on four nodes, and no constraint is generated. The states of u, w, z are uniquely determined from that of v, which means that 4 nodes are eliminated.

(b4) path of length more than 4.

For example, suppose that all edges are bidirectional (and thus of type $(-, -)$). Let z be an endpoint from which u, v, and w follow. If $v = 0$ is assigned, $u = w = 1$ and $z = 0$ hold and thus 4 nodes are eliminated. Otherwise, a clause of $\overline{u} \vee \overline{w}$ is added and the value of z is uniquely determined from the value of u (i.e., $z = \overline{u}$), which means that three nodes are eliminated and one clause is added. The other cases can be handled within the same complexity.

Consequently, we have the following recurrence on $f(k)$

$$f(k) \leq \max \begin{cases} f(k-2), \\ 2 \cdot f(k-3), \\ 2 \cdot f(k-4), \\ 1.234 \cdot f(k-3) + f(k-4), \end{cases}$$

from which $f(k) = O(1.266^k)$ follows. Therefore, the time complexity of eliminating paths with a total of k nodes is $O(1.266^k)$.

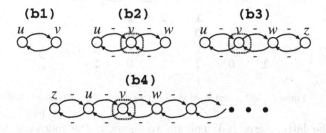

Fig. 5.4   Four types of fragments in elimination of paths.

Elimination of cycles is partitioned into two cases: cycles consisting of bidirectional edges and cycles containing unidirectional edges. For the former one, it is enough to consider the following three cases (Fig. 5.5) since the graph is bipartite and thus there is no odd cycle.

(c1) cycle of length 4.

There exist two possible assignments on four nodes.

(c2) cycle of length 6.

There exist five possible assignments on six nodes.

(c3) cycle of length 8 or more.

We transform the cycle into a path by selecting a set of consecutive nodes as shown in Fig. 5.5 (c3).

Consequently, we have the following recurrence on $f(k)$

$$f(k) \leq \max \begin{cases} 2 \cdot f(k-4), \\ 5 \cdot f(k-6), \\ f(k-3) + f(k-5) + 2 \cdot f(k-6), \end{cases}$$

from which $f(k) = O(1.338^k)$ follows.

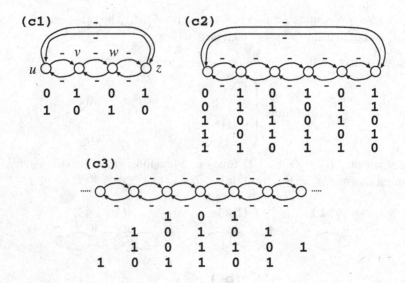

Fig. 5.5   Three cases for elimination of cycles consisting of bidirectional edges.

For the latter case, it is enough to consider the following two cases (Fig. 5.6) since there is no node with indegree 0.

(d1) two consecutive unidirectional edges.

Suppose that both edges are of type '-'. Then, there are two consisting assignments: one eliminates two variables and the other eliminates three variables. The other cases can be treated analogously.

(d1) one unidirectional edge outgoing from a bidirectional edge.

Suppose that all edges are of type '-'. Then, there are two consisting assignments: one eliminates two variables and the other eliminates three variables. The other cases can be treated analogously.

Consequently, we have the following recurrence on $f(k)$

$$f(k) \leq f(k-2) + f(k-3),$$

from which $f(k) = O(1.338^k)$ follows.

Putting all cases together, we have:

Lemma 5.1. *STEP 5 works in* $O(1.338^{2n})$ *time per execution.*

Finally, in order to guarantee that a singleton attractor of $N^2(V^2, F^2)$ corresponds to a periodic attractor of $N(V, F)$ of period p, the following constraint must be satisfied: $x_i(1) \neq x_i(2)$ holds for some $x_i \in V$. In order

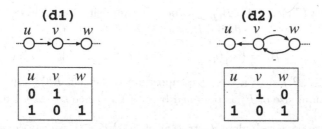

Fig. 5.6 Two types of fragments for elimination of cycles containing unidirectional edges.

to guarantee this constraint, it is enough to solve the singleton attractor detection problem for $N^2(V^2, F^2)$ under $2n$ different constraints; $(x_i(1) = 0, x_i(2) = 1)$ and $(x_i(1) = 1, x_i(2) = 0)$ for each $x_i \in V$. Since it is straightforward to cope with this constraint without increasing the order of the time complexity and it is enough to examine singleton attractor detection for $2n$ time, we have the following.

Theorem 5.1. *The problem of detection of a 2-periodic attractor of an AND/OR BN can be solved in $O(1.985^n)$ time.*

Proof. The correctness follows from the discussion above, Therefore, we analyze the total complexity. Since the number of times that each of STEP 4 and STEP 5 is executed is $O(1.381^H)$, the total time complexity is

$$O(1.381^H) \cdot \left[O^*(2^{n-(H/2)}) + O(1.338^{2n}) \right]$$

from Proposition. 5.3 and Lemma 5.1. The base of the exponential factor is minimized when $H = 0.3196n$, from which the total complexity of $O(1.985^n)$ follows. □

5.3 Periodic Attractor Detection for nc-BNs

We can extend **SattKtree** in Section 4.3 for p-periodic attractor detection for an nc-BN with bounded treewidth by making use of $N^p(V^p, F^p)$.

First, we note that a tree-decomposition of $N^p(V^p, F^p)$ can be obtained from that of $N(V, F)$.

Proposition 5.5. *If the graph $G(V, E)$ associated with $N(V, F)$ has treewidth w, then the graph $G^p(V^p, E^p)$ associated with $N^p(V^p, F^p)$ has a decomposition whose treewidth is less than $p(w + 1)$, and is such that for each $x \in V$ all $x(1), \cdots, x(p)$ are included in the same bag.*

Proof. Let $\langle \mathcal{T}(\mathcal{V}_\mathcal{T}, \mathcal{E}_\mathcal{T}), (B_t)_{t \in \mathcal{V}_\mathcal{T}} \rangle$ be a decomposition of $G(V, E)$. For each $B_t = \{x_{i_1}, \ldots, x_{i_k}\}$, we define B_t^p for $G^p(V^p, E^p)$ by

$$B_t^p = \{x_{i_1}(q), \ldots, x_{i_k}(q) \mid q = 1, \ldots, p\}.$$

Then, these B_t^ps give a tree decomposition of $G^p(V^p, E^p)$. Furthermore, the maximum size of B_t^p is bounded by $p(w+1)$ since $k \leq w+1$ holds. $\square$

Once we have a singleton attractor of $N^p(V^p, F^p)$, we can construct an attractor of $N(V, F)$. However, its period is not necessarily p. We can only say that its period divides p. Therefore, we need to modify the algorithm for singleton attractor detection so that it is ensured that the corresponding attractor for $N(V, F)$ has exactly period p.

Algorithm **SattKtree** can be modified so as to generate all possible singleton attractors. Therefore, we can find a p-periodic attractor by checking each of singleton attractors for $N^p(V^p, F^p)$ whether its period as an attractor in $N(V, F)$ is exactly p. However, this approach does not lead to an efficient algorithm since the number of singleton attractors for $N^p(V^p, F^p)$ may be too large. In order to ensure that the constraint on the period is satisfied, it is sufficient to know that for each i, $2 \leq i \leq p$, there is some node x in the network such that its values in the attractor satisfy $x(i) \neq x(1)$. To this end, we employ a table representing a set of available periodicity patterns, where each pattern is a 0-1 bit vector in which 1 at position i corresponds to $x(i) \neq x(1)$ for some $x \in V$.

Definition 5.1. The partial assignment $\alpha \in \mathcal{A}_t$ is *consistent* with the 0-1 vector $T[2 \ldots p]$ if there is a refinement ρ of α such that for all $2 \leq i \leq p$

$$T[i] = 1 \iff \text{there is } x \in \cup_{t'} B_{t'} \text{ such that } (\rho)_{x(1)} \neq (\rho)_{x(i)},$$

where t' ranges over t and its descendants.

Recall that α and ρ are partial assignments, ρ is called a refinement of α if $\rho \subseteq \alpha$, and $(\alpha)_i$ and $(\rho)_i$ denote the ith element of α and ρ, respectively, where $(\alpha)_i, (\rho)_i \in \{\emptyset, \{0\}, \{1\}, \{0, 1\}\}$.

We can see that there exists a p-periodic attractor if and only if there exists a partial assignment $\alpha \in \mathcal{A}_r$ that is consistent with the vector T such that $T[i] = 1$ for all $i = 2, \ldots, p$. We can also see that there exist 2^{p-1} possible vectors T. We use T_ℓ to denote each vector, where $\ell \in \{0, \ldots, 2^{p-1} - 1\}$ and a binary representation ℓ corresponds to T_ℓ. For example, consider the case of $p = 4$. Then, we have $T_0 = [0, 0, 0]$, $T_1 = [0, 0, 1]$, $T_2 = [0, 1, 0]$, $T_3 = [0, 1, 1]$, $T_4 = [1, 0, 0]$, $T_5 = [1, 0, 1]$, $T_6 =$

$[1, 1, 0]$, and $T_7 = [1, 1, 1]$, where the first and last elements in each vector corresponds to $T_\ell[2]$ and $T_\ell[p]$, respectively. In order to keep and update information on available periodicity patterns in the dynamic programming procedure, we introduce a *consistency vector* defined as below.

Definition 5.2. $\mathbf{C}_\alpha$ is a 0-1 vector of length 2^{p-1} in which each element value is determined by

$$\mathbf{C}_\alpha[\ell] = 1 \iff \alpha \text{ is consistent with } T_\ell.$$

We can see from this definition that there exists a p-periodic attractor if and only if there exists a partial assignment $\alpha \in \mathcal{A}_r$ such that $\mathbf{C}_\alpha[2^{p-1}-1] = 1$ holds. Note that $T_{2^{p-1}-1}$ denotes the vector consisting of 1s in all its elements.

In order to define $\mathbf{C}_\alpha$ for the bottom case of the dynamic programming procedure, we define $\mathbf{C}_\alpha^0$ as below.

Definition 5.3. For a partial assignment α, $\mathbf{C}_\alpha^0$ is the consistency vector defined as follows: $\mathbf{C}_\alpha^0[i] = 0$ except that $\mathbf{C}_\alpha^0[\ell] = 1$ where ℓ is the index of a 0-1 vector with which α is consistent, i.e., T_ℓ satisfies the property that

$$T_\ell[i] = 1 \iff |(\alpha)_{x(1)}| = |(\alpha)_{x(i)}| = 1 \text{ and}$$
$$(\alpha)_{x(1)} \neq (\alpha)_{x(i)} \text{ for some } x \in B_t$$

In order to update $\mathbf{C}_\alpha$ during the bottom-up dynamic programming procedure, we introduce an operation between consistency vectors. For 0-1 vectors T, T' and T'', we write $T = T' \vee T''$ if

$$T[i] = 1 \iff T'[i] = 1 \text{ or } T''[i] = 1.$$

Definition 5.4. For consistency vectors $\mathbf{C}_\alpha$ and $\mathbf{C}_\beta$, the consistency vector $\mathbf{C}_\alpha \otimes \mathbf{C}_\beta$ has values

$$(\mathbf{C}_\alpha \otimes \mathbf{C}_\beta)[\ell] = 1 \iff (\exists j)(\exists k)(T_\ell = T_j \vee T_k \text{ and } \mathbf{C}_\alpha[j] = \mathbf{C}_\beta[k] = 1).$$

Since this operator is commutative and associative, it is not necessary to indicate the order of computation for expressions and thus we can use such notation as $\mathbf{C}_\alpha \otimes \mathbf{C}_\beta \otimes \mathbf{C}_\gamma$. We also define $\mathbf{C}_\gamma = \mathbf{C}_\alpha \vee \mathbf{C}_\beta$ by $\mathbf{C}_\gamma[\ell] = 1$ iff (if and only if) $\mathbf{C}_\alpha[\ell] = 1$ or $\mathbf{C}_\beta[\ell] = 1$.

Here we present a procedure to compute $\mathbf{C}_\alpha$.

(1) For each node $t \in \mathcal{V}_\mathcal{T}$ and each $\alpha \in \mathcal{A}_t$, compute $\mathbf{C}_\alpha^0$.
(2) For each leaf node $t \in \mathcal{V}_\mathcal{T}$ and each $\alpha \in \mathcal{A}_t$, $\mathbf{C}_\alpha \leftarrow \mathbf{C}_\alpha^0$.

(3) For each non-leaf node t with children $t_1, \dots, t_d$, and for each $\alpha \in \mathcal{A}_t$, do (in a bottom-up manner)

    (a) for each t_i, $\mathbf{D}_{\alpha, t_i} \leftarrow \bigvee_{\beta \in \mathcal{A}_{t_i}(\alpha)} \mathbf{C}_\beta$, where $\mathcal{A}_{t_i}(\alpha) = \{\beta \in \mathcal{A}_{t_i} \mid \beta \cap \alpha \neq \emptyset\}$.

    (b) $\mathbf{C}_\alpha \leftarrow \mathbf{C}_\alpha^0 \otimes \mathbf{D}_{\alpha, t_1} \otimes \cdots \otimes \mathbf{D}_{\alpha, t_d}$.

As explained previously, we can check the existence of a p-periodic attractor by testing whether or not there exists an $\alpha \in \mathcal{A}_r$ such that $\mathbf{C}_\alpha[2^{p-1} - 1] = 1$. The resulting algorithm is denoted by **PattKtree**.

Example 5.2. Suppose that $\mathcal{V}_\mathcal{T} = \{t_A, t_B, t_C\}$ and $\mathcal{E}_\mathcal{T} = \{(t_A, t_B), (t_A.t_C)\}$ in $\mathcal{T}(\mathcal{V}_\mathcal{T}, \mathcal{E}_\mathcal{T})$ for $N^p(V^p, F^p)$ where $p = 4$, $\mathcal{A}_{t_A} = \{\alpha_{t_A}^1, \alpha_{t_A}^2\}$, $\mathcal{A}_{t_B} = \{\alpha_{t_B}^1, \alpha_{t_B}^2, \alpha_{t_B}^3\}$, and $\mathcal{A}_{t_C} = \{\alpha_{t_C}^1, \alpha_{t_C}^2\}$. Suppose also that $\alpha_{t_A}^1 \cap \alpha_{t_B}^1 \neq \emptyset$, $\alpha_{t_A}^1 \cap \alpha_{t_B}^2 \neq \emptyset$, $\alpha_{t_A}^1 \cap \alpha_{t_C}^1 \neq \emptyset$, $\alpha_{t_A}^2 \cap \alpha_{t_B}^2 \neq \emptyset$, $\alpha_{t_A}^2 \cap \alpha_{t_B}^3 \neq \emptyset$, and $\alpha_{t_A}^2 \cap \alpha_{t_C}^2 \neq \emptyset$, whereas $\alpha_{t'}^i \cap \alpha_{t''}^j = \emptyset$ for the other pairs. Furthermore, suppose that C_t^0s are given as follows

$$C_{\alpha_{t_A}^1}^0 = [1, 1, 0, 0, 0, 0, 0, 0],$$

$$C_{\alpha_{t_A}^2}^0 = [0, 0, 1, 0, 0, 0, 0, 0],$$

$$C_{\alpha_{t_B}^1}^0 = [0, 1, 0, 0, 0, 0, 0, 0],$$

$$C_{\alpha_{t_B}^2}^0 = [0, 0, 0, 0, 1, 0, 0, 0],$$

$$C_{\alpha_{t_B}^3}^0 = [0, 1, 1, 0, 0, 0, 0, 0],$$

$$C_{\alpha_{t_C}^1}^0 = [1, 0, 0, 0, 0, 1, 0, 0],$$

$$C_{\alpha_{t_C}^2}^0 = [0, 0, 0, 0, 1, 0, 0, 0],$$

where $p = 4$. Then, we have

$$D_{\alpha_{t_A}^1, t_B} = [0, 1, 0, 0, 1, 0, 0, 0],$$

$$D_{\alpha_{t_A}^1, t_C} = [1, 0, 0, 0, 0, 1, 0, 0],$$

$$C_{\alpha_{t_A}^1} = [0, 1, 0, 0, 1, 1, 0, 0],$$

$$D_{\alpha_{t_A}^2, t_B} = [0, 1, 1, 0, 1, 0, 0, 0],$$

$$D_{\alpha_{t_A}^2, t_C} = [0, 0, 0, 0, 1, 0, 0, 0],$$

$$C_{\alpha_{t_A}^2} = [0, 0, 0, 0, 0, 1, 1, 1].$$

Since $C_{\alpha_{t_A}^2}[7] = 1$, $N^p(V^p, f^p)$ has an attractor of period 4.

Theorem 5.2. *Periodic Attractor Detection for an nc-BN with bounded treewidth w and period p can be solved in $O(n^{2p(w+1)} poly(n))$ time for any* *constants p and w, where $poly(n)$ is a polynomial of n whose degree does not depend on p or w.*

Proof. Since the correctness of **PattKtree** is obvious, we analyze the time complexity.

From Proposition 5.5, the treewidth of $N^p(V^p, E^p)$ is less than $p(w+1)$ and thus the size of $\mathcal{A}_t$ is $O(n^{p(w+1)})$. As in **SattKtree**, for each non-leaf node $t \in \mathcal{V}_\mathcal{T}$, we examine the compatibility for $O(n^{p(w+1)} \times n^{p(w+1)} \times d)$ pairs of partial assignments. Therefore, the total computation time for constructing $\mathcal{A}_r$ is $O(n^{2p(w+1)}poly(n))$.

Since p and w are assumed to be a constant, each operation on $\mathbf{C}_\alpha$ can be done in constant time. Therefore, the total time for computing $\mathbf{C}_\alpha$s is $O(n^{2p(w+1)}poly(n))$. $\square$

If the maximum indegree is bounded by a constant d, the number of possible partial assignment per B_t is bounded by $(d+2)^{p(w+1)}$, which implies that **PattKtree** gives a fixed-parameter algorithm when p, w and d are parameters, where a fixed-parameter algorithm is an algorithm for which the exponential factor of the time complexity depends only on some parameter(s) [Flum and Grohe (2006); Fomin and Kratsch (2010)]. Furthermore, for a general Boolean function with at most d inputs, it is enough to consider 2^d partial assignments, instead of $m+1$ partial assignments. Therefore, **PattKtree** also gives a fixed-parameter algorithm for a BN with general Boolean functions when p, w and d are parameters.

5.4 Additional Remarks and Bibliographical Notes

Not much is known about the computational complexity of Periodic Attractor Detection. As mentioned at the beginning of this chapter, Periodic Attractor Detection seems to be PSPACE-complete following from the results in [Barrett *et al.* (2006)]. This chapter is based on [Akutsu *et al.* (2012a)]. Polynomial-time algorithms are known some special cases of Periodic Attractor Detection. A BN is called a positive OR-BN if every function assigned to a node is OR of input nodes. It is known that detection of a 2-periodic attractor for a positive OR-BN can be done in polynomial time [Akutsu *et al.* (2012a)], which was obtained based on some properties on this special class of BNs [Akutsu *et al.* (2012b); Goles and Salinas (2010)]. On the other hand, the problem remains NP-hard for a positive BN in which each function is AND or OR of input nodes [Just (2006)]. Practical algorithms for enumerating singleton and periodic attractors for moderate size BNs were proposed using a combination of partial states and predecessors [Irons *et al.* (2006)]. and a combination of partial states and path-decomposition [Tamaki (2010)].

Chapter 6

Identification of Boolean Networks

In 1990s, DNA microarray and DNA chip technologies were developed, which enabled us to observe time series data of expression of several thousands (or more) of genes to some extent. Recently, the next generation DNA sequencing technology can also be used for the same purpose. Motivated by these innovations, extensive studies have been done on inference of gene regulatory networks from gene expression time series data. The BN model has also been employed for solving this inference problem. In this chapter, we review some fundamental algorithms for inferring a BN from Boolean time series data and fundamental results on the number of expression data that are required to uniquely identify the underlying BN. Although time series data can be obtained as mentioned above, it is difficult to get a lot of time series data and time series data usually contain large noise. Instead, it is much easier to obtain gene expression data in steady states, which may correspond to attractors. Therefore, some studies have been done on inference of gene regulatory networks from attractors. In the latter sections of this chapter, we review some of theoretical results on this problem.

6.1 Identification from Samples

6.1.1 *Problem Definition*

Although time series data are usually obtained by biological experiments using DNA microarrays, we divide time series data as a set of input/output pairs.

Let $(\mathbf{a}^j, \mathbf{b}^j)$ $(j = 1, \ldots, m)$ be a pair of 0-1 vectors length n, where 0-1 value of the ith coordinate corresponds to the expression level (active or inactive) of the ith gene. If $\mathbf{a}^j$ corresponds to a gene activity profile at time

t for some t, $\mathbf{b}^j$ corresponds to a gene activity profile at time $t+1$. For the sake of convenience, $\mathbf{a}^j[i]$ and $\mathbf{b}^j[i]$ are called input and output values (of the ith gene), respectively.

We say that a node x_i in a BN $N(V, F)$ is *consistent* with a sample $(\mathbf{a}^j, \mathbf{b}^j)$ if $\mathbf{b}^j[i] = f_i(\mathbf{a}^j)$ holds. We say that $N(V, F)$ is *consistent* with $(\mathbf{a}^j, \mathbf{b}^j)$ if $\mathbf{b}^j[i] = f_i(\mathbf{a}^j)$ holds for all $i = 1, \ldots, n$. For a set of samples $S = \{(\mathbf{a}^1, \mathbf{b}^1), \ldots, (\mathbf{a}^m, \mathbf{b}^m)\}$, we say that $N(V, F)$ (resp., x_i) is *consistent* with S if $N(V, F)$ (resp., x_i) is consistent with all $(\mathbf{a}^j, \mathbf{b}^j) \in S$. Then, the inference and identification problems are defined as below (see also Fig. 6.1).

Definition 6.1.   [Inference of BN]
Instance: a set of n-dimensional samples $S = \{(\mathbf{a}^1, \mathbf{b}^1), \ldots, (\mathbf{a}^m, \mathbf{b}^m)\}$,
Problem: decide whether or not there exists a BN consistent with S, and output one if it exists.

Definition 6.2.   [Identification of BN]
Instance: a set of n-dimensional samples $S = \{(\mathbf{a}^1, \mathbf{b}^1), \ldots, (\mathbf{a}^m, \mathbf{b}^m)\}$,
Problem: decide whether or not there exists a unique BN consistent with S, and output it if it exists.

Note that both problems are very similar: the difference lies only in a point that the uniqueness of the solution should be verified in the identification problem. Note also that information about the number of nodes n is included in samples (n is equal to the number of dimensions of each vector).

6.1.2   *Sample Complexity*

In this section, we consider the number of samples required to uniquely identify a BN. First, we show a simple result.

Proposition 6.1. *2^n samples are required to uniquely identify a BN if there is no restriction on a BN.*

Proof. As we saw in Chapter 2, BNs correspond to state-transition tables in a one-to-one manner. This means that all rows of a state-transition table are required in order to uniquely specify a BN. Since there are 2^n rows in a state-transition table and each row corresponds to a sample, the proposition holds. $\square$

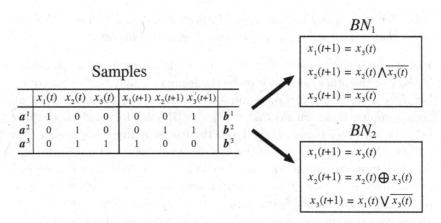

Fig. 6.1 Difference between Inference of BN and Identification of BN. In this example, BNs consistent with given samples are not determined uniquely because both BN_1 and BN_2 are consistent with samples. Therefore, Inference of BN has a solution whereas Identification of BN does not have a solution.

This proposition implies that an exponential number of gene expression data are required, which is not realistic. However, if the maximum indegree is bounded by a constant K, the situation drastically changes. We begin with a lower bound on the sample complexity.

Proposition 6.2. $\Omega(2^K + K \log n)$ *samples are necessary in the worst case to uniquely identify a BN of maximum indegree* K.

Proof. We estimate the number of mutually distinct Boolean networks. The number of Boolean functions that exactly depend on K input variable is $2^{2^K} - K2^{2^{K-1}}$, which is $\Theta(2^{2^K})$ because the number of Boolean functions with K input variables is 2^{2^K}. Since there are $\Omega(n^K)$ possible combinations of input nodes and $\Theta(2^{2^K})$ possible Boolean functions per node, there are $\Omega((2^{2^K} \cdot n^K)^n)$ BNs whose maximum indegree is K. Therefore, $\Omega(2^K n + nK \log n)$ bits are required to specify a BN. On the other hand, each sample gives information quantity of n bits because only $\mathbf{b}^i$ in $(\mathbf{a}^i, \mathbf{b}^i)$ gives information on a BN. Therefore, $\Omega(2^K + K \log n)$ samples are required in the worst case. $\qquad\square$

In order to show an upper bound of the sample complexity, we need the following lemma.

Lemma 6.1. *If all assignments (i.e., 2^{2K} assignments) of Boolean values to all subsets of V with $2K$ nodes (i.e., $\binom{n}{2K}$ subsets) appear in* $\mathbf{a}^j s$, *there* *exists for each node x_i at most one Boolean functions together with input nodes that is assigned to x_i and is consist with all samples.*

Proof. Since the output value of each node is determined independently of those of the other nodes, we prove the lemma for only one node, say x_1. Let f be a Boolean function whose output values are consistent with all given samples, which means that $f(\mathbf{a}^j) = \mathbf{b}^j[1]$ holds for all given samples. Let g be any other Boolean function with at most K input nodes. Let $U = IN(f) \cup IN(g)$. Let f_U and g_U be the restriction of f and g, respectively, in which input variables are restricted to U. Since both f and g depend on variables in U and $f \neq g$, there must exist an 0-1 assignment $\mathbf{u} = (u_1, \ldots, u_{|U|})$ such that $f_U(\mathbf{u}) \neq g_U(\mathbf{u})$. Since $|U| \leq 2K$, such $\mathbf{u}$ must appear as a subsequence of some $\mathbf{a}^j$. g is not consistent with such a sample because $\mathbf{b}^j[1] = f(\mathbf{a}^j) = f_U(\mathbf{u}) \neq g_U(\mathbf{u}) = g(\mathbf{a})$ holds for any such $\mathbf{a}^j$. $\quad\square$

Example 6.1. Consider two sets of samples S_1 and S_2 shown in the table below, where $n = 4$, $K = 1$, and only columns corresponding to $\mathbf{a}^j$s are shown for each set. S_1 satisfies the condition of Lemma 6.1, whereas S_2 does not satisfy it since $[x_2, x_3] = [0, 0]$ does not appear in S_2.

	S_1				S_2			
	x_1	x_2	x_3	x_4	x_1	x_2	x_3	x_4
$\mathbf{a}^1$	0	1	1	1	1	1	0	0
$\mathbf{a}^1$	1	0	1	1	0	0	1	1
$\mathbf{a}^1$	1	1	0	1	1	0	1	0
$\mathbf{a}^1$	1	1	1	0	0	1	0	1
$\mathbf{a}^1$	0	0	0	0	1	1	1	1

In the following, we assume that all $\mathbf{a}^j$s are given uniformly at random, whereas there is no restriction on $\mathbf{b}^j$s: $\mathbf{b}^j$ can be random or can be determined according to $\mathbf{b}^j[i] = f_i(\mathbf{a}^j)$ where f_i is a Boolean function assigned to node x_i in the underlying BN.

Theorem 6.1. *If $O(2^{2K} \cdot (2K + \alpha) \cdot \log n)$ samples are given uniformly at random, the following holds with probability at least $1 - \frac{1}{n^\alpha}$: there exists at most one BN of n nodes with maximum indegree $\leq K$ which is consistent with given samples.*

Proof. We derive the number of samples satisfying the condition of Lemma 6.1. For that purpose, we consider the probability that the condition is not satisfied when m random samples are given.

For any fixed set of nodes $\{x_{i_1}, \ldots, x_{i_{2K}}\}$, the probability that a sub-assignment $x_{i_1} = x_{i_2} = \cdots = x_{i_{2K}} = 1$ does not appear in one random $\mathbf{a}^j$ is

$$1 - \frac{1}{2^{2K}}.$$

Thus, the probability that $x_{i_1} = \cdots = x_{i_{2K}} = 1$ does not appear in any of m random a^js is

$$(1 - \frac{1}{2^{2K}})^m.$$

Since the number of combinations of $2K$ nodes is less than n^{2K}, the probability that there exists a combination of $2K$ nodes for which an assignment $x_{i_1} = \cdots = x_{i_{2K}} = 1$ does not appear in any of m random $\mathbf{a}^j$s is at most

$$n^{2K} \cdot (1 - \frac{1}{2^{2K}})^m.$$

Since there are 2^{2K} possible assignments to $2K$ variables, the probability that the condition of Lemma 6.1 is not satisfied is at most

$$2^{2K} \cdot n^{2K} \cdot (1 - \frac{1}{2^{2K}})^m.$$

It is not difficult to see that

$$2^{2K} \cdot n^{2K} \cdot (1 - \frac{1}{2^{2K}})^m < p$$

holds for

$$m > \ln 2 \cdot 2^{2K} \cdot (2K + 2K \log n + \log \frac{1}{p}).$$

Letting $p = \frac{1}{n^{\alpha}}$, we obtain the theorem. $\qquad\qquad \square$

6.1.3 *Computational Complexity*

In order to infer/identify a BN consistent with given samples, we can use the following quite simple algorithm.

Procedure IdentBN(S)
for all nodes x_i **do**
   let $F_i \leftarrow \emptyset$;
   for all Boolean functions f_i with at most K input nodes **do**
      if f_i is consistent with all $(\mathbf{a}^j, \mathbf{b}^j) \in S$ **then** $F_i \leftarrow F_i \cup \{f_i\}$;
   if $|F_i| \neq 1$ **then return** FALSE;
   return TRUE.

The following proposition is straightforward from this algorithm.

Proposition 6.3. IdentBN *works in* $O(2^{2^K} \cdot n^K \cdot poly(n, m))$ *time.*

Proof. We analyze **IdentBN**, where its correctness is obvious because this algorithm examines consistency of all possible Boolean functions with at most K input nodes for each node.

As for the time complexity, it examines for each node all Boolean functions with at most K input nodes, the number of which is $O(2^{2^K} \cdot n^K)$. Since the total number of consistency tests is $O(2^{2^K} \cdot n^K \cdot mn)$ and the time needed for any other parts is $O(poly(m, n))$, the proposition holds. $\square$

This algorithm takes long time for large K. Therefore, it is reasonable to ask whether there exists an efficient algorithm that works in time polynomial to m, n, and K. However, the following proposition implies that it is not plausible to develop such an algorithm.

Proposition 6.4. *Inference of BN with the maximum indegree K is NP-hard if K is a part of input.*

Proof. It is enough to prove that it is NP-hard to decide whether there exists a Boolean function for node x_1 with K inputs which is consistent with a given set of samples $(\mathbf{a}^j, \mathbf{b}^j[1])$.

We use a polynomial-time reduction from Set Cover. Let $(\mathcal{S} = \{S_1, \ldots, S_n\}, K)$ be an instance of Set Cover over $U = \{u_1, \ldots, u_m\}$. Recall that Set Cover is to decide whether there exist K-sets $S_{i_1}, \ldots, S_{i_K}$ such that $S_{i_1} \cup \ldots \cup S_{i_K} = U$. From $(\mathcal{S}, K)$, we construct $m + 1$ samples as follows:

$$\mathbf{a}^j[i] = 1, \quad \text{if } j \leq m \text{ and } u_j \in S_i,$$
$$\mathbf{a}^j[i] = 0, \quad \text{otherwise,}$$
$$\mathbf{b}^j[1] = 1, \quad \text{for } j = 1, \ldots, m,$$
$$\mathbf{b}^{m+1}[1] = 0.$$

Suppose that there exists a set cover $\{S_{i_1}, \ldots, S_{i_K}\}$. Then, $f_1(x_{i_1}, \ldots, x_{i_K}) = x_{i_1} \vee \cdots \vee x_{i_K}$ is consistent with all samples.

Conversely, suppose that there exists $f_1(x_{i_1}, \ldots, x_{i_K})$ which is consistent with all samples and depends on all of $x_{i_1}, \ldots, x_{i_K}$. Then, for each $j = 1, \ldots, m$, there must exist i_k such that $(\mathbf{a}^j)_{i_k} = 1$ holds because otherwise $f_1(\mathbf{a}^j) = f_1(\mathbf{a}^{m+1}) = 0$ would hold, which contradicts $f_1(\mathbf{a}^j) = \mathbf{b}^j[1] = 1$. It means that u_j is covered by such S_{i_k}. Therefore, $\{S_{i_1}, \ldots, S_{i_m}\}$ is a cover of $\mathcal{S}$.

Since the reduction can be done in polynomial time, the proposition holds. □

In this proposition, we have used a reduction from Set Cover to Inference of BN. Conversely, we can apply a well-known greedy algorithm for Set Cover to Inference of BN, where it is called here **SC-Greedy**. The following is a pseudo-code of **SC-Greedy**, which repeatedly selects a set that covers the maximum number of uncovered elements.

Procedure SC-Greedy($\mathcal{S}$)
$\mathcal{S}_r \leftarrow \mathcal{S}$;
$\mathcal{S}_c \leftarrow \emptyset$;
$U \leftarrow S_1 \cup \cdots \cup S_m$;
while $U \neq \emptyset$ **do**
$\quad S_k \leftarrow \mathrm{argmax}\{|S_i \cap U| \mid S_i \in \mathcal{S}_r\}$;
$\quad U \leftarrow U - S_i$;
$\quad \mathcal{S}_r \leftarrow \mathcal{S}_r - \{S_k\}$;
$\quad \mathcal{S}_c \leftarrow \mathcal{S}_c \cup \{S_k\}$;
return $\mathcal{S}_c$.

We can reduce Inference of BNto Set Cover as follows. Since a Boolean function assigned to each node can be inferred independently, we only consider inference of a Boolean function assigned to x_1. Then, from a set of samples $S = \{(\mathbf{a}^j, \mathbf{b}^j) \mid j = 1, \ldots, m\}$, we construct an instance of a set cover by letting

$$U = \{(\mathbf{a}^j, \mathbf{a}^k) \mid 1 \leq j < k \leq m,\ \mathbf{b}^j[1] \neq \mathbf{b}^k[1]\},$$
$$S_i = \{(\mathbf{a}^j, \mathbf{a}^k) \in U \mid \mathbf{a}^j[i] \neq \mathbf{a}^k[i]\}.$$

We denote the resulting algorithm by **GreedyIdent**.

It is well-known that **SC-Greedy** outputs a set cover whose number of elements is at most $\ln(m) + 1$ times that of the minimum set cover. Using this fact, we have the following for **GreedyIdent**.

Proposition 6.5. *Suppose that there exists a BN with the maximum indegree K which is consistent with a given set of samples S. Then, **GreedyIdent** find in polynomial time a BN with the maximum indegree $(2\ln(m) + 1)K$ which is consistent with S.*

Proof. Since it is straightforward to see the correctness and polynomial time complexity, we analyze the approximation ratio. As mentioned above, the approximation ratio of **SC-Greedy** is upper bounded by

$\ln(|U|) + 1$. Since $|U| \leq m^2/2$ in **GreedyIdent**, the approximation ratio of **GreedyIdent** is upper bounded by

$$\ln(|U|) + 1 \leq \ln(m^2/2) + 1 = 2\ln(m) - \ln(2) + 1 < 2\ln(m) + 1.$$

$\square$

This proposition shows that **GreedyIdent** outputs a BN that is not too large compared with the underlying BN. However, we can show that **GreedyIdent** can find the exact solution with high probability if Boolean functions are restricted to be simple ones and samples are given at uniformly random. Before considering the general case, we explain the basic idea using an example.

Example 6.2. As discussed before, we focus on identification of a Boolean function assigned to x_1. Suppose that a BN has three nodes x_1, x_2, x_3 and $x_1(t+1) = x_1(t) \wedge x_2(t)$ is assigned to x_1 in the underlying BN. Then, we have 8 possible assignments on x_1, x_2, x_3 as shown in Fig. 6.2. In this case, U, S_1, S_2, S_3 are given by

$$U = \{(a^1, a^7), (a^1, a^8), (a^2, a^7), (a^2, a^8), (a^3, a^7), (a^3, a^8), (a^4, a^7), (a^4, a^8),$$
$$(a^5, a^7), (a^5, a^8), (a^6, a^7), (a^6, a^8)\},$$
$$S_1 = \{(a^1, a^7), (a^1, a^8), (a^2, a^7), (a^2, a^8), (a^3, a^7), (a^3, a^8), (a^4, a^7), (a^4, a^8)\},$$
$$S_2 = \{(a^1, a^7), (a^1, a^8), (a^2, a^7), (a^2, a^8), (a^5, a^7), (a^5, a^8), (a^6, a^7), (a^6, a^8)\},$$
$$S_3 = \{(a^1, a^8), (a^2, a^7), (a^3, a^8), (a^4, a^7), (a^5, a^8), (a^6, a^7)\}.$$

Since $|S_1| = |S_2| = 8 > |S_3| = 6$, either S_1 or S_2 is selected in the first iteration of **GreedyIdent**. Suppose that S_1 is selected. Then, U, S_2, and S_3 are updated as

$$U = \{(a^5, a^7), (a^5, a^8), (a^6, a^7), (a^6, a^8)\},$$
$$S_2 = \{(a^5, a^7), (a^5, a^8), (a^6, a^7), (a^6, a^8)\},$$
$$S_3 = \{(a^5, a^8), (a^6, a^7)\}.$$

Since $|S_2| = 4 > |S_3| = 2$, S_2 is selected in the second iteration and then U is updated as $U = \emptyset$. Therefore, we can see that the correct input node set $\{x_1, x_2\}$ is selected for a Boolean function assigned to x_1.

We generalize the above discussion to a general case of AND of inputs, where it can be further generalized to cases of AND/OR of literals in a straightforward way. Suppose that $x_1(t+1) = x_1(t) \wedge x_2(t) \wedge \cdots \wedge x_K(t)$ is assigned to x_1 in the underlying BN and m random samples are given.

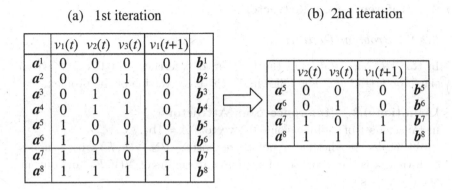

Fig. 6.2   Illustration for average case analysis of **GreedyIdent**.

Then, it is expected that $|U| \approx \frac{1}{2^K} \cdot \frac{2^K-1}{2^K} \cdot m^2$ holds because approximately $\frac{1}{2^K} \cdot m$ samples have output value 1 (i.e., $\mathbf{b}^j[1] = 1$) whereas approximately $\frac{2^K-1}{2^K} \cdot m$ samples have output value 0. Similarly, $|S_i| \approx \frac{1}{2 \cdot 2^K} \cdot m^2 \approx \frac{2^{K-1}}{2^K-1} \cdot |U|$ holds for each of relevant nodes (i.e., $i \in \{1, \dots, K\}$) because approximately $\frac{1}{2} \cdot m$ samples satisfy $\mathbf{a}^j[i] = 0$ and $\mathbf{b}^j[1] = 0$ whereas approximately $\frac{1}{2^K} \cdot m$ samples satisfy $\mathbf{a}^j[i] = 1$ and $\mathbf{b}^j[1] = 1$. On the other hand, it is expected that $|S_i| \approx \frac{1}{2} \cdot |U|$ holds for each of non-relevant nodes (i.e., $i > K$). Since $\frac{2^{K-1}}{2^K-1} \cdot |U| > \frac{1}{2} \cdot |U|$ holds, it is expected that one of the relevant input nodes is selected at the first iteration of **GreedyIdent**.

Suppose that x_1 is selected at the first iteration. Then, at the beginning of the second iteration, it is expected that $|S_i| \approx \frac{2^{K-2}}{2^{K-1}-1} \cdot |U|$ holds for each of the remaining relevant nodes and $|S_i| \approx \frac{1}{2} \cdot |U|$ holds for each of non-relevant nodes. Therefore, it is expected that one of the relevant input nodes is also selected at the second iteration.

We can repeat this discussion until all relevant K input nodes are identified. By carefully analyzing the success probability, the following theorem can be obtained [Akutsu *et al.* (2003a)].

Theorem 6.2. *Suppose that the underlying BN consists Boolean functions each of which is AND or OR of at most K literals, where K is a constant. Suppose that $\mathbf{a}^j$'s are generated uniformly at random. Then, for sufficiently large m ($m = \Omega((\alpha + 1)n)$), **GreedyIdent** outputs the correct BN with probability no smaller than $1 - \frac{1}{n^\alpha}$.*

6.2   Inference from Attractors

6.2.1   *Problem Definitions*

In this section, we discuss the problem of inference of a BN from given singleton attractors. The following is the basic version of the problem.

Definition 6.3.   [**Inference from Attractors**]
Instance: a set of n-dimensional 0-1 vectors $A = \{\mathbf{b}_1, \ldots, \mathbf{b}_m\}$,
Problem: decide whether or not there exists a BN $N(V, F)$ with n nodes such that $\mathcal{A}$ is the whole set of singleton attractors of $N(V, F)$, and output one if it exists.

The uniqueness in the above definition is important because if the uniqueness is not required, there is a trivial solution: $x_i(t+1) = x_i(t)$ for all x_i. Since there are too many Boolean functions in general but biologically meaningful Boolean functions are limited, we focus on AND/OR BNs. Then, a sign can be assigned to each edge: if input variable occurs as a positive (resp., negative) literal in an AND or OR function, the corresponding edge is positive (resp., negative). Until the end of this section, it is assumed that BNs are restricted to be AND/OR BNs unless otherwise stated.

As variants of the inference problem, we consider network completion problems from singleton attractors. We define the edge completion problem and the function completion problem as follows.

Definition 6.4. [Edge Completion]
Instance: a BN $G(V, F)$ and a set of n-dimensional 0-1 vectors $A = \{\mathbf{b}_1, \ldots, \mathbf{b}_m\}$,
Problem: decide whether or not there exists a minimum set of additional edges with possible negations to all nodes in V which makes $\mathcal{A}$ the exact set of singleton attractors of the resulting BN, and output one if it exists.

Definition 6.5. [Function Completion]
Instance: a direct graph $G(V, E)$ and a set of n-dimensional 0-1 vectors $\mathcal{A} = \{\mathbf{b}_1, \mathbf{b}_2, \ldots, \mathbf{b}_m\}$, where $n = |V|$.
Problem: decide whether or not there exists a Boolean function assignment to all nodes in V which makes $\mathcal{A}$ the exact set of singleton attractors of the resulting BN, where the set of input nodes of each Boolean function must be the same as those provided by the directed graph, and output one if it exists.

Example 6.3.

- Edge Completion.
  Suppose that a BN defined by

$$\begin{cases} x_1(t+1) = \overline{x_2(t)}, \\ x_2(t+1) = x_3(t), \\ x_3(t+1) = x_1(t). \end{cases}$$

and $\mathcal{A} = \{[1,0,0]\}$ are given, where all nodes are assumed to be AND nodes. Then, we have a desired BN by adding a positive edge (x_2, x_3), which means that the function assigned to x_3 becomes $x_3(t+1) = x_1(t) \wedge x_2(t)$,

- Function Completion.
  Suppose that $G(V, E)$ defined by

$$\begin{cases} x_1(t+1) = f_1(x_2(t)), \\ x_2(t+1) = f_2(x_3(t)), \\ x_3(t+1) = f_3(x_1(t), x_2(t)). \end{cases}$$

and $\mathcal{A} = \{[1,0,0]\}$ are given. Then, we have a desired BN by assigning Boolean functions as follows.

$$x_1(t+1) = \overline{x_2(t)},$$
$$x_2(t+1) = x_3(t),$$
$$x_3(t+1) = x_1(t) \wedge x_2(t).$$

6.2.2 *Algorithms for Inference from Attractors*

In this subsection, we describe algorithms for inferring BNs from attractors. For one or two singleton attractors (i.e., $m = |\mathcal{A}| \in \{1, 2\}$), we show linear time algorithms for inferring AND/OR BNs. For three or more singleton attractors (i.e., $m \geq 2$), we show a polynomial time algorithm for inferring general BNs, where the algorithm for the case of $m = 1$ is used as a subroutine.

We begin with the case of $m = 1$. Before presenting the algorithm, we give an example for illustration of the main idea. Suppose that $[1, 1, 0]$ is given as the unique singleton attractor. Then, we begin with a BN

$$\begin{cases} x_1(t+1) = x_2(t), \\ x_2(t+1) = \overline{x_3(t)}, \\ x_3(t+1) = x_1(t), \end{cases}$$

which means that x_i is determined from x_{i+1} where x_{n+1} is identified with x_1. This guarantees that $[1, 1, 0]$ is a singleton attractor. However, there exists another singleton attractor, $[0, 0, 1]$. In order to prevent $[0, 0, 1]$ from being a singleton attractor, we assign $x_3(t+1) = x_1(t) \wedge \overline{x_2(t)}$ to x_3. Then, $[0, 0, 1]$ becomes the unique singleton attractor.

The following is a formal description of algorithm, **InfFrom1Att**, for solving Inference from Attractors for AND/OR BNs with $m = 1$, where $\mathbf{b} = [b_1, b_2, \ldots, b_n]$ is a given singleton attractor, and $n > 1$.

Procedure InfFrom1Att(b)

(1) For $i = 1, \ldots, n - 1$, assign Boolean functions by:

$$x_i(t+1) = \begin{cases} x_{i+1}(t), \text{ if } b_i = b_{i+1}, \\ \\ \overline{x_{i+1}(t)}, \text{ if } b_i \neq b_{i+1}, \end{cases}$$

where $i = 1, 2, \ldots, n - 1$.

(2) Assign a Boolean function for $x_n(t)$ by: If $b_n = 0$,

$$\begin{cases} x_n(t+1) = \overline{x_1(t)} \wedge x_2(t), \text{ if } b_1 = 0, b_2 = 0, \\ x_n(t+1) = \overline{x_1(t)} \wedge \overline{x_2(t)}, \text{ if } b_1 = 0, b_2 = 1, \\ x_n(t+1) = x_1(t) \wedge x_2(t), \text{ if } b_1 = 1, b_2 = 0, \\ x_n(t+1) = x_1(t) \wedge \overline{x_2(t)}, \text{ if } b_1 = 1, b_2 = 1. \end{cases}$$

Otherwise,

$$\begin{cases} x_n(t+1) = x_1(t) \vee \overline{x_2(t)}, \text{ If } b_1 = 0, b_2 = 0, \\ x_n(t+1) = x_1(t) \vee x_2(t), \text{ If } b_1 = 0, b_2 = 1, \\ x_n(t+1) = \overline{x_1(t)} \vee x_2(t), \text{ If } b_1 = 1, b_2 = 0, \\ x_n(t+1) = \overline{x_1(t)} \vee x_2(t), \text{ If } b_1 = 1, b_2 = 1. \end{cases}$$

Example 6.4. Suppose the given unique singleton attractor is $[0, 1, 0]$. Then, **InfFrom1Att** constructs the BN defined by

$$\begin{cases} x_1(t+1) = \overline{x_2(t)}, \\ x_2(t+1) = x_3(t), \\ x_3(t+1) = x_1(t) \wedge \overline{x_2(t)}, \end{cases}$$

where the first two functions are determined in Step 1 and the last one is determined in Step 2.

Theorem 6.3. InfFrom1Att *solves Inference from Attractors for AND/OR BNs with $m = 1$ in linear time and the obtained network has $n + 1$ edges, where $n > 1$.*

Proof. First, we show the correctness of the algorithm. Step 1 guarantees that either $[b_1, b_2, \ldots, b_n]$ or $[\overline{b_1}, \overline{b_2}, \ldots, \overline{b_n}]$ can be a singleton attractor because all the values of x_i with $i = 1, \ldots, n - 1$ are determined uniquely from the value of x_n. Suppose that $b_1 = 0$, $b_2 = 0$, and $b_n = 1$; the other cases can be proved in an analogous way. Then, the latter state is not any more a singleton attractor due to Step 2 and thus the former one becomes the unique singleton attractor.

Next, we can see that the total number of edges in this BN is $n + 1$ because each x_i for $i = 1, \ldots, n - 1$ has one incoming edge and x_n has two incoming edges.

Finally, we analyze the time complexity. The assigned Boolean function f_i depends on only b_i and b_{i+1} for $i = 1, \ldots, n - 1$ and f_n on only b_1, b_2, and b_n. Thus, each Boolean function can be constructed in a constant time. Since the number of nodes is n, the total computation time is $O(n)$. $\square$

In order to extend **InfFrom1Att** to the case of $m = 2$, we divide the state vectors of two given attractors into the common parts (i.e., common bits) and the non-common parts. Let $\mathbf{b} = [b_1, b_2, \ldots, b_n]$ and $\mathbf{c} = [c_1, c_2, \ldots, c_n]$ be two given attractors. For the common parts, we construct a BN by **InfFrom1Att** because these parts are identical (i.e., $c_i = b_i$). For the non-common parts, we construct a BN as in Step 1 of **InfFrom1Att** because these parts are complementary (i.e., $c_i = \overline{b_i}$). Recall that there exist two complementary attractors after Step 1 of **InfFrom1Att**. The following is a formal description of the resulting algorithm, **InfFrom2Att**, for solving Inference from Attractors for AND/OR BNs with $m = 2$, where $n > 2$.

Procedure InfFrom2Att(b, c)

(1) Let $(i_1, i_2, \ldots, i_k)$ be the indices such that $b_{i_j} \neq c_{i_j}$.
(2) Construct a sub-BN BN_1 for nodes $x_{i_1}, x_{i_2}, \ldots, x_{i_k}$ by

$$x_{i_j}(t+1) = \begin{cases} x_{i_{j+1}}(t), & \text{if } b_{i_j} = b_{i_{j+1}}, \\ \\ \overline{x_{i_{j+1}}(t)}, & \text{if } b_{i_j} \neq b_{i_{j+1}}, \end{cases} \quad \text{for } j = 1, \ldots, k-1,$$

$$x_{i_k}(t+1) = \begin{cases} x_{i_1}(t), & \text{if } b_{i_1} = b_{i_k}, \\ \\ \overline{x_{i_1}(t)}, & \text{if } b_{i_1} \neq b_{i_k}, \end{cases} \quad \text{if } k > 1,$$

$$x_{i_1}(t+1) = x_{i_1}(t), \text{otherwise (i.e., } k = 1).$$

(3) Let $T = \{1, 2, \ldots, n\} \setminus \{i_1, i_2, \ldots, i_k\}$.

- If $T = \emptyset$, we are done.
- If $|T| = 1$, let M be the only element of T.

  - If $b_M = 0$, and $\max(b_{i_1}, b_{i_2}, \ldots, b_{i_k}) = \min(b_{i_1}, b_{i_2}, \ldots, b_{i_k})$, let
    $$x_M(t+1) = \overline{x_{i_1}(t)} \wedge x_{i_2}(t) \wedge \ldots \wedge x_{i_k}(t).$$

  - If $b_M = 0$, and $\max(b_{i_1}, b_{i_2}, \ldots, b_{i_k}) \neq \min(b_{i_1}, b_{i_2}, \ldots, b_{i_k})$, let
    $$x_M(t+1) = x_{i_1}(t) \wedge x_{i_2}(t) \wedge \ldots \wedge x_{i_k}(t).$$

  - If $b_M = 1$, and $\max(b_{i_1}, b_{i_2}, \ldots, b_{i_k}) = \min(b_{i_1}, b_{i_2}, \ldots, b_{i_k})$, let
    $$x_M(t+1) = \overline{x_{i_1}(t)} \vee x_{i_2}(t) \vee \ldots \vee x_{i_k}(t).$$

  - If $b_M = 1$, and $\max(b_{i_1}, b_{i_2}, \ldots, b_{i_k}) \neq \min(b_{i_1}, b_{i_2}, \ldots, b_{i_k})$, let
    $$x_M(t+1) = x_{i_1}(t) \vee x_{i_2}(t) \vee \ldots \vee x_{i_k}(t).$$

- If $|T| \geq 2$, construct a sub-BN by
  $$BN_2 = \mathbf{InfFrom1Att}([b_{j_1}, b_{j_2}, \ldots, b_{j_{n-k}}])$$
  where $j_l \in \{1, 2, \ldots, n\} \setminus \{i_1, i_2, \ldots, i_k\}$ and then concatenate BN_1 and BN_2.

Example 6.5. Suppose that $\{[0, 1, 1, 1], [1, 0, 1, 1]\}$ is given as the exact set of singleton attractors. In Step 1 of **InfFrom2Att**, 4 nodes are divided into two groups: x_1, x_2, and x_3, x_4. Then, the sub-BN defined by
$$\begin{cases} x_1(t+1) = \overline{x_2(t)}, \\ x_2(t+1) = \overline{x_1(t)}, \end{cases}$$
is constructed in Step 2 and the sub-BN defined by
$$\begin{cases} x_3(t+1) = x_4(t), \\ x_4(t+1) = \overline{x_3(t)} \vee x_4(t). \end{cases}$$
is constructed in Step 3.

Theorem 6.4. InfFrom2Att *solves Inference from Attractors for AND/OR BNs with $m = 2$ in linear time and the obtained network has at most $2n - 2$ edges, where $n > 2$.*

Proof. First, we show the correctness of the algorithm. Note that Step 3 constructs a sub-network having two complementary singleton attractors, $[b_{i_1}, b_{i_2}, \ldots, b_{i_k}]$ and $[c_{i_1}, c_{i_2}, \ldots, c_{i_k}]$. If $T = \emptyset$, these are clearly unique singleton attractors. If $|T| = 1$, $x_M = b_M = c_M$ holds both for $[b_{i_1}, b_{i_2}, \ldots, b_{i_k}]$ and for $[c_{i_1}, c_{i_2}, \ldots, c_{i_k}]$ since $k > 1$ holds from $n >$

2. Otherwise, it is guaranteed by **InfFrom1Att** that $[b_{j_1}, b_{j_2}, \ldots, b_{j_{n-k}}]$ is the unique singleton attractor for $[x_{j_1}, x_{j_2}, \ldots, x_{j_{n-k}}]$ and thus the concatenated network has the required two unique singleton attractors.

Next, it is seen that Step 2 creates k edges. Step 3 creates 0 edges if $k = n$, $n - 1$ edges if $k = n - 1$, or $n - k + 1$ edges otherwise. Hence, at most $2n - 2$ edges are created.

Finally, we analyze the time complexity. It is straightforward to see that each step can be done in $O(n)$ time. Therefore, the total computation time is $O(n)$. □

In the above, we considered the cases with one or two unique singleton attractors. It is unclear whether or not we can extend the results to three or more unique singleton attractors for AND/OR BNs. However, it is possible to construct in polynomial time a BN whose set of singleton attractors is exactly the same as a given one if more general types of Boolean functions can be used in which the recursive use of "if then else" type rules is allowed.

Let $\mathcal{A} = \{\mathbf{b}^1, \mathbf{b}^2, \ldots, \mathbf{b}^m\}$ be a given set of unique singleton attractors. Recall that $\mathbf{b}^i[j]$ denote the Boolean value of node x_j for $\mathbf{b}^i$. The algorithm is based on simple divide and conquer. Let k be the maximum index such that there exist two attractors $\mathbf{b}^{i_1}$ and $\mathbf{b}^{i_2}$ such that $\mathbf{b}^{i_1}[k] = 0$ and $\mathbf{b}^{i_2}[k] = 1$. If there is no such k, $\mathcal{A}$ should be a singleton set and thus we can apply **InfFrom1Att**. Otherwise, we divide $\mathcal{A}$ into $\mathcal{A}_0$ and $\mathcal{A}_1$ so that $\mathbf{b}^i \in \mathcal{A}_d$ satisfies $\mathbf{b}^i[k] = d$. Then, we recursively construct BNs for $\mathcal{A}_0$ and $\mathcal{A}_1$ and merge the resulting two BNs.

The following is a formal description of algorithm, **InfFromAtt**, for solving Inference from Attractors for general BNs with an arbitrary m, where it is invoked as **InfFromAtt**$(\mathcal{A}, n)$ and $n > 1$.

Procedure InfFromAtt$(\mathcal{A}, h)$

(1) If $\mathcal{A} = \{\mathbf{b}\}$, return **InfFrom1Att**$(\mathbf{b})$.
(2) Let k be the maximum number such that both $\mathcal{A}_0 = \{\mathbf{b}^i | \mathbf{b}^i \in \mathcal{A}, \mathbf{b}^i[k] = 0\}$ and $\mathcal{A}_1 = \{\mathbf{b}^i | \mathbf{b}^i \in \mathcal{A}, \mathbf{b}^i[k] = 1\}$ are non-empty and $k \leq h$.
(3) Let $BN_0 =$**InfFromAtt**$(\mathcal{A}_0, k-1)$ and $BN_1 =$**InfFromAtt**$(\mathcal{A}_1, k-1)$.
(4) Construct BN_2 by merging BN_0 and BN_1 so that it simulates BN_0 if $x_k(t) = 0$, otherwise it simulates BN_1.
(5) Return BN_2.

In Step 4, construction of BN_2 can be done by assigning a Boolean function $f_i = (\overline{x_k(t)} \rightarrow f_i^0) \wedge (x_k(t) \rightarrow f_i^1)$ to each node x_i $(i = 1, \ldots, n)$ where f_i^j is a Boolean function assigned to node x_i in BN_j $(j = 0, 1)$.

Example 6.6. Suppose that $\mathcal{A} = \{[0, 1, 0, 1], [0, 1, 1, 0], [1, 0, 0, 1]\}$ is a given set of three singleton attractors. At the initial call of **InfFromAtt**$(\mathcal{A}, 4)$, $\mathcal{A}$ is decomposed into:

$$\mathcal{A}_0 = \{[0, 1, 1, 0]\}, \quad \mathcal{A}_1 = \{[0, 1, 0, 1], [1, 0, 0, 1]\}.$$

at $k = 4$. Then, **InfFromAtt**$(\mathcal{A}_0, 3)$ is called and it returns

$$BN_0 = \begin{cases} x_1(t+1) = \overline{x_2(t)}, \\ x_2(t+1) = x_3(t), \\ x_3(t+1) = \overline{x_4(t)}, \\ x_4(t+1) = \overline{x_1(t)} \wedge \overline{x_2(t)}. \end{cases}$$

Next, **InfFromAtt**$(\mathcal{A}_1, 3)$ is called and $\mathcal{A}_1$ is further decomposed into:

$$\mathcal{A}'_0 = \{[1, 0, 0, 1]\}, \quad \mathcal{A}'_1 = \{[0, 1, 0, 1]\}.$$

at $k = 2$. Then, **InfFromAtt**$(\mathcal{A}'_0, 1)$ and **InfFromAtt**$(\mathcal{A}'_1, 1)$ are called and the following BNs are constructed:

$$BN'_0 = \begin{cases} x_1(t+1) = \overline{x_2(t)}, \\ x_2(t+1) = x_3(t), \\ x_3(t+1) = \overline{x_4(t)}, \\ x_4(t+1) = \overline{x_1(t)} \vee x_2(t), \end{cases}$$

$$BN'_1 = \begin{cases} x_1(t+1) = \overline{x_2(t)}, \\ x_2(t+1) = \overline{x_3(t)}, \\ x_3(t+1) = \overline{x_4(t)}, \\ x_4(t+1) = x_1(t) \vee x_2(t). \end{cases}$$

Then, BN_1 is obtained by merging BN'_0 and BN'_1 as:

$$BN_1 = \begin{cases} \begin{cases} x_1(t+1) = \overline{x_2(t)}, \\ x_2(t+1) = x_3(t), \\ x_3(t+1) = \overline{x_4(t)}, \\ x_4(t+1) = \overline{x_1(t)} \vee x_2(t), \end{cases} & \text{if } x_2(t) = 0, \\ \begin{cases} x_1(t+1) = \overline{x_2(t)}, \\ x_2(t+1) = \overline{x_3(t)}, \\ x_3(t+1) = \overline{x_4(t)}, \\ x_4(t+1) = x_1(t) \vee x_2(t), \end{cases} & \text{if } x_2(t) = 1. \end{cases}$$

Finally, BN_2 is obtained by merging BN_0 and BN_1 as:

$$BN_2 = \begin{cases} \begin{cases} x_1(t+1) = \overline{x_2(t)}, \\ x_2(t+1) = x_3(t), \\ x_3(t+1) = \overline{x_4(t)}, \\ x_4(t+1) = \overline{x_1(t)} \wedge \overline{x_2(t)}, \end{cases} & \text{if } x_4(t) = 0, \\[2em] \begin{cases} x_1(t+1) = \overline{x_2(t)}, \\ x_2(t+1) = x_3(t), \\ x_3(t+1) = \overline{x_4(t)}, \\ x_4(t+1) = \overline{x_1(t)} \vee \overline{x_2(t)}, \end{cases} & \begin{aligned} &\text{if } x_4(t) = 1 \\ &\text{and } x_2(t) = 0, \end{aligned} \\[2em] \begin{cases} x_1(t+1) = \overline{x_2(t)}, \\ x_2(t+1) = \overline{x_3(t)}, \\ x_3(t+1) = \overline{x_4(t)}, \\ x_4(t+1) = x_1(t) \vee x_2(t), \end{cases} & \begin{aligned} &\text{if } x_4(t) = 1 \\ &\text{and } x_2(t) = 1. \end{aligned} \end{cases}$$

Theorem 6.5. **InfFromAtt** *solves Inference from Attractors for general BNs in polynomial time with respect to n and m, where $n > 1$ and $m > 0$.*

Proof. First, we show the correctness of the algorithm by mathematical induction on the size (i.e., cardinality) of $\mathcal{A}$. As the base step of the induction, we consider the case of $|\mathcal{A}| = 1$. Then, **InfFromAtt** returns a correct solution because it simply calls **InfFrom1Att**. As the inductive step, assuming that **InfFromAtt** returns a correct solution for any $\mathcal{A}$ of size at most m_0, we consider tha case $|\mathcal{A}| = m_0 + 1$. Then, there must exist an index k satisfying the conditions of Step 2 because $|\mathcal{A}| \geq 2$ holds and $\mathbf{b}^i[k'] = \mathbf{b}^j[k']$ holds for all $k' \geq h + 1$ and all $\mathbf{b}^i, \mathbf{b}^j \in \mathcal{A}$ $(i \neq j)$, where $\mathcal{A}$ means the current one (not the original one). Since $|\mathcal{A}_0| \leq m_0$ and $|\mathcal{A}_1| \leq m_0$ hold from the assumption and BN_2 correctly simulates BN_0 (if $x_k(t) = 0$) and BN_1 (otherwise), **InfFromAtt** returns a correct solution.

Next, we analyze the time complexity. For the simplicity, we assume that m is bounded by a polynomial of n, where the same argument holds even if this assumption does not hold. Note that the number of recursive calls is $2m - 1$ (including the initial call) because $\mathcal{A}$ is divided into two disjoint non-empty sets at Step 2 and thus the recursive call structure corresponds to a binary tree with m leaves. Now, we show that each recursive step can be done in polynomial time of n and m. The critical issue is the size of f_i because the other parts clearly work in polynomial time. If $|\mathcal{A}| = 1$, the size of f_i is $O(n)$ from Theorem 6.3. Otherwise, it is seen from the construction that the size of f_i is bounded by the sum of the size of f_i^0, the size of f_i^1, and a constant. Since $\mathcal{A}$ is always divided into two disjoint sets whenever BN_2 is constructed and the number of recursive calls is $2m - 1$, we can see that the size of f_i is $O(mn)$. Therefore, the algorithm works in polynomial time and the theorem follows.   □

Note that disjunctive or conjunctive normal form representation of f_i may be of exponential size. Note also that if m is exponential of n (e.g., m can be 2^n), the size of f_i may be exponential of n and thus representation of the resulting BN may need exponential space of n although the required space and time remain polynomial of m.

6.2.3   *Network Completion Problems for AND/OR BNs*

In this subsection, we consider Edge Completion and Function Completion for AND/OR BNs.

For Edge Completion, since a general case seems to be very difficult, we consider a special case in which $m = 1$ and the uniqueness of a singleton attractor is not necessarily ensured.

Before presenting the algorithm, we explain the basic idea using an example. Suppose that

$$\begin{cases} x_1(t+1) = x_3(t) \vee \overline{x_2(t)}, \\ x_2(t+1) = x_1(t), \\ x_3(t+1) = x_1(t) \vee \overline{x_2(t)}, \end{cases}$$

is a given BN where x_2 is an AND node, and $[1, 0, 1]$ is the desired singleton attractor. Then, this BN has a state transition from $[1, 0, 1]$ to $[1, 1, 1]$, from which we know that the Boolean function for x_2 must be modified. In order to make $[1, 0, 1]$ a singleton attractor by addition of a minimum number of edges, f_1 and f_3 should be kept as they are and an edge to x_2 should be added by revising the Boolean function for x_2 into $x_2(t+1) = x_1(t) \wedge x_2(t)$ or $x_2(t+1) = x_1(t) \wedge \overline{x_3(t)}$.

The following is a formal description of algorithm, **EdgeCmpl1**, for solving Edge Completion for general BNs with $m = 1$.

Procedure EdgeCmpl1($[b_1, b_2, \ldots, b_n]$)

(1) Let $[x_1(t), x_2(t), \ldots, x_n(t)] = [b_1, b_2, \ldots, b_n]$ and compute $[x_1(t+1), x_2(t+1), \ldots, x_n(t+1)]$ according to F.
(2) For all nodes x_i such that $x_i(t+1) \neq b_i$, do Steps 3-5.

(3) If x_i is an AND node and $indeg(x_i) < n$ and $b_i = 0$, select an arbitrary node $x_j \notin IN(x_i)$ and add a positive edge from x_j to x_i if $b_j = 0$, and add a negative edge from x_j to x_i otherwise.

(4) Else if x_i is an OR node and $indeg(x_i) < n$ and $b_i = 1$, select an arbitrary node $x_j \notin IN(x_i)$ and add a positive edge from x_j to x_i if $b_j = 1$, and add a negative edge from x_j to x_i otherwise.

(5) Else output 'None' and stop.

Theorem 6.6. **EdgeCmpl1** *solves Edge Completion for an AND/OR BN in polynomial time if $m = 1$ and the uniqueness of a singleton attractor is not required to be ensured.*

Proof. First, we show the correctness of the algorithm. Since we do not modify the Boolean function of any node x_i such that $x_i(t+1) = b_i$, this property still holds for x_i after the completion. If x_i is an AND node (resp., OR node) and $x_i(t+1) = 0$ (resp., $x_i(t+1) = 1$), it is impossible to change the value of $x_i(t+1)$ by addition of any edge(s). If $indeg(x_i) = n$, it is impossible to add an edge and thus the value of $x_i(t+1)$ can not be changed. Otherwise, it is possible to change the value of $x_i(t+1)$ by adding only one edge as described by the algorithm. This completes the proof of the correctness.

Next, we analyze the time complexity. Step 1 can be done in $O(n^2)$ time because computation of $x_i(t+1)$ can be done in $O(n)$ time for each x_i. It is also seen that Steps 3-5 can be done in $O(n)$ time per execution. Since at most n nodes are examined, Steps 2-5 take $O(n^2)$ time in total. Therefore, the total computation time is $O(n^2)$. □

The following example shows that that the uniqueness of the singleton attractor is not guaranteed by **EdgeCmpl1**.

Example 6.7. Suppose that

$$\begin{cases} x_1(t+1) = x_3(t) \wedge \overline{x_2(t)}, \\ x_2(t+1) = x_1(t) \wedge x_3(t). \\ x_3(t+1) = x_1(t) \wedge \overline{x_2(t)}, \end{cases}$$

is a given BN and $[1, 0, 1]$ is the desired singleton attractor. Then, **EdgeCmpl1** revises the Boolean function for x_2 into

$$x_2(t+1) = x_1(t) \wedge x_2(t) \wedge x_3(t).$$

However, $[0, 0, 0]$ is also a singleton attractor both before and after the modification. Therefore, the uniqueness of the singleton attractor is not guaranteed.

For Function Completion, no positive result is known. The following negative result was proven in [Jiang *et al.* (2013)].

Theorem 6.7. *Function Completion for AND/OR BNs cannot be solved in polynomial time unless P=NP.*

6.3   Additional Remarks and Bibliographical Notes

Inference of a genetic network from time series gene expression data using the BN model was first studied in [Liang *et al.* (1998)]. Independently and almost simultaneously, inference of a genetic network by strategic gene disruptions and gene overexpressions was studied in a preliminary version of [Akutsu *et al.* (2003b)]. After these studies, many methods have been proposed for inference of genetic networks using the BN model and its variants. For details of such developments, see survey/comparison papers [Berestovsky and Nakhleh (2013); Hickman and Hodgman (2009)] and some recent papers [Atias *et al.* (2014); Haider and Pal (2012); Barman and Kwon (2017); Sharan and Karp (2013)]. The sample complexity result and the simple identification algorithm in Section 6.1 are based on [Akutsu *et al.* (1999)]. Another analysis of the sample complexity was done in [Perkins and Hallett (2010)] with focusing on reducing the factor on K. NP-hardness of Inference of BN was given in [Akutsu *et al.* (2000b)], where many similar results had already been known in various fields. The greedy algorithm and its analyses in Section 6.1.3 are based on [Akutsu *et al.* (2003a)], where the identifiable class by the greedy algorithm was extended to more general classes [Arpe and Reischuk (2003); Fukagawa and Akutsu (2005)]. Furthermore, deep theoretical analyses have been done on inference of a Boolean function with the minimum number of relevant attributes [Mossel *et al,* (2004); O'Donnell (2014)].

Inference a BN from attractors was first proposed in [Pal *et al.* (2005)] and was also studied in [Zou (2010)]. The results in Section 6.2 are based on [Jiang *et al.* (2013)]. Although network completion from singleton attractors was studied in this chapter, theoretical aspects of network completion of a BN with observed data were also studied in [Akutsu *et al.* (2009)].

Chapter 7

Control of Boolean Networks

One of the major goals of systems biology is to develop control theory for biological systems [Kitano (2002, 2004)]. Such a development is important both from a theoretical viewpoint and from a practical viewpoint. From a theoretical viewpoint, biological systems are complex and contain highly non-linear components and thus existing methods in control theory cannot be directly applied to control of biological systems. From a practical viewpoint, control of cells may be useful for systems-based drug discovery and cancer treatment [Kitano (2002, 2004)]. Therefore, it is an important and interesting challenge to develop theory and methods for control of biological systems. Since BNs are highly non-linear systems, it is reasonable to try to develop methods for control of BNs. In this chapter, we describe algorithms and complexity results on control of BNs.

7.1 Basic Control Problem

7.1.1 *Problem Definition*

There are several ways of formalization on control problems for BNs. The concept of controllability in linear systems can be applied to BNs, which requires that BNs with an arbitrary initial state must be driven to an arbitrary target state. However, most of BNs would be uncontrollable under such a definition. For example, consider two nodes x_1 and x_2 regulated as

$$x_1(t+1) = x_3(t) \wedge x_4(t),$$
$$x_2(t+1) = x_3(t) \wedge \overline{x_4(t)}.$$

Then, it is impossible to let $[x_1(t), x_2(t)] = [1, 1]$ by giving any control to x_4. Therefore, we consider a specific case in which it is required to find a control strategy that drives a given BN with a specified set of control nodes from a given initial state to a given target state.

In this formalism, each BN has two types of nodes: *internal nodes* and *external nodes*, where internal nodes correspond to usual nodes (e.g., genes) in a BN and external nodes correspond to control nodes (e.g., drugs). Let $V = \{x_1, \ldots, x_n\}$ and $U = \{u_1, \ldots, u_m\}$ be a set of internal nodes and a set of external nodes, respectively. The state of each internal node is determined by

$$x_i(t+1) = f_i(x_1(t), \ldots, x_n(t), u_1(t), \ldots, u_m(t)),$$

where some input nodes may be irrelevant. We use $\mathbf{x}(t)$ and $\mathbf{u}(t)$ to denote the states of V and U, respectively. Then, the dynamics of this modified BN can be described as

$$\mathbf{x}(t+1) = \mathbf{f}(\mathbf{x}(t), \mathbf{u}(t)),$$

where $\mathbf{u}(t)$s are determined externally. Then, the control problem for a BN (BN Control) is defined as follows.

Definition 7.1. [BN Control]
Instance: a BN with a set of internal nodes $V = \{x_1, \ldots, x_n\}$ and a set of external nodes $U = \{u_1, \ldots, u_m\}$, an initial state of internal nodes $\mathbf{x}^0$, and the desired state of internal nodes $\mathbf{x}^M$ at the M-th time step,
Problem: decide whether or not there exists a sequence of 0-1 vectors $\langle \mathbf{u}(0), \ldots, \mathbf{u}(M-1) \rangle$ such that $\mathbf{x}(0) = \mathbf{x}^0$ and $\mathbf{x}(M) = \mathbf{x}^M$, and output one if it exists.

Example 7.1. Consider a BN defined by

$$x_1(t+1) = \overline{u_1(t)},$$
$$x_2(t+1) = x_1(t) \wedge u_2(t),$$
$$x_3(t+1) = x_1(t) \vee x_2(t).$$

Suppose that $\mathbf{x}^0 = [0, 0, 0]$, $\mathbf{x}^M = [0.1.1]$, and $M = 3$. Then, we have a solution $\langle \mathbf{u}(0), \mathbf{u}(1), \mathbf{u}(2) \rangle$ with

$$\mathbf{u}(0) = [0, 1],$$
$$\mathbf{u}(1) = [0, 1],$$
$$\mathbf{u}(2) = [1, 1],$$

which drives the BN as in Fig. 7.1.

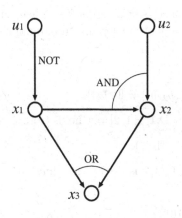

initial (x^0)	0	0	0
desired (x^M)	0	1	1

(M=3)

t	x_1	x_2	x_3	u_1	u_2
0	0	0	0	0	1
1	1	0	0	0	1
2	1	1	1	1	1
3	0	1	1	-	-

Fig. 7.1   Example of BN Control. In this problem, it is required to compute a sequence of states of external nodes $[u_1, u_2]$ that drives the BN from the initial state to the desired state. '-' in a table means that the corresponding value is not relevant.

7.1.2 *Dynamic Programming Algorithm*

BN Control can be solved by a dynamic programming algorithm, which is obtained by simplifying the algorithm for PBN Control (to be shown in Chapter 13).

In this algorithm, we use a 0-1 table $D[b_1, \ldots, b_n, t]$ where each $[b_1, \ldots, b_n]$ corresponds to a global state of internal nodes and t is the time step. $D[b_1, \ldots, b_n, t]$ takes 1 if there exists a control sequence $\langle \mathbf{u}(t), \ldots, \mathbf{u}(M-1) \rangle$ which drives the BN to the target state $\mathbf{x}^M$ at time M beginning from the state $[b_1, \ldots, b_n]$ at time t. This table is computed backwards (from $t = M$ to $t = 0$) by using the following procedure:

$$D[b_1, \ldots, b_n, M] = \begin{cases} 1, \text{ if } [b_1, \ldots, b_n] = \mathbf{x}^M, \\ 0, \text{ otherwise,} \end{cases}$$

$$D[b_1, \ldots, b_n, t-1] = \begin{cases} 1, \text{ if there exists } (\mathbf{c}, \mathbf{u}) \text{ such that } D[c_1, \ldots, c_n, t] = 1 \\ \quad \text{and } \mathbf{c} = \mathbf{f}(\mathbf{b}, \mathbf{u}), \\ 0, \text{ otherwise,} \end{cases}$$

where $\mathbf{b} = [b_1, \ldots, b_n]$ and $\mathbf{c} = [c_1, \ldots, c_n]$. Then, there exists a desired control sequence if and only if $D[a_1, \ldots, a_n, 0] = 1$ holds for $\mathbf{x}^0 = [a_1, \ldots, a_n]$. Once the table is constructed, a desired control sequence can be obtained using the standard *traceback technique*.

Example 7.2. We consider the same instance as in Example 7.1. Then, the following table is constructed at the beginning of the dynamic programming procedure:

$$D[0, 1, 1, 3] = 1,$$
$$D[b_1, b_2, b_3, 3] = 0, \text{ for } [b_1, b_2, b_3] \neq [0, 1, 1].$$

Then, we fill $D[b_1, b_2, b_3, 2]$s. For example, $D[1, 1, 1, 2] = 1$ holds from

$$[0, 1, 1] = \mathbf{f}([1, 1, 1], [1, 1]).$$

On the other hand, $D[0, 0, 0, 2] = 0$ holds since for any $\mathbf{u} \in \{[0, 0], [0, 1], [1, 0], [1, 1]\}$, we have

$$[0, 1, 1] \neq \mathbf{f}([0, 0, 0], \mathbf{u}).$$

By repeating this procedure, we have

$$D[1, 0, 0, 1] = 1, \text{from } [1, 1, 1] = \mathbf{f}([1, 0, 0], [0, 1]),$$
$$D[0, 0, 0, 0] = 1, \text{from } [1, 0, 0] = \mathbf{f}([0, 0, 0], [0, 1]).$$

Since $\mathbf{x}^0 = [0, 0, 0]$, there exists a required control sequence.

Theorem 7.1. *Suppose that each of Boolean functions appearing in a BN can be evaluated in polynomial time. Then, BN Control can be solved in $O^*(M \cdot 2^{n+m})$ time.*

Proof. Since the correctness is straightforward from the dynamic programming algorithm, we analyze the time complexity. The size of table $D[b_1, \ldots, b_n, t]$ is clearly $O(M \cdot 2^n)$. In order to fill the table at each t, we need to examine all pairs $(\mathbf{b}, \mathbf{u})$, whose number is $O(2^n \cdot 2^m)$. Since we assume that each Boolean function can be evaluated in polynomial time, the total computation time is $O^*(M \cdot 2^{n+m})$. □

It is also possible to obtain the same complexity result by making the state transition diagram and then finding a path of length M from the initial state to the target state.

The above dynamic programming algorithm takes exponential time even if M is a constant. To be shown later, this result is reasonable since BN Control is NP-hard even for a small constant M. However, we might be able to obtain a polynomial-time algorithm if the structure of a BN is restricted. Indeed, we can show that BN Control can be solved in polynomial time if a BN has a tree structure (i.e., the graph is connected and there is no cycle). Since the algorithm for a general tree structured case is a bit complicated, we present here a simple algorithm for BNs with rooted tree structure (i.e., all paths are directed from leaves to the root). Although dynamic programming is also employed in this algorithm, it is used in a different way.

We use a 0-1 table $S[x_i, t, b]$ where x_i is a node in a BN, t is a time step, and b is a Boolean value (i.e., 0 or 1). We assume here that u_i is represented as x_{n+i}. $S[x_i, t, b]$ takes 1 if there exists a control sequence (up to time t) that makes $x_i(t) = b$. Precisely, $S[x_i, t, b]$ is defined as follows.

$$S[x_i, t, 1] = \begin{cases} 1, \text{ if there exists } \langle \mathbf{u}(0), \ldots, \mathbf{u}(t) \rangle \text{ such that } x_i(t) = 1, \\ 0, \text{ otherwise.} \end{cases}$$

$$S[x_i, t, 0] = \begin{cases} 1, \text{ if there exists } \langle \mathbf{u}(0), \ldots, \mathbf{u}(t) \rangle \text{ such that } x_i(t) = 0, \\ 0, \text{ otherwise.} \end{cases}$$

Then, there exists a control sequence that drives the BN to the desired state $\mathbf{x}^M = [a_1, \ldots, a_n]$ at time step M if and only if $S[x_i, M, a_i] = 1$ holds for each $x_i \in V$.

The table $S[x_i, t, b]$ can be computed by applying the following dynamic programming procedure from $t = 0$ to $t = M$.

$$S[x_i, t+1, 1] = \begin{cases} 1, \text{ if there exists } [b_{i_1}, \ldots, b_{i_k}] \text{ such that } f_i(b_{i_1}, \ldots, b_{i_k}) = 1 \\ \quad \text{holds and } S[x_{i_j}, t, b_{i_j}] = 1 \text{ holds for all } j = 1, \ldots, k, \\ 0, \text{ otherwise,} \end{cases}$$

$$S[x_i, t+1, 0] = \begin{cases} 1, \text{ if there exists } [b_{i_1}, \ldots, b_{i_k}] \text{ such that } f_i(b_{i_1}, \ldots, b_{i_k}) = 0 \\ \quad \text{holds and } S[x_{i_j}, t, b_{i_j}] = 1 \text{ holds for all } j = 1, \ldots, k, \\ 0, \text{ otherwise.} \end{cases}$$

It should be noted that each leaf is either a constant node or an external node. For a constant node, $S[x_i, t, 1] = 1$ and $S[x_i, t, 0] = 0$ hold for all t, or $S[x_i, t, 1] = 0$ and $S[x_i, t, 0] = 1$ hold for all t. For an external node, $S[x_i, t, 1] = 1$ and $S[x_i, t, 0] = 1$ hold for all t since we can assign an arbitrary value to this node at each time step. It should also be noted that dynamic programming is applied from $t = 0$ to $t = M$, whereas it is applied from $t = M$ to $t = 0$ in the algorithm for Theorem 7.1.

Example 7.3. Suppose that a BN with rooted tree structure is defined as

$$x_1(t+1) = 1,$$
$$x_2(t+1) = x_1(t) \wedge u_1(t),$$
$$x_3(t+1) = x_2(t) \vee u_2(t).$$

Suppose also that the initial state is given as $[1, 1, 1]$ and the desired state at time $M = 2$ is given as $[1, 1, 0]$ (see also Fig. 7.2). Then, $S[x_i, t, b]$s

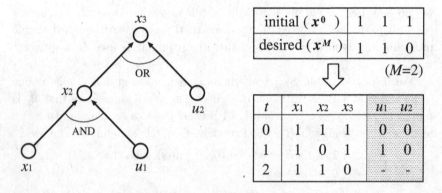

Fig. 7.2   Example of BN Control for a BN with rooted tree structure. x_1 is a constant node with $x_1(t) = 1$ for all t. '-' in a table means that the corresponding value is not relevant.

for $t = 0, \ldots, 2$ are determined as follows by the dynamic programming algorithm, where p/q means that $S[x_i, t, 0] = p$ and $S[x_i, t, 1] = q$.

t	x_1	x_2	x_3	u_1	u_2
0	0/1	0/1	0/1	1/1	1/1
1	0/1	1/1	0/1	1/1	1/1
2	0/1	1/1	1/1	1/1	1/1

Since $S[x_1, 2, 1] = 1$, $S[x_2, 2, 1] = 1$, and $S[x_3, 2, 0] = 1$ hold, there exists a required control sequence. Furthermore, we can get such a control sequence as $\langle \mathbf{u}(0), \mathbf{u}(1) \rangle$ with $\mathbf{u}(0) = [0, 0]$ and $\mathbf{u}(1) = [1, 0]$ from this table by using a traceback procedure.

Theorem 7.2. *BN Control can be solved in $O((n+m)M)$ time if a BN has rooted tree structure and its maximum indegree is bounded by a constant.*

Proof. Since the correctness is straightforward from the dynamic programming algorithm, we analyze the time complexity. The size of table $S[x_i, t, b]$ is clearly $O((n+m)M)$. In order to fill each entry of $S[x_i, t, b]$, we need to examine 2^k combinations of $[b_{i_1}, \ldots, b_{i_k}]$, whose number is constant because we assume ·that the maximum indegree is bounded by a constant. Therefore, each entry of $S[x_i, t, b]$ can be filled in a constant time, and thus the total time complexity is $O((n+m)M)$. $\qquad \square$

To be shown in the next subsection, the indegree bound is essential in this theorem.

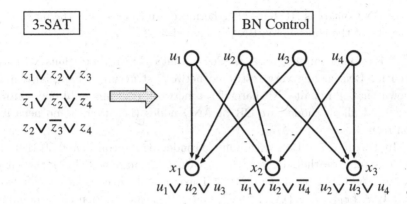

Fig. 7.3 Example of reduction from 3-SAT to BN Control. In this case, 3-SAT instance has a solution of $z_1 = 1, z_2 = 0, z_3 = 1, z_4 = 4$ and BN Control has the corresponding solution $\langle \mathbf{u}(0) \rangle$ such that $\mathbf{u}(0) = [1, 0, 1, 1]$. Arrows with '-' correspond to negative inputs.

7.1.3   *NP-hardness*

As mentioned in Section 7.1.2, the dynamic programming algorithm for control of general BNs takes exponential time and thus is not efficient. However, the following theorem suggests that it is not plausible to develop a polynomial-time algorithm for the general case.

Theorem 7.3. *BN Control is NP-hard even for $M = 1$ and BNs with the maximum indegree 3.*

Proof. We present a simple polynomial-time reduction from 3-SAT. Recall that 3-SAT is a problem of asking whether or not there exists a 0-1 assignment to Boolean variables which satisfies all the clauses (i.e., the values of all clauses are 1). Let $\{c_1, \ldots, c_L\}$ be a set of clauses over a set of variables $\{z_1, \ldots, z_N\}$ in a 3-SAT instance.

From this instance, we construct a BN as follows (see also Fig. 7.3). We construct the set of nodes of the BN by $V = \{x_1, \ldots, x_L\}$ and $U = \{u_1, \ldots, u_N\}$ where each x_i corresponds to c_i, and each u_j corresponds to z_j. Suppose that $c_i = f_i(z_{i_1}, z_{i_2}, z_{i_3})$ in a 3-SAT instance. Then, we assign $x_i(t + 1) = f_i(u_{i_1}(t), u_{i_2}(t), u_{i_3}(t))$ to x_i in the BN. Finally, we let $M = 1$, $\mathbf{x}^0 = [0, 0, \ldots, 0]$ and $\mathbf{x}^M = [1, 1, \ldots, 1]$.

It is straightforward to see that there exists a control sequence $\langle \mathbf{u}(0) \rangle$ which makes $\mathbf{x}(1) = [1, 1, \ldots, 1]$ if and only if there exists an assignment which satisfies all the clauses. Since the reduction can be done in linear time, BN Control is NP-hard. Furthermore, we can see that the maximum indegree of the constructed BN is bounded by 3.   □

It is also known [Akutsu *et al.* (2007)] that BN Control remains NP-hard even for BNs having very restricted network structures. Especially, it is shown that it remains NP-hard if the network contains only one control node and all the nodes are OR or AND nodes (i.e., there is no negative control).

In Theorem 7.3, BNs with bounded indegree are considered. If there is no constraint on the indegree, the proof can be simplified. From the same instance of 3-SAT as in the proof of Theorem 7.3, we construct a BN such that $V = \{x_1\}$, $U = \{u_1, \ldots, u_N\}$, and a Boolean function corresponding to $c_1 \wedge c_2 \wedge \cdots \wedge c_L$ is assigned to x_1. It is straightforward to see that there exists a control sequence $\langle \mathbf{u}(0) \rangle$ if and only if there exists an assignment which satisfies all the clauses. Furthermore, this BN has a rooted tree structure consisting of the root x_1 and leaves $u_1, \ldots, u_N$.

Corollary 7.1. *BN Control is NP-hard even for BNs with rooted tree structure unless the indegree is bounded.*

If M is not bounded, BN Control is PSPACE-hard because it is known that the reachability problem on a BN is PSPACE-hard [Barrett *et al.* (2006)] and the reachability problem is considered as a special case of the control problem in which the number of external nodes is 0.

Proposition 7.1. *BN Control is PSPACE-hard if M is not bounded.*

7.1.4   *ILP-based Method for BN Control*

In Section 3.4, we saw that integer linear programming (ILP) can be applied to solving Singleton Attractor Detection. We can also apply ILP to BN Control. Since time steps need be handled in BN Control, we need to introduce the notion of time. Accordingly, we introduce integer variables $x_{i,t}$ to represent the Boolean value of $x_i(t)$ and use $x_{i,t,b_1\ldots b_k}$ in place of $x_{i,b_1\ldots b_k}$ in Attractor Detection. Then, based on the ILP-formulation for Attractor Detection, we have the following ILP-formulation for BN Control.

Maximize $\sum_{i=1}^{n} x_{i,M}$,
Subject to
$$x_{i,t+1,b_{i_1}\ldots b_{i_k}} \geq \left(\sum_{j=1}^{k} \tau_{b_{i_j}}(x_{i_j,t}) \right) - (k-1),$$
$$x_{i,t+1,b_{i_1}\ldots b_{i_k}} \leq \frac{1}{k} \sum_{j=1}^{k} \tau_{b_{i_j}}(x_{i_j,t}),$$

for all $i \in \{1, \ldots, n\}$, $t \in \{0, \ldots, M-1\}$ and
$[b_{i_1}, \ldots, b_{i_k}] \in \{0,1\}^k$ such that $f_i(b_{i_1}, \ldots, b_{i_k}) = 1$,

$x_{i,t+1,b_{i_1} \ldots b_{i_k}} = 0$,

for all $i \in \{1, \ldots, n\}$, $t \in \{0, \ldots, M-1\}$ and
$[b_{i_1}, \ldots, b_{i_k}] \in \{0,1\}^k$ such that $f_i(b_{i_1}, \ldots, b_{i_k}) = 0$,

$x_{i,t} \leq \sum_{[b_{i_1}, \ldots, b_{i_k}] \in \{0,1\}^k} x_{i,t,b_{i_1} \ldots b_{i_k}}$,

$x_{i,t} \geq \frac{1}{2^k} \sum_{[b_{i_1}, \ldots, b_{i_k}] \in \{0,1\}^k} x_{i,t,b_{i_1} \ldots b_{i_k}}$,

for all $i \in \{1, \ldots, n\}$ and $t \in \{1, \ldots, M\}$,

$x_{i,0} = \mathbf{x}^0[i]$, $x_{i,M} = \mathbf{x}^M[i]$, for all $i \in \{1, \ldots, n\}$,

$x_{i,t} \in \{0,1\}$,

for all $i \in \{1, \ldots, n+m\}$ and $t \in \{0, \ldots, M\}$,

$x_{i,t,b_{i_1} \ldots b_{i_k}} \in \{0,1\}$,

for all $i \in \{1, \ldots, n\}$, $t \in \{1, \ldots, M\}$ and $[b_{i_1}, \ldots, b_{i_k}] \in \{0,1\}^k$.

The correctness of this formulation is almost obvious. Note that, as in Singleton Attractor Detection, we do not need an objective function and thus "maximize ..." is used as a dummy function. Of course, we may use some objective function if some appropriate score is assigned to control sequences. The efficiency of this ILP-based method against artificially generated BNs was examined in [Akutsu *et al.* (2012c)].

7.2 Minimum Driver Sets

7.2.1 *Problem Definition and NP-hardness*

We have assumed so far that external nodes are given in advance. However, it might be better not to have such an assumption because control of cells is often achieved by enforcing activation and/or knockout of several genes [Takahashi *et al.* (2007)]. Furthermore, since it is difficult to control many genes, the minimum number of genes should be selected as control nodes. Indeed, in the field of complex networks, extensive studies have been done on selecting and analyzing the minimum set of control nodes using linear models and certain types of non-linear models [Liu *et al.* (2011); Liu and Barabási (2016); Nacher and Akutsu (2016)]. In this context, a set of control nodes is often called as a set of *driver nodes*. In this section, we discuss the problem of selecting a minimum driver set for controlling a BN from a specified initial state to a specified target state, which is referred as Minimum Driver Set.

We begin with a formal definition of Minimum Driver Set. Let $N(V, F)$

be a BN where $V = \{x_1, \ldots, x_n\}$. Let $U = \{x_{i_1}, \ldots, x_{i_N}\}$ be a subset of V. Let $V' = V \setminus U = \{x_{j_1}, \ldots, x_{j_{n-N}}\}$. For a state $\mathbf{x}(t) = [x_1(t), \ldots, x_n(t)]$, we define $\mathbf{w}(t)$ and $\mathbf{u}(t)$ by

$$\mathbf{w}(t) = [w_1(t), \ldots, w_{n-N}(t)] = [x_{j_1}(t), \ldots, x_{j_{n-N}}(t)],$$
$$\mathbf{u}(t) = [u_1(t), \ldots, u_N(t)] = [x_{i_1}, \ldots, x_{i_N}(t)].$$

We assume that we can arbitrarily assign 0-1 values to $\mathbf{u}(t)$ for any t. By renaming variables in f_i appropriately, we assume that $w_i(t+1)$ is determined by

$$w_i(t+1) = f_i(\mathbf{w}(t), \mathbf{u}(t)).$$

Accordingly, the dynamics of the whole BN is represented as

$$\mathbf{w}(t+1) = \mathbf{f}(\mathbf{w}(t), \mathbf{u}(t)).$$

Definition 7.2.   [Minimum Driver Set]
Instance: a BN $N(V, F)$, an initial state $\mathbf{x}^0$, and the desired state $\mathbf{x}^M$ at the Mth time step,
Problem: find a set of driver nodes $U \subseteq V$ with the minimum cardinality such that there exists a sequence of states $\langle \mathbf{u}(0), \mathbf{u}(1), \ldots, \mathbf{u}(M) \rangle$ which satisfies $\mathbf{x}(M) = \mathbf{x}^M$.

Recall that it is assumed that $\mathbf{u}(t)$ is set arbitrarily for any $t > 0$. Therefore, it is enough to drive a BN so that $\mathbf{w}(M)$ coincides with $\mathbf{x}^M$ for the variables in W. It should be noted that there always exists a solution because it is possible to satisfy $\mathbf{x}(M) = \mathbf{x}^M$ at any $M > 0$ by letting $U = V$ (i.e., letting all nodes to be driver nodes).

Example 7.4. Consider a BN $N(V, F)$ defined by $V = \{x_1, x_2, x_3, x_4, x_5\}$ and

$$x_1(t+1) = x_1(t),$$
$$x_2(t+1) = x_1(t),$$
$$x_3(t+1) = x_1(t),$$
$$x_4(t+1) = x_2(t) \lor x_3(t),$$
$$x_5(t+1) = x_2(t) \land x_3(t).$$

Suppose that $\mathbf{x}^0 = [0,0,0,0,0]$, $\mathbf{x}^M = [1,1,1,1,1]$, and $M = 3$ (see also Fig. 7.4). If $U = \{x_1, x_5\}$ is selected as a set of driver nodes, the BN can be driven to the desired state $\mathbf{x}^M$ at $M = 3$ as below.

t	x_2	x_3	x_4	x_1	x_5
0	0	0	0	0	0
1	0	0	0	1	0
2	1	1	0	1	1
3	1	1	1	1	1

Therefore, $\{x_1, x_5\}$ is a set of driver nodes.

If $U = \{x_1\}$ is selected as a set of driver nodes, the BN can also be driven to the desired state $\mathbf{x}^M$ at $M = 3$ as below.

t	x_2	x_3	x_4	x_5	x_1
0	0	0	0	0	0
1	0	0	0	0	1
2	1	1	1	0	1
3	1	1	1	1	1

Therefore, $\{x_1\}$ is a set of driver nodes.

If x_1 is not included in a set of driver nodes, $x_1(t) = 0$ holds for all $t \geq 0$. Therefore, $\{x_1\}$ is the minimum set of driver nodes.

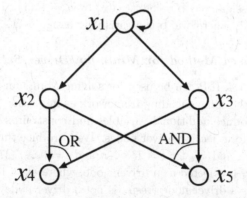

Fig. 7.4 Example of a Boolean network for Minimum Driver Set. For $\mathbf{x}^0 = [0, 0, 0, 0, 0]$ and $\mathbf{x}^M = [1, 1, 1, 1, 1]$ with $M = 3$, $U = \{x_1\}$ is the minimum set of driver nodes.

By modifying the proof of Theorem 7.3, Minimum Driver Set is shown to be NP-hard.

Theorem 7.4. *Minimum Driver Set is NP-hard even for $M = 2$ and BNs with the maximum indegree 3.*

Proof. We modify the reduction used in the proof of Theorem 7.3.

From a given 3-SAT instance, we construct a BN as in the proof of Theorem 7.3. However, in this case, $V = \{x_1, \ldots, x_L, u_1, \ldots, u_N\}$ holds and thus we need to assign Boolean functions also to u_is. We assign the following Boolean function to each u_i $(i = 1, \ldots, N)$:

$$u_i(t+1) = u_i(t).$$

Then, we let $\mathbf{x}^0 = [0, \ldots, 0]$, $\mathbf{x}^2 = [1, \ldots, 1]$, and $M = 2$. We show that the minimum set of driver nodes is $U = \{u_1, \ldots, u_N\}$ if and only if there exists a satisfying 0-1 assignment to $[x_1, \ldots, x_N]$.

First note that if u_i is not included in a set of driver nodes, $u_i(t) = 0$ would hold for all $t \geq 0$. Therefore, all u_is must be included in a minimum set of driver nodes.

Suppose that there exists a satisfying 0-1 assignment $\mathbf{b} = [b_1, \ldots, b_N]$. We let

$$u_i(1) = b_i, \quad u_i(2) = 1,$$

Then, $\mathbf{x}(2) = [1, \ldots, 1]$ holds. Therefore, U is the minimum set of driver nodes.

Conversely, suppose that U is the minimum set of driver nodes. We define the 0-1 assignment $\mathbf{b} = [b_1, \ldots, b_N]$ by $b_i = u_i(1)$. Then, all clauses must be satisfied. Therefore, $\mathbf{b}$ is a satisfying assignment. $\square$

7.2.2   *ILP-based Method for Minimum Driver Set*

As in Section 7.1.4, ILP can be used for solving Minimum Driver Set.

We employ the same encoding framework as in Section 7.2.2. However, we need to introduce additional variables and constraints in order to add the mechanism for selecting driver nodes. We introduce three kinds of new variables $y_{i,t}$, w_i, and $z_{i,t}$ for $i = 1, \ldots, n$ and $t = 0, \ldots, M$. w_i represents whether node x_i is selected as a driver node, where $w_i = 1$ (resp., $w_i = 0$) means that x_i is a driver node (resp., is not a driver node), $y_{i,t}$ represents the 0-1 state of node x_i at time t when x_i is not a driver node. $z_{i,t}$ represents the 0-1 state of node x_i at time t when x_i is a driver node. Then, $x_{i,t}$ (state of node x_i at time t) is determined by

$$y_{i,t} - w_i \leq x_{i,t} \leq y_{i,t} + w_i,$$

$$z_{i,t} - (1 - w_i) \leq x_{i,t} \leq z_{i,t} + (1 - w_i).$$

Note that our aim is to minimize the number of driver nodes, which can be represented as $\min \sum_{i=1}^{n} w_i$.

By putting all constraints together, we have the following ILP-formalization for Minimum Driver Set.

Minimize $\sum_{i=1}^{n} w_i$,
Subject to
$$x_{i,t+1,b_{i_1}...b_{i_k}} \geq (\sum_{j=1}^{k} \tau_{b_{i_j}}(x_{i_j,t})) - (k-1),$$
$$x_{i,t+1,b_{i_1}...b_{i_k}} \leq \frac{1}{k}\sum_{j=1}^{k} \tau_{b_{i_j}}(x_{i_j,t})$$
for all $i \in \{1,...,n\}$, $t \in \{0,...,M-1\}$ and
$[b_{i_1},...,b_{i_k}] \in \{0,1\}^k$ such that $f_i(b_{i_1},...,b_{i_k}) = 1$,
$$x_{i,t+1,b_{i_1}...b_{i_k}} = 0$$
for all $i \in \{1,...,n\}$, $t \in \{0,...,M-1\}$ and
$[b_{i_1},...,b_{i_k}] \in \{0,1\}^k$ such that $f_i(b_{i_1},...,b_{i_k}) = 0$,
$$y_{i,t} \leq \sum_{[b_{i_1},...,b_{i_k}]\in\{0,1\}^k} x_{i,t,b_{i_1}...b_{i_k}},$$
$$y_{i,t} \geq \frac{1}{2^k} \sum_{[b_{i_1},...,b_{i_k}]\in\{0,1\}^k} x_{i,t,b_{i_1}...b_{i_k}}$$
for all $i \in \{1,...,n\}$, $t \in \{0,...,M\}$,
$$y_{i,t} - w_i \leq x_{i,t} \leq y_{i,t} + w_i,$$
$$z_{i,t} - (1-w_i) \leq x_{i,t} \leq z_{i,t} + (1-w_i)$$
for all $i \in \{1,...,n\}$, $t \in \{0,...,M\}$,
$$x_{i,t}, y_{i,t}, z_{i,t}, w_i \in \{0,1\} \qquad \text{for all } i \in \{1,...,n\},$$
$$x_{i,0} = \mathbf{x}^0[i], \ x_{i,M} = \mathbf{x}^M[i], \quad \text{for all } i \in \{1,...,n\},$$
$$x_{i,t,b_{i_1}...b_{i_k}} \in \{0,1\}$$
for all $i \in \{1,...,n\}$, $t \in \{0,...,M\}$ and $[b_{i_1},...,b_{i_k}] \in \{0,1\}^k$.

The efficiency of this ILP-based method against artificially generated BNs and some realistic BN models was examined in [Hou *et al.* (2016)].

7.3 Control of Attractors

In the previous sections, we assumed that the desired state at a specific time setp is given. However, the desired states should often be stable states (e.g., singleton attractors). Furthermore, it is not easy to dynamically control states of control nodes, especially when nodes correspond to genes. Based on this idea, we consider the following control problem.

Let $N(V, F)$ be a Boolean network. We select m nodes from V and fix 0-1 values of these m nodes. Suppose that $x_{i_1},...,x_{i_m}$ are selected as control nodes and Boolean values of $b_{i_1},...,b_{i_m}$ are assigned to these nodes. Then, $\mathbf{x}$ is called a *forced singleton attractor* if the following conditions are satisfied:

- $x_i = b_i$ if $i \in \{i_1, \ldots, i_m\}$,
- $x_i = f_i(\mathbf{x})$ otherwise.

In addition, we introduce a score function g from $\{0,1\}^n$ to the set of real numbers for evaluating how appropriate each attractor state is. Since there is no established score function, we assume for simplicity that g is given as a linear combination of 0-1 values of internal nodes:

$$g(\mathbf{x}) = \sum_{i=1}^{n} \alpha_i \cdot (1 - w_i) \cdot x_i,$$

where α_is are real constants. A large α_i means that the gene corresponding to x_i should be expressed in a desired state. w_i is a 0-1 variable meaning that w_i is 1 if node x_i is selected as a control node, otherwise w_i is 0. This means that the scores of selected control nodes are not taken into account for $g(\mathbf{x})$. Since singleton attractors need not be uniquely determined even if the values of $x_{i_1}, \ldots, x_{i_m}$ are fixed, we may want to maximize the minimum score of singleton attractors, considering the worst case. However, to be mentioned later, it is very difficult to maximize the minimum score. Therefore, we introduce a threshold Θ of the minimum score and then define the problem of control of attractors (Attractor Control) as follows.

Definition 7.3.   [Attractor Control]
Instance: a BN, a score function g, the number of control nodes m, and a threshold Θ,
Problem: decide whether or not there exist m nodes and a 0-1 assignment to these control nodes for which the minimum score of singleton attractors is no less than Θ, and output one if it exists.

Example 7.5. Consider a BN in Fig. 7.5. Let $\alpha_1 = 3$, $\alpha_2 = 2$, $\alpha_3 = 1$, $\Theta = 2$, and $m = 1$. Then, there exist the following possibilities.

control node/assignment	attractor/score	minimum score
$x_1 = 0$	$[0,0,1]/1$	1
$x_1 = 1$	$[1,1,0]/2$	2
$x_2 = 0$	$[0,0,1]/1$	1
$x_2 = 1$	$[0,1,0]/0$	0
$x_3 = 0$	$[0,0,0]/0$	0
$x_3 = 1$	$[0,0,1]/0,[1,1,1]/5$	0

Since the minimum score is no less than $\Theta = 2$ only in the case of $x_1 = 1$, this node-assignment pair is the solution.

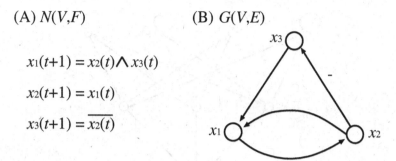

Fig. 7.5   Example of a BN for Attractor Control, where (A) and (B) show the BN and its underlying graph structure, respectively. An arrow with '-' corresponds to a negative input.

As shown below, Attractor Control is harder than NP-hard,

Theorem 7.5. *Attractor Control is* $\sum_2^P$*-hard.*

Proof. Let $\psi(\mathbf{y}, \mathbf{z})$ be a 3-DNF (disjunction of conjunctions each of which consisting of 3 literals) over variables $\mathbf{y} = [y_1, \ldots, y_{n_1}]$ and $\mathbf{z} = [z_1, \ldots, z_{n_2}]$. It is known that deciding whether or not $(\exists \mathbf{y})(\forall \mathbf{z})\psi(\mathbf{y}, \mathbf{z})$ is true is $\sum_2^P$-complete [Stockmeyer (1976)]. We show a polynomial-time reduction from this problem to Attractor Control.

From a given $\psi(\mathbf{y}, \mathbf{z})$, we construct a BN as follows (see also Fig. 7.6). Let m_1 be the number of terms in $\psi(\mathbf{y}, \mathbf{z})$. Then, we let $V = \{x_1, x_2, \ldots, x_{n_1+n_2+m_1+1}\}$. For $i = 1, \ldots, n_1$, x_i corresponds to y_i. For $i = 1, \ldots, n_2$, x_{n_1+i} corresponds to z_i. For $i = 1, \ldots, m_1$, $x_{n_1+n_2+i}$ corresponds to the ith term of $\psi(\mathbf{y}, \mathbf{z})$, where the ith term is represented as $\ell_{i_1} \wedge \ell_{i_2} \wedge \ell_{i_3}$. In the following, corresponding variables in 3-SAT and nodes in the BN are identified in ℓ_{i_j}.

Then, we assign the following functions to V:

$$x_i(t+1) = \overline{x_i(t)}, \quad \text{for } i = 1, \ldots, n_1,$$

$$x_{n_1+i}(t+1) = x_{n_1+i}(t), \quad \text{for } i = 1, \ldots, n_2,$$

$$x_{n_1+n_2+i}(t+1) = \ell_{i_1}(t) \wedge \ell_{i_2}(t) \wedge \ell_{i_3}(t), \quad \text{for } i = 1, \ldots, m_1,$$

$$x_{n_1+n_2+m_1+1}(t+1) = \bigvee_{i \in \{1, \ldots, m_1\}} x_{n_1+n_2+i}(t).$$

Finally, we let $m = n_1$, $\alpha_{n_1+n_2+m_1+1} = 1$, $\alpha_i = 0$ for $i < n_1 + n_2 + m_1 + 1$, and $\Theta = 1$.

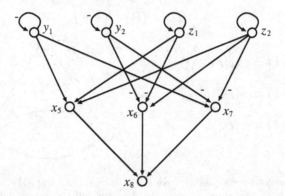

Fig. 7.6   Reduction from $(\exists \mathbf{y})(\forall \mathbf{z})((y_1 \wedge z_1 \wedge z_2) \vee (\overline{y}_2 \wedge \overline{z}_1 \wedge z_2) \vee (y_1 \wedge \overline{y}_2 \wedge \overline{z}_2))$ to Attractor Control. In this figure, y_1, y_2, z_1 and z_2 are identified with x_1, x_2, x_3 and x_4, respectively. Arrows with '-' correspond to negative inputs. In this case, Attractor Control has a solution by selecting y_1 and y_2 as control nodes with assigning $[y_1, y_2] = [1, 0]$.

Then, we can see that Attractor Control has a solution if and only if $(\exists \mathbf{y})(\forall \mathbf{z})\psi(\mathbf{y}, \mathbf{z})$ is true. First, suppose that $(\exists \mathbf{y})(\forall \mathbf{z})\psi(\mathbf{y}, \mathbf{z})$ is true for an assignment of $\mathbf{y} = [b_1, \ldots, b_{n_1}]$. Then, it is straightforward to see that Attractor Control has a solution by an assignment of $[x_1, \ldots, x_{n_1}] = [b_1, \ldots, b_{n_1}]$.

Next, suppose that Attractor Control has a solution. Then, we can see that $x_1, \ldots, x_{n_1}$ must be selected as control nodes since $x_i(t + 1) = \overline{x_i(t)}$ are assigned to these nodes. Furthermore, for any assignment on $x_{n_1+1}, \ldots, x_{n_2}$, the states of $x_{n_1+n_2+1}, \ldots, x_{n_1+n_2+m_1+1}$ satisfying the condition of a singleton attractor are uniquely determined. Since $g(\mathbf{x})$ is determined only by the value of $x_{n_1+n_2+m_1+1}$ and $g(\mathbf{x}) \geq 1$ must hold, $x_{n_1+n_2+m_1+1}$ takes 1 (in a singleton attractor) for each assignment on $x_{n_1+1}, \ldots, x_{n_2}$. It means that for any $\mathbf{y}$, at least one term becomes true. Therefore, $(\exists \mathbf{y})(\forall \mathbf{z})\psi(\mathbf{y}, \mathbf{z})$ is true.

Since the reduction can obviously be done in polynomial time, we have the theorem.   □

This theorem still holds for BNs with the maximum indegree 3, by encoding the large OR node (i.e., $x_{n_1+n_2+m+1}$) using a binary tree. Since ILP belongs to NP and it is widely believed that $\sum_2^P$ is not equal to NP [Garey and Johnson (1979)], it is not plausible that Attractor Control is directly reduced to ILP in polynomial time. However, it is possible to solve Attractor Control by using ILP repeatedly, as shown below.

We consider a subproblem of finding a singleton attractor with the maximum score by selecting and controlling m nodes. This subproblem can be solved by using an ILP formulation that is similar to those for Attractor Detection and BN Control. Different from those cases, we need to consider the following two possibilities for each variable x_i:

- x_i is selected as a control node (i.e., x_i corresponds to an external node),
- x_i is not selected as a control node (i.e., x_i becomes an internal node).

In order to choose one from these two, we introduce additional variables and constraints. Let x_i be given by $x_i = \begin{cases} y_i \text{ if } w_i = 0, \\ z_i \text{ if } w_i = 1. \end{cases}$ Note that y_i, z_i are newly introduced variables here and are different from those in the proof of Theorem 7.5. This relation is represented by ILP formula:

$$y_i - w_i \ \leq x_i \leq \ y_i + w_i,$$
$$z_i - (1 - w_i) \ \leq x_i \leq \ z_i + (1 - w_i).$$

$w_i = 1$ corresponds to the case that x_i is selected as a control node and z_i gives 0-1 assignment on it. $w_i = 0$ corresponds to the case that x_i is an internal node and the value of x_i is determined by y_i.

In Attractor Control, we need to maximize the score for non-control nodes. This objective function can be represented as $\max \sum_i \alpha_i \cdot (1 - w_i) \cdot x_i$., We can assume without loss of generality that $\alpha_i \geq 0$ (otherwise, we can use $1 - x_i$ instead of x_i). Since this objective function is not linear, we introduce additional 0-1 variables u_i and add constraints $u_i \leq x_i$ and $u_i \leq 1 - w_i$, and let the objective function be $\max \sum_i \alpha_i \cdot u_i$. Then, the following is the ILP formation for the subproblem, which is denoted by ILP-A.

Maximize $\sum_{i=1}^n \alpha_i u_i$,
Subject to
$$x_{i,b_{i_1}\ldots b_{i_k}} \ \geq \ \left(\sum_{j=1}^k \tau_{b_{i_j}}(x_{i_j}) \right) - (k-1),$$
$$x_{i,b_{i_1}\ldots b_{i_k}} \ \leq \ \frac{1}{k} \sum_{j=1}^k \tau_{b_{i_j}}(x_{i_j}),$$
$$\text{for all } i \in \{1, \ldots, n\} \text{ and } [b_{i_1}, \ldots, b_{i_k}] \in \{0,1\}^k$$
$$\text{such that } f_i(b_{i_1}, \ldots, b_{i_k}) = 1,$$
$$x_{i,b_{i_1}\ldots b_{i_k}} = 0,$$
$$\text{for all } i \in \{1, \ldots, n\} \text{ and } [b_{i_1}, \ldots, b_{i_k}] \in \{0,1\}^k$$
$$\text{such that } f_i(b_{i_1}, \ldots, b_{i_k}) = 0,$$

$$y_i \leq \sum_{[b_{i_1},\ldots,b_{i_k}]\in\{0,1\}^k} x_{i,b_{i_1}\ldots b_{i_k}},$$

$$y_i \geq \frac{1}{2^k}\sum_{[b_{i_1},\ldots,b_{i_k}]\in\{0,1\}^k} x_{i,b_{i_1}\ldots b_{i_k}},$$

$$y_i - w_i \leq x_i \leq y_i + w_i,$$

$$z_i + w_i - 1 \leq x_i \leq z_i - w_i + 1,$$

$$u_i \leq x_i, \quad u_i \leq 1 - w_i,$$

$$x_i, y_i, z_i, w_i, u_i \in \{0,1\},$$

$$\text{for all } i \in \{1,\ldots,n\},$$

$$x_{i,b_{i_1}\ldots b_{i_k}} \in \{0,1\},$$

$$\text{for all } i \in \{1,\ldots,n\} \text{ and } [b_{i_1},\ldots,b_{i_k}] \in \{0,1\}^k,$$

$$\sum_{i=1}^n w_i = m.$$

In order to solve Attractor Control, we repeatedly use this ILP formulation. Suppose that $V' = \{x_{i_1},\ldots,x_{i_m}\}$ are selected as control nodes with a 0-1 assignment $\mathbf{b}' = [b_{i_1},\ldots,b_{i_m}]$, by using ILP-A. Then, we find the attractor of the minimum score under these control nodes. This can also be formalized as ILP by modifying ILP-A as follows. Let $I = \{i_1,\ldots,i_m\}$. We replace the objective function by "Minimize $\sum_{i\notin I} \alpha_i x_i$" and the constraints using u_i by

$$x_i = z_i, \ w_i = 1 \qquad \text{for all } i \in I,$$
$$w_i = 0, \qquad\qquad \text{for all } i \notin I.$$

The resulting ILP is denoted by ILP-B.

We repeatedly apply ILP-A and ILP-B until the required condition is satisfied. In order to examine different control node sets at each iteration, we need to modify ILP-A. To this end, we introduce some linear inequalities stating that the solution must be different from the previously obtained solutions. Let $\mathbf{x}^j = [x_1^{(j)}, x_2^{(j)},\ldots,x_n^{(j)}]$ be the jth control previously found, where we let $x_i^{(j)} = z_i$ if $w_i = 1$, otherwise $x_i^{(j)} = -1$. Then, for each j, we add the following linear constraint:

$$\sum_{x_i^{(j)}\neq -1} \left(\delta(x_i^{(j)},1)(-z_i - w_i) + \delta(x_i^{(j)},0)(z_i - w_i) \right)$$

$$\geq 1 - \sum_{x_i^{(j)}\neq -1} (1 + x_i^{(j)}),$$

where $\delta(x,y)$ is the delta function (i.e., $\delta(x,y) = 1$ if and only if $x = y$). This inequality means that the following must hold for at least one i:

- if $x_i^{(j)} = 1$, either $z_i = 0$ or $w_i = 0$ holds,
- otherwise, either $z_i = 1$ or $w_i = 0$ holds.

This modified ILP formulation is denoted by ILP-A'. Note that using ILP-A', it is guaranteed that a set of control nodes determined by w_is is different from any of previously examined sets of control nodes.

The following is the main procedure for solving Attractor Control.

Procedure AttCtrl$(N(V, F), g, m, \Theta)$

(1) Repeat Steps 2-3.
(2) Find $(V', \mathbf{b}')$ which maximizes the score of a singleton attractor using ILP-A' under the condition that $(V', \mathbf{b}')$ is different from any of previously examined nodes/values pairs. If the maximum score is less than Θ, output "None" and halt.
(3) Compute the minimum score of singleton attractors for $(V', \mathbf{b}')$ using ILP-B. If the minimum score is no less than Θ, output $(V', \mathbf{b}')$ and halt.

It is straightforward to see that **AttCtrl** exactly solves Attractor Control. **AttCtrl** may repeat exponentially many times in the worst case, which is reasonable from $\sum_2^P$-hardness of the problem. However, it is expected that this procedure does not repeat so many times because the expected number of singleton attractors (per $(V', \mathbf{b}')$) is small regardless of n for a random BN (recall Proposition 2.1). The efficiency and the number of repetitions of **AttCtrl** against artificially generated BNs were examined in [Akutsu *et al.* (2012c)].

7.4   Additional Remarks and Bibliographical Notes

The formalization and NP-hardness of BN Control, and the algorithm for tree-structured BNs in Section 7.1 are based on [Akutsu *et al.* (2007)]. ILP-based methods in Sections 7.1 and 7.3 are given in [Akutsu *et al.* (2012c)], which also gives the formalization and hardness result of Attractor Control. Attractor Control was extended for handling multiple networks [Qiu *et al.* (2014)]. The formalization, hardness, and ILP-based method for Minimum Driver Set are based on [Hou *et al.* (2016)].

For solving BN Control and related problems, several methods have been proposed, which include a model checking-based method [Langmead and Jha (2009)] and Petri net-based methods [Kobayashi and Hiraishi (2013)]. To be discussed in Chapter 9, extensive studies and various extensions have been done on BN Control under the semi-tensor product framework [Cheng *et al.* (2011, 2012)].

As mentioned in Section 7.2, extensive studies have been done on the minimum driver set problem under various mathematical models in the field of complex networks [Liu *et al.* (2011); Liu and Barabási (2016); Nacher and Akutsu (2016)].

Chapter 8

Predecessor and Observability Problems

In this chapter, we consider two other important problems on BNs, predecessor detection and minimum observer detection for attractors, both of which are related to BN Control. The problem of predecessor detection is, given a BN and its state, to find its predecessor, a state that transits into the given state. This problem can be used as a pre-process of BN Control because if the desired state does not have a predecessor, there is no control sequence for driving the BN to this state. It may also be useful to identify the basin of attraction for a given attractor by enumerating predecessor states recursively [Wuensche (2000)]. Observability is an important concept in control theory and is a dual of controllability. A system with observer nodes is called observable if the system's complete internal state at any given time step can be reconstructed from time-series data of observer nodes. Although extensive studies have been done on the observability of BN and related models using semi-tensor product [Cheng *et al.* (2009, 2011); Laschov *et al.* (2013); Wu *et al.* (2017); Zhang and Zhang (2013)], it is also known that many nodes are required to observe previous states in a BN [Li *et al,* (2015)]. Therefore, in this chapter, we consider the problem of finding a minimum set of nodes using which given attractors are discriminated. Since attractors are often regarded as cell types, this problem has a potential application in finding marker genes for discriminating cell types.

8.1 Predecessor Detection

Given a BN and a state of the BN $\mathbf{w}$, $\mathbf{x}$ is called a *predecessor* of $\mathbf{w}$ if $\mathbf{w} = \mathbf{f}(\mathbf{x})$ holds. The predecessor detection problem is defined as below.

Definition 8.1.   [Predecessor Detection]
Instance: a BN $N(V, F)$ and a state $\mathbf{w}$ of $N(V, F)$.
Problem: decide whether or not there exists a state (predecessor) $\mathbf{x}$ of $N(V, F)$ such that $\mathbf{w} = \mathbf{f}(\mathbf{x})$, and output one if it exists.

Example 8.1. Consider the following BN, which is the same as that in Example 2.1:

$$x_1(t+1) = x_3(t),$$
$$x_2(t+1) = x_1(t) \wedge \overline{x_3(t)},$$
$$x_3(t+1) = x_1(t) \wedge \overline{x_2(t)}.$$

The structure and state transition diagram of this BN are shown in Fig. 8.1. Each directed edge in the state transition diagram corresponds to a state-predecessor relationship, where the source and target vertices correspond to a state and its predecessor, respectively. The following table shows all state-predecessor relations, where '-' means that there does not exist a predecessor.

state	predecessor(s)
$[0, 0, 0]$	$[0, 0, 0], [0, 1, 0]$
$[0, 0, 1]$	-
$[0, 1, 0]$	$[1, 1, 0]$
$[0, 1, 1]$	$[1, 0, 0]$
$[1, 0, 0]$	$[0, 0, 1], [0, 1, 1], [1, 1, 1]$
$[1, 0, 1]$	$[1, 0, 1]$
$[1, 1, 0]$	-
$[1, 1, 1]$	-

This problem has a similarity with Singleton Attractor Detection. As in Singleton Attractor Detection, Predecessor Detection is NP-hard.

Proposition 8.1. *Predecessor Detection is NP-hard even for $K = 3$.*

Proof. We use a simple polynomial-time reduction from 3-SAT to Predecessor Detection.

Let $C = \{c_1, \ldots, c_M\}$ be a set of clauses over a set of Boolean variables $Z = \{z_1, \ldots, z_N\}$, where each clause is a disjunction (OR) of at most three literals. Recall that 3-SAT is to ask whether or not there exists an assignment of 0-1 values to $z_1, \ldots, z_N$ that satisfies all the clauses (i.e., the values of all clauses are 1).

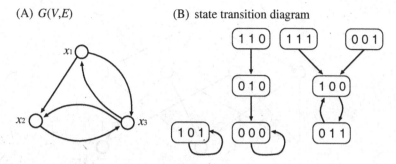

Fig. 8.1 Structure (A) and state transition diagram (B) of BN in Example 8.1. For example, $[1, 1, 0]$ is the predecessor of $[0, 1, 0]$, and $[0, 0, 1]$, $[0, 1, 1]$, and $[1, 1, 1]$ are the predecessors of $[1, 0, 0]$.

From this instance of 3-SAT, we construct an instance of Predecessor Detection (see also Fig. 8.2). Let $V = \{x_1, \ldots, x_{N+M+1}\}$, where each x_i for $i = 1, \ldots, N$ corresponds to z_i, each x_{N+j} for $j = 1, \ldots, M$ corresponds to c_j, and x_{N+M+1} is a special node which does not have any input variables and takes always value 1 (i.e., $x_{N+M+1}(t) = 1$ for all t). For each x_i $(i = 1, \ldots, N)$, we assign the following function:

$$x_i(t+1) = x_{N+M+1}(t).$$

Let $c_j = g_j(z_{j_1}, z_{j_2}, z_{j_3})$. Then, for each x_{N+j} $(j = 1, \ldots, M)$, we assign the following function:

$$x_{N+j}(t+1) = g_j(x_{j_1}(t), x_{j_2}(t), x_{j_3}(t)).$$

Finally, we let $\mathbf{w} = [1, 1, \ldots, 1]$.

Then, it is straightforward to see that $\mathbf{x}$ satisfying $\mathbf{w} = \mathbf{f}(\mathbf{x})$ corresponds to a satisfying assignment for 3-SAT. That is, there exists a predecessor $\mathbf{x}$ if and only if there exists a satisfying assignment for 3-SAT. Since the reduction can be done in polynomial time, the proposition holds. $\square$

In the above, 3-SAT was reduced to Predecessor Detection. Conversely, Predecessor Detection with the maximum indegree K can be reduced to K-SAT as follows.

Proposition 8.2. *Predecessor Detection with n nodes and the maximum indegree K can be reduced to K-SAT with n variables in polynomial time for a fixed K.*

Proof. Let $N(V, F)$ be a BN with the maximum indegree K and $V = \{x_1, \ldots, x_n\}$. Let $\mathbf{w} = [w_1, \ldots, w_n]$ be the state for which predecessor should be obtained.

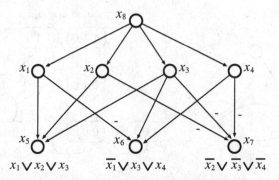

$$x_1 \vee x_2 \vee x_3 \qquad \overline{x_1} \vee x_3 \vee x_4 \qquad \overline{x_2} \vee \overline{x_3} \vee \overline{x_4}$$

Fig. 8.2   Example of a reduction from 3-SAT to Predecessor Detection for $K = 3$. An instance of 3-SAT $\{z_1 \vee z_2 \vee z_3, \overline{z_1} \vee z_3 \vee z_4, \overline{z_2} \vee \overline{z_3} \vee \overline{z_4}\}$ is transformed into this Boolean network. Arrows with '-' correspond to negative inputs.

Recall that the state of $x_i(t + 1)$ is determined by

$$x_i(t + 1) = f_i(x_{i_1}(t), \dots, x_{i_k}(t)),$$

where $k \leq K$. For each f_i, let $A_{POS}(f_i)$ denote the set of 0-1 assignments $[a_{i_1}, \dots, a_{i_k}]$ on $[x_{i_1}, \dots, x_{i_k}]$ each of which makes $f_i = 1$. We define $\ell_i(a)$ by

$$\ell_i(a) = \begin{cases} x_i, & \text{if } a = 1, \\ \overline{x_i}, & \text{otherwise,} \end{cases}$$

where x_is represent both nodes and their values in a predecessor. Then, f_i is represented as

$$f_i(x_{i_1}, \dots, x_{i_k}) = \bigvee_{[a_{i_1}, \dots, a_{i_k}] \in A_{POS}(f_i)} \ell_{i_1}(a_{i_1}) \wedge \cdots \wedge \ell_{i_k}(a_{i_k}).$$

If $w_i = 1$, we let

$$\bigvee_{[a_{i_1}, \dots, a_{i_k}] \in A_{POS}(f_i)} \ell_{i_1}(a_{i_1}) \wedge \cdots \wedge \ell_{i_k}(a_{i_k}) = 1.$$

Although the left-hand side of the above is not in the SAT form, it can be represented as a conjunction of clauses each of which consists of at most k literals, by applying the distributive law of Boolean algebra. Therefore, the above constraint can be represented as a part of K-SAT. Furthermore, the size of this representation is $O(1)$ per node for a fixed K.

If $w_i = 0$, we let

$$\bigvee_{[a_{i_1}, \dots, a_{i_k}] \in A_{POS}(f_i)} \ell_{i_1}(a_{i_1}) \wedge \cdots \wedge \ell_{i_k}(a_{i_k}) = 0,$$

which is equivalent to

$$\bigvee_{[a_{i_1},\ldots,a_{i_k}]\in A_{POS}(f_i)} \ell_{i_1}(a_{i_1}) \wedge \cdots \wedge \ell_{i_k}(a_{i_k}) = 1,$$

It is seen from De Morgan's laws that this constraint can be represented as a part of K-SAT. Again, the size of this representation is $O(1)$ per node for a fixed K.

Accordingly, all constraints are combined into a K-SAT formula and thus Predecessor Detection can be reduced to K-SAT in polynomial time. □

Example 8.2. Consider a BN defined by $V = \{x_1, x_2, x_3\}$ and $f_1 = x_2 \vee x_3$, $f_2 = x_1 \vee \overline{x_3}$, and $f_3 = x_1 \oplus x_2$. Note that $K = 2$ for this BN. Let $\mathbf{w} = [1, 0, 1]$ be the state for which a predecessor should be obtained. Then, we have

$$x_2 \vee x_3 = 1,$$
$$x_1 \vee \overline{x_3} = 0,$$
$$x_1 \oplus x_2 = 1.$$

Note that the second constraint is transformed as follows

$$\overline{x_1 \vee \overline{x_3}} = 1,$$
$$\overline{x_1} \wedge x_3 = 1,$$

and the third constraint is transformed as follows

$$(x_1 \wedge \overline{x_2}) \vee (\overline{x_1} \vee x_2) = 1,$$
$$(x_1 \vee \overline{x_1}) \wedge (x_1 \vee x_2) \wedge (\overline{x_2} \vee \overline{x_1}) \wedge (\overline{x_2} \vee x_2) = 1,$$
$$(x_1 \vee x_2) \wedge (\overline{x_2} \vee \overline{x_1}) = 1.$$

Therefore, the original instance of Predecessor Detection is transformed into an instance of 2-SAT:

$$(x_2 \vee x_3) \wedge (\overline{x_1}) \wedge (x_3) \wedge (x_1 \vee x_2) \wedge (\overline{x_2} \vee \overline{x_1}).$$

This SAT instance has the unique solution of $[x_1, x_2, x_3] = [0, 1, 1]$. Therefore, Predecessor Detection has the unique solution of $[0, 1, 1]$.

Although Singleton Attractor Detection is similar to Predecessor Detection, there are some differences in the computational complexity.

- For $K = 2$, Singleton Attractor Detection is NP-hard whereas Predecessor Detection is solvable in polynomial time (because 2-SAT is polynomially solvable).

- Singleton Attractor Detection with the maximum indegree K is reduced to $(K+1)$-SAT whereas Predecessor Detection with the maximum indegree K is reduced to K-SAT.

In Example 8.2, there was a unique solution. However, in general, K-SAT may have multiple solutions and thus there may exist multiple predecessors. For enumeration of singleton attractors, a simple recursive algorithm was presented in Section 3.6. This algorithm can be modified for enumeration of all predecessors of a given state $\mathbf{w} = [w_1, \ldots, w_n]$. To this end, it is enough to replace the condition of

$$f_i(\mathbf{x}) \neq x_i$$

in **RecursiveEnumSatt** with

$$f_i(\mathbf{x}) \neq w_i.$$

Then, the same average case time complexity result holds. Recall also that in Section 2.2, the expected number of singleton attractors was shown to be 1 regardless of the size of a BN. We have a similar result on the expected number of predecessors.

Proposition 8.3. *For any BN, the average number of predecessors per state is 1.*

Proof. The number of outgoing edges from each node in a state transition diagram is 1. Thus, the total number of edges in a state transition diagram is 2^n where $n = |V|$. Since each edge corresponds to a predecessor and there exist 2^n nodes in the state transition diagram, the average number of incoming edges (i.e., predecessors) per state is 1.   □

Since the average number of predecessors is 1 and some state may have multiple predecessors, some state may not have a predecessor. If a general BN is considered, we can obtain the following precise result on the number of such states.

Proposition 8.4. *Suppose that all possible BNs with n nodes are given at uniformly random. Then, the expected number of states with no predecessor converges to $2^n/e$ as n grows, where e is the base of natural log.*

Proof. Since each state $\mathbf{w}$ of a BN has exactly one outgoing edge in a state transition diagram, the probability that a specified $\mathbf{x}$ is a predecessor of $\mathbf{w}$

is $1/N$ where $N = 2^n$. Hence the probability that each state $\mathbf{w}$ has no predecessor is

$$\left(1 - \frac{1}{N}\right)^N,$$

which approaches to $1/e$ as N grows. Since there exist $N = 2^n$ states in a BN, we have the proposition. □

For BNs with the maximum indegree K, we have the following result.

Proposition 8.5. *Suppose that all possible BNs with n nodes and the maximum indegree K are given at uniformly random. Then, the expected number of states with no predecessor is no less than $2^n(1 - (1 - \frac{1}{2^{2^K}}))$.*

Proof. We assume w.l.o.g. that a randomly chosen state is $\mathbf{w} = [1, 1, \ldots, 1]$. If a Boolean function always outputting 0 is assigned to some node, $\mathbf{w}$ has no predecessor. Since there are 2^{2^K} Boolean functions with at most K inputs, the probability that such a function is not assigned to any of n nodes is $(1 - \frac{1}{2^{2^K}})^n$, which gives an upper bound of the probability that a randomly chosen state state has at least one predecessor. Therefore, the probability that a randomly chosen state does not have a predecessor is lower bounded by $(1 - (1 - \frac{1}{2^{2^K}})^n)$ and thus the proposition follows. □

8.2 Observation of Attractors

In this section, we consider the problem of determining the minimum set of nodes by which all given singleton and periodic attractors can be discriminated.

8.2.1 *Observation of Singleton Attractors*

Let B be an $m \times n$ binary matrix, where each column corresponds to a node and each row corresponds to a singleton attractor in a BN. $B[i, j]$ denotes the element at ith row and jth column, $B[i, -]$ denotes the ith row, and $B[-, j]$ denotes the jth column, Let $J = \{j_1, \ldots, j_k\}$ be a set of column indices. Then, B_J denotes the submatrix of B consisting of the $j_1, j_2, \cdots, j_k$th columns. The minimum observer for singleton attractors is defined as follows.

Definition 8.2. [**Minimum Observer for Singleton Attractors**]
Instance: an $m \times n$ binary matrix where each column corresponds to a node

and each row corresponds to a singleton attractor.

Problem: find a minimum cardinality set J of columns such that $B_J[i_1, -] \neq B_J[i_2, -]$ holds for all i_1, i_2 with $1 \leq i_1 < i_2 \leq m$.

In this definition, a BN is not given as a part of the input. It is reasonable from the motivation that we consider a situation in which gene expression data of different cell types are given, which correspond to attractors. Note also that Minimum Observer for Singleton Attractors always has a solution since all given attractors are differentiated by using all columns.

Example 8.3. Consider a 7×6 matrix B defined by

$$B = \begin{pmatrix} 0\ 1\ 1\ 1\ 0\ 1 \\ 1\ 1\ 1\ 1\ 0\ 0 \\ 1\ 0\ 1\ 1\ 0\ 1 \\ 0\ 0\ 1\ 0\ 1\ 1 \\ 1\ 0\ 1\ 0\ 1\ 1 \\ 0\ 1\ 1\ 1\ 0\ 0 \\ 0\ 0\ 0\ 0\ 1\ 1 \end{pmatrix}.$$

Then, $B[1, -] = [0, 1, 1, 1, 0, 1]$ and $B[-, 2] = [1, 1, 0, 0, 1, 0]^{\top}$, where $A^{\top}$ denotes the transposed matrix of A. $J = \{1, 3, 5, 6\}$ is a solution of Minimum Observer for Singleton Attractors for B because any pair of rows are different in

$$B_{\{1,3,5,6\}} = \begin{pmatrix} 0\ 1\ 0\ 1 \\ 1\ 1\ 0\ 0 \\ 1\ 1\ 0\ 1 \\ 0\ 1\ 1\ 1 \\ 1\ 1\ 1\ 1 \\ 0\ 1\ 0\ 0 \\ 0\ 0\ 1\ 1 \end{pmatrix}$$

and there is no such index set of size 3.

This problem is essentially the same as Minimum Test Collection [Garey and Johnson (1979)]. The following is a modified version of the proof for NP-hardness of Minimum Test Collection in [Garey and Johnson (1979)].

Theorem 8.1. *Minimum Observer for Singleton Attractors is NP-hard.*

Proof. We prove the theorem by showing a polynomial-time reduction from the three dimensional matching problem (3DM). 3DM is, given a set of tuples $T \subseteq W \times Y \times Z$ where $W = \{w_1, \ldots, w_n\}$, $Y = \{y_1, \ldots, y_n\}$, $Z = \{z_1, \ldots, z_n\}$, and $T = \{t_1, \ldots, t_m\}$, to find $M \subseteq S$ such that $|M| = n$, $\{w | (w, y, z) \in M\} = W$, $\{y | (w, y, z) \in M\} = Y$, and $\{z | (w, y, z) \in M\} = Z$ hold.

From an instance of 3DM, we construct a $(3n + 3) \times (m + 2)$ binary matrix B as follows. We encode the set of tuples T by a $3n \times m$ submatrix of B as

$$B[i, j] = \begin{cases} 1, & \text{if } w_i \text{ appears in } t_j, \\ 0, & \text{otherwise,} \end{cases}$$

$$B[n + i, j] = \begin{cases} 1, & \text{if } y_i \text{ appears in } t_j, \\ 0, & \text{otherwise,} \end{cases}$$

$$B[2n + i, j] = \begin{cases} 1, & \text{if } z_i \text{ appears in } t_j, \\ 0, & \text{otherwise,} \end{cases}$$

where $i = 1, \ldots, n$ and $j = 1, \ldots, m$. Sets of rows $\{1, \ldots, n\}$, $\{n + 1, \ldots, 2n\}$, and $\{2n + 1, \ldots, 3n\}$ correspond to W, Y, and Z, respectively. Columns $1, \ldots, m$ correspond to tuples $t_1, \ldots, t_m$, respectively. In addition, we let

$$B[i, m + 1] = 1,$$
$$B[n + i, m + 2] = 1,$$

for $i = 1, \ldots, n$, and

$$B[3n + 1, m + 1] = 1,$$
$$B[3n + 2, m + 2] = 1.$$

All other elements of B are set to 0. Note that all elements of the $(3n+3)$th row are 0.

We prove that 3DM has a solution if and only if Minimum Observer for Singleton Attractors has a solution of size $n + 2$.

Suppose that 3DM has a solution M. Let $J = \{j | t_j \in M\}$. Then, for any pair (i_1, i_2) of rows such that $1 \leq i_1 < i_2 \leq n$, there exists a column $j \in J$ such that $B[i_1, j] = 1$ and $B[i_2, j] = 0$ and $t_j \in M$. Indeed, t_j is the unique element in M that contains w_{i_1}. Similarly, for any pair (i_1, i_2) of rows such that $1 \leq i_1 < i_2 \leq n$, there exist columns $j', j'' \in J$ such that $B[n + i_1, j'] = 1$ and $B[n + i_2, j'] = 0$ and $t_{j'} \in M$, and $B[2n + i_1, j''] = 1$ and $B[2n + i_2, j''] = 0$ and $t_{j''} \in M$. Furthermore, the following hold:

- for any pair (i_1, i_2) such that $1 \leq i_1 \leq n$ and $n + 1 \leq i_2 \leq 3n$, $B[i_1, m + 1] = 1$ and $B[i_2, m + 1] = 0$ hold.
- for any pair (i_1, i_2) such that $n + 1 \leq i_1 \leq 2n$ and $3n + 1 \leq i_2 \leq 3n$, $B[i_1, m + 2] = 1$ and $B[i_2, m + 2] = 0$ hold.

- for any pair $(i_1, 3n+i)$ such that $1 \le i_1 \le 3n$ and $1 \le i \le 3$, $B[i_1, j] = 1$ and $B[3n + i, j] = 0$ hold for some j.
- $B[3n + 1, m + 1] = 1$ and $\dot{B}[3n + 2, m + 2] = 1$ hold, whereas $B[3n + 2, m + 1] = 0$, $B[3n + 3, m + 1] = 0$, and $B[3n + 3, m + 2] = 0$ hold.

It is seen from the above that all rows can be differentiated by a set of columns $J \cup \{m+1, m+2\}$. Therefore, if 3DM has a solution J, Minimum Observer for Singleton Attractors has a solution $J \cup \{m + 1, m + 2\}$.

Conversely, suppose that Minimum Observer for Singleton Attractors has a solution J of size $n+2$. Then, J must contain columns $m+1$ and $m+2$ because otherwise rows $3n + 1$, $3n + 2$, and $3n + 3$ cannot be differentiated. Furthermore, it is straightforward to see that $J \setminus \{m+1, m+2\}$ corresponds to a solution of 3DM.

Since the reduction can be done in polynomial time, the theorem holds.

□

Example 8.4. We show an example of a reduction from 3DM to Minimum Observer for Singleton Attractors. Let $T = \{(a, B, \gamma), (a, A, \beta), (b, C, \alpha), (b, A, \gamma), (c, A, \beta)\}$ be an instance of 3DM. It has a solution $M = \{(a, B, \gamma), (b, C, \alpha), (c, A, \beta)\}$.

From this instance, the following binary matrix is constructed.

$$
B = \begin{pmatrix}
1 & 1 & 0 & 0 & 0 & 1 & 0 \\
0 & 0 & 1 & 1 & 0 & 1 & 0 \\
0 & 0 & 0 & 0 & 1 & 1 & 0 \\
0 & 1 & 0 & 1 & 1 & 0 & 1 \\
1 & 0 & 0 & 0 & 0 & 0 & 1 \\
0 & 0 & 1 & 0 & 0 & 0 & 1 \\
0 & 0 & 1 & 0 & 0 & 0 & 0 \\
0 & 1 & 0 & 0 & 1 & 0 & 0 \\
1 & 0 & 0 & 1 & 0 & 0 & 0 \\
0 & 0 & 0 & 0 & 0 & 1 & 0 \\
0 & 0 & 0 & 0 & 0 & 0 & 1 \\
0 & 0 & 0 & 0 & 0 & 0 & 0
\end{pmatrix}.
$$

Then, $J = \{1, 3, 5, 6, 7\}$ is a solution of Minimum Observer for Singleton Attractors, where columns 1, 3, and 5 correspond to tuples (a, B, γ), (b, C, α), and (c, A, β), respectively.

From Theorem 8.1, it is not plausible that there exists a polynomial-time algorithm for Minimum Observer for Singleton Attractors. On the other hand, Minimum Observer for Singleton Attractors can be solved in $O(2^n poly(m,n))$ time by examining all possible 2^n subsets of columns. In many practical cases, n is large and m is small because n and m correspond to the number of genes and the number attractors (e.g., the number of cell types), respectively. In the following, we describe an $O(m^m poly(m,n))$ time algorithm. Of course, m^m is a large number. However, if the number of relevant cell types is relatively small (e.g., $m \approx 10$), it is expected to be faster than the naive enumeration based algorithm.

Let $\mathbf{s}$ be an m-dimensional vector of integers between 0 to $m-1$, which is referred to as a *signature vector*. Recall that $\mathbf{s}[i]$ denotes the ith element of $\mathbf{s}$, and $\mathbf{0}$ denotes the signature vector consisting only of 0's.

If $\mathbf{s}[i] \leq 2^k - 1$ holds for all $i = 1, \ldots, m$ for some integer k (i.e., each element of $\mathbf{s}$ is represented using k bits), $\mathbf{s}$ is called a *k-bit signature vector*. We identify such $\mathbf{s}$ with an $m \times k$ binary matrix by regarding the ith element of $\mathbf{s}$ as the ith row consisting of k bits. Let $M(\mathbf{s})$ denote such a matrix. Conversely, a k-bit signature vector $\mathbf{s}$ can be constructed from a given $m \times k$ binary matrix M by identifying each row with a k bit integer number. However, we do not use such $\mathbf{s}$, instead use a compact form of $\mathbf{s}$ by renaming elements of $\mathbf{s}$ (with the ordering being kept) so that only consecutive numbers beginning from 0 are used. The resulting vector is denoted by $\mathbf{v}(M)$. For an $m \times k_1$ matrix M_1 and an $m \times k_2$ matrix M_2, $M_1 \cdot M_2$ denotes the $m \times (k_1 + k_2)$ matrix obtained by concatenating M_1 and M_2. The compact form is useful to reduce the size of the table in a dynamic programming algorithm for Minimum Observer for Singleton Attractors.

Example 8.5. Consider the matrix B given in Example 8.3. Then, the signature vector is $\mathbf{s} = [29, 60, 45, 11, 43, 28, 3]$, meaning that $M(\mathbf{s}) = B$. The compact form of $\mathbf{s}$ is $\mathbf{v}(B) = [3, 6, 5, 1, 4, 2, 0]$ (i.e., 29 is replaced by 3, 60 is replaced by 6, ...). The signature vector and its compact form for $B_{\{1,3,5\}}$ are $\mathbf{s} = [2, 6, 6, 3, 7, 2, 1]$ and $\mathbf{v}(B_{\{1,3,5\}}) = [1, 3, 3, 2, 4, 1, 0]$, respectively. $M(\mathbf{s}) \cdot B[-, 6] = B_{\{1,3,5,6\}}$ holds for this $\mathbf{s}$. The signature vector and its compact form for $B_{\{1,3,5,6\}}$ are $\mathbf{s} = [5, 12, 13, 7, 15, 4, 3]$ and $\mathbf{v}(B_{\{1,3,5,6\}}) = [2, 4, 5, 3, 6, 1, 0]$, respectively.

Here we describe a dynamic programming algorithm **MinObsSatt** for solving Minimum Observer for Singleton Attractors. It is common in dynamic programming algorithms to use a table. In **MinObsSatt**, we use a binary table $D[\mathbf{s}, k]$ that is defined by: $D[\mathbf{s}, k] = 1$ if and only if there exists J with $|J| = k$ such that $\mathbf{v}(B_J) = \mathbf{s}$. $D[\mathbf{s}, k]$ can be computed by the following dynamic programming procedure, where all $D[\mathbf{s}, k]$s are initialized to be 0. Although it returns only the minimum size of J, such J can be obtained by using the standard *traceback* procedure.

Procedure MinObsSatt(B)
$D[\mathbf{0}, 0] \leftarrow 1;$
for $k = 1$ **to** n **do**
   for all $\mathbf{s}$ such that $D[\mathbf{s}, k - 1] = 1$ **do**
      for all column j of B **do**
         $M' \leftarrow M(\mathbf{s}) \cdot B[-, j];$
         $\mathbf{s}' \leftarrow \mathbf{v}(M');$
         $D[\mathbf{s}', k] \leftarrow 1;$
         if $\mathbf{s}'[i_1] \neq \mathbf{s}'[i_2]$ holds for all i_1, i_2 with $1 \leq i_1 < i_2 \leq m$ **then**
            return k.

Theorem 8.2. *Minimum Observer for Singleton Attractors can be solved in $O(m^m poly(m, n))$ time.*

Proof. Since it is straightforward to see the correctness of **MinObsSatt**, we analyze the time complexity. First, note that $D[\mathbf{s}, k]$ is defined only for the compact forms of signature vectors and $k = 0, \ldots, n$. The number of compact forms is bounded by m^m per k because each element in $\mathbf{s}$ is between 0 to $m - 1$ and the length of each $\mathbf{s}$ is m. Therefore, the size of $D[\mathbf{s}, k]$ is $O(m^m n)$. For each $D[\mathbf{s}, k - 1]$ such that $D[\mathbf{s}, k - 1] = 1$, **for all** loop on j will be executed. Clearly, it takes $O(poly(m, n))$ time per execution. Therefore, the total time complexity is $O(m^m poly(m, n))$. $\qquad\square$

In **MinObsSatt**, equivalent signatures are discriminated, where two signatures are called *equivalent* if one is obtained by substitution of the elements. For example, $[0, 0, 1, 2, 2, 3]$ and $[3, 3, 0, 1, 1, 2]$ are equivalent because the latter vector is obtained from the former one by substituting 0, 1, 2, and 3 by 3, 0, 1, and 2, respectively. However, we do not need to discriminate equivalent signatures because our purpose is to find $D[\mathbf{s}, k] = 1$ for which all elements of $\mathbf{s}$ are mutually distinct. Therefore, it is possible to improve the result of Theorem 8.2.1 by identifying equivalent signatures. Since the number of non-equivalent signatures is shown to be $O((m/1.146)^m)$ [Cheng *et al.* (2017b)], we obtain an improved $O((m/1.146)^m poly(m, n))$ time algorithm.

8.2.2 Observation of Singleton and Periodic Attractors

In the above, attractors are limited to singleton attractors. Here, we consider all attractors, that is, singleton and periodic attractors. Before discussing details, we show that simple application of the approach in Section 8.2.1 does not work. For example, suppose that two periodic attractors $A_1 = \{[0, 1], [1, 0]\}$ and $A_2 = \{[0, 0], [1, 1]\}$ are given. If we focus on $[1, 0]$ and $[1, 1]$, the solution of Minimum Observer for Singleton Attractors would be $\{x_2\}$. However, the corresponding infinite time series data are $(1, 0, 1, 0, \cdots)$ and $(0, 1, 0, 1, \cdots)$ for A_1 and A_2, respectively. Since these two time series are identical except the starting states and we cannot know which is the starting state, we cannot discriminate A_1 from A_2 by looking at time series data for x_2. The situation is the same for x_1. However, if we look at both x_1 and x_2, the time series are $([0, 1], [1, 0], [0, 1], [1, 0], \cdots)$ and $([0, 0], [1, 1], [0, 0], [1, 1], \cdots)$ for A_1 and A_2. These two sequences are clearly different and thus we can discriminate A_1 from A_2.

Before describing the algorithm, we formally define the problem. In Chapter 2, an attractor is define as a set of states. However, in this section, an attractor is defined as a sequence of states because the underlying BN is not given as a part of an input and thus the ordering on states must be specified. Recall that for a set $U \subseteq V$ and a 0-1 vector $\mathbf{x}$ for $V = \{x_1, \ldots, x_n\}$, $\mathbf{x}_U$ denotes the $|U|$-dimensional vector consisting of elements of $\mathbf{x}$ that correspond to U. For example, for $\mathbf{x} = [0, 1, 0, 1, 1, 0]$, $\mathbf{x}_U = [0, 1, 0]$ for $U = \{x_1, x_2, x_3\}$, and $\mathbf{x}_U = [1, 1, 1, 0]$ for $U = \{x_2, x_4, x_5, x_6\}$.

Let

$$A_h = (\mathbf{x}(0), \mathbf{x}(1), \ldots, \mathbf{x}(p(A_h) - 1))$$

be an attractor of period $p(A_h)$ (i.e., $\mathbf{x}(0) = \mathbf{x}(p(A_h))$) on an underlying BN. Then, $Ser(A_h, U, t)$ denotes the infinite sequence of vectors defined by

$$Ser(A_h, U, t) = (\mathbf{x}_U(t), \mathbf{x}_U(t + 1), \mathbf{x}_U(t + 2), \cdots).$$

Two periodic attractors A_h and A_k are *identical* if and only if $Ser(A_h, V, 0) = Ser(A_k, V, t)$ holds for some $t \geq 0$.

Definition 8.3. [Minimum Observer for Attractors]
Instance: a set of attractors $\mathcal{A} = \{A_1, A_2, \ldots, A_m\}$, where each A_h consists of $p(A_h)$ states represented as a sequence of $p(A_h)$ binary vectors, $p(A_h)$ denotes the period of A_h, $n > 0$ denotes the number of nodes, and $m > 1$. Problem: find a minimum cardinality set U of nodes such that $Ser(A_h, U, 0) \neq Ser(A_k, U, t)$ for any $t \geq 0$ when $h \neq k$.

Example 8.6. Let $\mathcal{A} = \{A_1, A_2, A_3, A_4, A_5\}$ be a set of attractors, where

$$A_1 = ([0,1,1,0,1]),$$
$$A_2 = ([0,0,1,0,1]),$$
$$A_3 = ([1,0,1,0,1]),$$
$$A_4 = ([0,1,0,0,0],[1,0,0,0,1],[0,1,0,1,0],[1,0,0,1,1]),$$
$$A_5 = ([1,0,0,0,0],[0,1,0,1,1],[1,0,0,1,0],[0,1,0,0,1]).$$

Then, $\{x_1, x_2, x_5\}$ is a solution of Minimum Observer for Attractors (see also Fig. 8.3). Note that $Ser(A_4, \{x_1, x_2\}, 0) = Ser(A_5, \{x_1, x_2\}, 1)$ holds and thus $\{x_1, x_2\}$ is not a solution, whereas $Ser(A_4, \{x_1, x_2, x_5\}, 0) \neq Ser(A_5, \{x_1, x_2, x_5\}, t)$ holds for any t.

Note that there always exists a solution for Minimum Observer for Attractors because every pair of attractors can be discriminated by $U = V$.

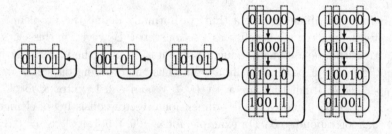

Fig. 8.3 Example of Minimum Observer for Attractors. A solution $\{x_1, x_2, x_5\}$ is shown by dotted boxes.

The following lemma plays a key role for solving Minimum Observer for Attractors. It is proved by using Chinese Remainder Theorem, where the proof is given in [Cheng *et al.* (2017b)].

Lemma 8.1. *For any two distinct (i.e., non-identical) attractors* $A_h = (\mathbf{x}(0), \ldots, \mathbf{x}(p_h - 1))$ *and* $A_k = (\mathbf{w}(0), \ldots, \mathbf{w}(p_k - 1))$, *there exists* $U \subseteq V$ *of* $|U| = 2$ *for which* $Ser(A_h, U, 0) \neq Ser(A_k, U, t)$ *holds for any* $t \geq 0$.

This lemma indicates that the minimum number of nodes for discriminating two different periodic attractors is at most two. Since the state of a singleton attractor does not change, a singleton attractor and a periodic attractor can be discriminated by looking at time series data of any single node whose state changes in the periodic attractor. Since

$2 \cdot \dbinom{m}{2} = m(m-1)$ holds, we can see that the size of U for Minimum Observer for Attractors is upper-bounded by $m \cdot (m-1)$.

Based on the above observation, a simple exhaustive-type algorithm can de designed for Minimum Observer for Attractors. Let $\mathcal{A} = \{A_1, \ldots, A_m\}$ be a set of singleton and periodic attractors. Let p be the longest period among $A_1, \ldots, A_m$. We modify $Ser(A_h, U, t)$ so that it does not consist of an infinite sequence. Let $Ser(A_h, U, t, p)$ be the sequence of vectors of length p defined by

$$Ser(A_h, U, t, p) = (\mathbf{x}_U(t), \mathbf{x}_U(t+1), \mathbf{x}_U(t+2), \cdots, \mathbf{x}_U(t+p-1)).$$

The following is a pseudocode of the algorithm **MinObsAtt**, which returns a minimum set of observer nodes U for Minimum Observer for Attractors.

Procedure MinObsAtt($\mathcal{A}$)
for $s = 1$ to $m(m-1)$ do
   for all $U \subseteq V$ such that $|U| = s$ do
      $flag \leftarrow 1$;
      for all (A_i, A_j) such that $i < j$ do
         if $Ser(A_i, U, 0, p) = Ser(A_j, U, t, p)$ holds for some $t \in \{0, \ldots, p-1\}$
         then $flag \leftarrow 0$; **break**;
      if $flag = 1$ return U.

Theorem 8.3. *Minimum Observer for Attractors can be solved in $O(n^{|U_{\min}|} poly(m, n, p))$ time, where $U_{\min}$ is an optimal solution of Minimum Observer for Attractors and p is the longest period of input attractors. Furthermore, $|U_{\min}| \leq m(m-1)$ holds.*

Proof. The correctness of **MinObsAtt** is obvious because the algorithm examines all subsets of V from smaller size to larger size.

Since the algorithm returns a minimum node set $U_{\min}$ as soon as it finds $U_{\min}$ and the exponential factor depends only on the number of Us examined in the algorithm, the time complexity of Minimum Observer for Attractors is $O(n^{|U_{\min}|} poly(m, n, p))$. Furthermore, it is seen from Lemma 8.1 that $|U_{\min}| \leq m(m-1)$ holds. $\qquad\square$

8.2.3 Relation with Feedback Vertex Sets

As seen in Chapter 3, attractors can be identified by looking at time series data of nodes in any feedback vertex set (FVS). Therefore, the minimum FVS (i.e., FVS with the minimum number of nodes) may give a solution to Minimum Observer for Attractors. Indeed, it gives a solution but does not necessarily give an optimal solution. Here we give a very simple example showing that the minimum FVS does not necessarily give an optimal solution of Minimum Observer for Singleton Attractors or Minimum Observer for Attractors.

Consider the following BN (see also Fig. 8.4):

$$x_1(t+1) = x_2(t) \oplus x_3(t),$$
$$x_2(t+1) = x_2(t) \vee \overline{x_1(t)},$$
$$x_3(t+1) = x_3(t) \wedge x_1(t).$$

In this BN, there exist two singleton attractors, $[1,0,1]$ and $[1,1,0]$, which can be discriminated by observing the state of x_2 (or x_3). Therefore, the size of the minimum observer node set is 1. On the other hand, $\{x_2, x_3\}$ is the minimum FVS. Therefore, it is seen that the minimum FVS does not necessarily give an optimal solution for Minimum Observer for Singleton Attractors. Since this BN does not have a periodic attractor, it also means that the minimum FVS does not necessarily give an optimal solution for Minimum Observer for Attractors.

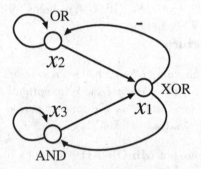

Fig. 8.4 Example of BN showing that the minimum FVS does not necessarily give an optimal solution for Minimum Observer for Singleton Attractors or Minimum Observer for Attractors. In this case, an optimal solution is $\{x_2\}$ (or $\{x_3\}$) but the minimum FVS is $\{x_2, x_3\}$. An arrow with '-' corresponds to a negative input.

Of course, there are cases in which the minimum FVS gives an optimal solution. For example, consider the following BN:

$$x_1(t+1) = x_2(t) \vee x_3(t).$$
$$x_2(t+1) = x_2(t) \vee \overline{x_1(t)},$$
$$x_3(t+1) = x_3(t) \wedge x_1(t).$$

Then, the singleton attractors of this BN are $[1, 0, 1]$, $[1, 1, 0]$, and $[1, 1, 1]$, and $\{x_2, x_3\}$ is the minimum FVS. Since at least two nodes are required to discriminate three attractors, this minimum FVS gives an optimal solution for this BN in both Minimum Observer for Singleton Attractors and Minimum Observer for Attractors.

8.3 Additional Remarks and Bibliographical Notes

The complexity of Predecessor Detection was extensively studied in [Barrett *et al.* (2007)]. Propositions 8.1, 8.2, 8.3, and 8.4 were given in [Coppersmith (2007)]. Proposition 8.5 was shown in [Akutsu *et al.* (2008)], where it was also shown that detection of a predecessor of a predecessor is NP-hard even for $K = 2$.

As mentioned at the beginning of this chapter, extensive studies have been done on the observability of BN and related models using semi-tensor product [Cheng *et al.* (2009, 2011); Laschov *et al.* (2013); Li *et al*, (2015); Wu *et al.* (2017); Zhang and Zhang (2013)]. It is shown in [Laschov *et al.* (2013)] that the original observability problem on BN is NP-hard. For a variant of Minimum Observer for Singleton Attractors, an ILP-based method was proposed [Cheng *et al.* (2017a)]. The results of Section 8.2 are based on [Cheng *et al.* (2017b)], where the proof of Theorem 8.1 is based on the proof of NP-hardness of Minimum Test Collection given in [Garey and Johnson (1979)].

Chapter 9

Semi-Tensor Product Approach

We have seen discrete and combinatorial approaches for analysis and control of BNs so far. On the other hand, many studies have also been done by using algebraic approaches. Extensive studies have been especially done using the *semi-tensor product* (STP) [Cheng (2009); Cheng *et al.* (2009, 2011, 2012)], which is a generalization of the conventional matrix product. In this chapter, we review the STP and some fundamental results on STP-based analysis of BNs.

9.1 Semi-Tensor Product of Matrices

Let $\mathcal{M}_{m \times n}$ denote the set of $m \times n$ real matrices (i.e., each element is a real number). For a matrix A, each of A_{ij} and $A_{i,j}$ denotes the element at the ith row and jth column of A, $A[i, -]$ (resp., $A[-, j]$) denotes the row (resp., column) vector consisting of the elements at the ith row (resp., jth column).

Definition 9.1. Let $A \in \mathcal{M}_{m \times n}$ and $B \in \mathcal{M}_{p \times q}$. Then, the *Kronecker product* $A \otimes B$ is the $mp \times nq$ block matrix

$$A \otimes B = \begin{pmatrix} A_{11}B & \cdots & A_{1n}B \\ \vdots & \ddots & \vdots \\ A_{m1}B & \cdots & A_{mn}B \end{pmatrix},$$

precisely $(A \otimes B)_{p(i-1)+r, q(j-1)+s} = A_{ij}B_{rs}$.

Definition 9.2. Let $A \in \mathcal{M}_{m \times n}$, $B \in \mathcal{M}_{p \times q}$, and c be the least common multiple of n and p. Then, the *semi-tensor product* (STP) $A \ltimes B$ is defined by

$$A \ltimes B = (A \otimes I_{\frac{c}{n}})(B \otimes I_{\frac{c}{p}}),$$

where I_k is the $k \times k$ identify matrix.

Note that tensor product is equivalent to conventional matrix multiplication, $A \ltimes B = AB$, if $n = p$.

Example 9.1.

(1)

$$\begin{pmatrix} 1 \\ 2 \end{pmatrix} \ltimes \begin{pmatrix} 3 \\ 4 \end{pmatrix} = \begin{pmatrix} 1 & 0 \\ 0 & 1 \\ 2 & 0 \\ 0 & 2 \end{pmatrix} \begin{pmatrix} 3 \\ 4 \end{pmatrix} = \begin{pmatrix} 3 \\ 4 \\ 6 \\ 8 \end{pmatrix}.$$

(2)

$$(1\ 2) \ltimes (3\ 4) = (1\ 2) \begin{pmatrix} 3 & 0 & 4 & 0 \\ 0 & 3 & 0 & 4 \end{pmatrix} = (3\ 6\ 4\ 8).$$

(3)

$$(1\ 2\ 3) \ltimes \begin{pmatrix} 1 \\ 2 \end{pmatrix} = \begin{pmatrix} 1 & 0 & 2 & 0 & 3 & 0 \\ 0 & 1 & 0 & 2 & 0 & 3 \end{pmatrix} \begin{pmatrix} 1 & 0 & 0 \\ 0 & 1 & 0 \\ 0 & 0 & 1 \\ 2 & 0 & 0 \\ 0 & 2 & 0 \\ 0 & 0 & 2 \end{pmatrix} = \begin{pmatrix} 1 & 6 & 2 \\ 4 & 1 & 6 \end{pmatrix}.$$

(4)

$$\begin{pmatrix} 1 & 2 & 3 & -1 \\ -1 & 0 & 1 & 2 \end{pmatrix} \ltimes \begin{pmatrix} 1 & 2 \\ 0 & -1 \end{pmatrix} = \begin{pmatrix} 1 & 2 & 3 & -1 \\ -1 & 0 & 1 & 2 \end{pmatrix} \begin{pmatrix} 1 & 0 & 2 & 0 \\ 0 & 1 & 0 & 2 \\ 0 & 0 & -1 & 0 \\ 0 & 0 & 0 & -1 \end{pmatrix}$$

$$= \begin{pmatrix} 1 & 2 & -1 & 5 \\ -1 & 0 & -3 & -2 \end{pmatrix}.$$

It is known that STP keeps many properties of the conventional matrix product as below [Cheng *et al.* (2011)].

Proposition 9.1. *Let a and b some reals. Then the followings hold.*

(1) (Distributive Law)

$$F \ltimes (aG + bH) = (aF \ltimes G) + (bF \ltimes H),$$
$$(aF + bG) \ltimes H = (aF \ltimes H) + (bG \ltimes H).$$

(2) (Associative Law)

$$(F \ltimes G) \ltimes H = F \ltimes (G \ltimes H).$$

Proposition 9.2. $(A \ltimes B)^{\mathsf{T}} = B^{\mathsf{T}} \ltimes A^{\mathsf{T}}$. *If A and B are invertible,* $(A \ltimes B)^{-1} = B^{-1} \ltimes A^{-1}$.

9.2   Matrix Representation of Boolean Functions

Let $\mathcal{L}_{m \times n}$ denote the set of $m \times n$ Boolean (i.e., 0-1) matrices. Let δ_n^i denote the column vector of size n such that the ith row has value 1 and the other rows have value 0. We represent Boolean values 1 and 0 by δ_2^1 and δ_2^2, respectively:

$$1 \iff \delta_2^1 = \begin{pmatrix} 1 \\ 0 \end{pmatrix},$$

$$0 \iff \delta_2^2 = \begin{pmatrix} 0 \\ 1 \end{pmatrix}.$$

Let $D = \delta_n[i_1, i_2, \ldots, i_k]$ denote the $n \times k$ Boolean matrix such that $D[-, j] = \delta_n^{i_j}$. For example, $\delta_2[1, 2, 2, 1] = \begin{pmatrix} 1 & 0 & 0 & 1 \\ 0 & 1 & 1 & 0 \end{pmatrix}$ and

$$\delta_4[1, 4, 3, 2, 1] = \begin{pmatrix} 1 & 0 & 0 & 0 & 1 \\ 0 & 0 & 0 & 1 & 0 \\ 0 & 0 & 1 & 0 & 0 \\ 0 & 1 & 0 & 0 & 0 \end{pmatrix}.$$ The following proposition states that any

n-ary Boolean function can be represented by a 2×2^n Boolean matrix.

Proposition 9.3. *Let $f(y_1, \ldots, y_n)$ be a Boolean function from $\{0, 1\}^n$ to $\{0, 1\}$. Then there exists a unique matrix $M \in \mathcal{L}_{2 \times 2^n}$ such that*

$$f(y_1, \ldots, y_n) = 1 \quad \textit{iff} \quad M \ltimes x = \delta_2^1,$$

where $x = \ltimes_{i=1}^n x_i = x_1 \ltimes x_2 \ltimes \cdots \ltimes x_n$, $x_i \in \{\delta_2^1, \delta_2^2\}$ for all $i \in \{1, \ldots, n\}$, and $x_i = \delta_2^1$ iff $y_i = 1$.

Proof. Let $z = 2^n - (2^{n-1} y_1 + 2^{n-2} y_2 + \cdots + 2 y_{n-1} + y_n)$. Then, $x = \delta_{2^n}^z$ holds. We define M by

$$M[-, z] = \begin{cases} \delta_2^1, & \text{if } f(y_1, \cdots, y_n) = 1, \\ \delta_2^2, & \text{otherwise.} \end{cases}$$

Then, the required property holds because $M \ltimes \delta_{2^n}^z = M[-, z]$ holds. $\square$

Example 9.2. Vectors $[0, 0]$, $[0, 1]$, $[1, 0]$, and $[1, 1]$ correspond to

$$\delta_4^4 = \begin{pmatrix} 0 \\ 0 \\ 0 \\ 1 \end{pmatrix}, \quad \delta_4^3 = \begin{pmatrix} 0 \\ 0 \\ 1 \\ 0 \end{pmatrix}, \quad \delta_4^2 = \begin{pmatrix} 0 \\ 1 \\ 0 \\ 0 \end{pmatrix}, \quad \text{and } \delta_4^1 = \begin{pmatrix} 1 \\ 0 \\ 0 \\ 0 \end{pmatrix}, \text{ respectively.}$$

Example 9.3.

(1) $f(x_1) = \overline{x_1}$ is represented by

$$M_{\neg} = \delta_2[2,1] = \begin{pmatrix} 0 & 1 \\ 1 & 0 \end{pmatrix}.$$

(2) $f(x_1, x_2) = x_1 \wedge x_2$ is represented by

$$M_{\wedge} = \delta_2[1,2,2,2] = \begin{pmatrix} 1 & 0 & 0 & 0 \\ 0 & 1 & 1 & 1 \end{pmatrix}.$$

(3) $f(x_1, x_2) = x_1 \vee x_2$ is represented by

$$M_{\vee} = \delta_2[1,1,1,2] = \begin{pmatrix} 1 & 1 & 1 & 0 \\ 0 & 0 & 0 & 1 \end{pmatrix}.$$

(4) $f(x_1, x_2) = x_1 \oplus x_2$ is represented by

$$M_{\oplus} = \delta_2[2,1,1,2] = \begin{pmatrix} 0 & 1 & 1 & 0 \\ 1 & 0 & 0 & 1 \end{pmatrix}.$$

Example 9.4.

(1) $M_{\wedge} \ltimes \delta_2^1 \ltimes \delta_2^2 = M_{\wedge} \ltimes \delta_4^2 = \begin{pmatrix} 1 & 0 & 0 & 0 \\ 0 & 1 & 1 & 1 \end{pmatrix} \begin{pmatrix} 0 \\ 1 \\ 0 \\ 0 \end{pmatrix} = \delta_2^2.$

(2) $M_{\vee} \ltimes \delta_2^1 \ltimes \delta_2^2 = M_{\vee} \ltimes \delta_4^2 = \begin{pmatrix} 1 & 1 & 1 & 0 \\ 0 & 0 & 0 & 1 \end{pmatrix} \begin{pmatrix} 0 \\ 1 \\ 0 \\ 0 \end{pmatrix} = \delta_2^1.$

(3)

$$M_{\oplus} \ltimes \delta_2^1 = \begin{pmatrix} 0 & 1 & 1 & 0 \\ 1 & 0 & 0 & 1 \end{pmatrix} \ltimes \begin{pmatrix} 1 \\ 0 \end{pmatrix} = \begin{pmatrix} 0 & 1 & 1 & 0 \\ 1 & 0 & 0 & 1 \end{pmatrix} \begin{pmatrix} 1 & 0 \\ 0 & 1 \\ 0 & 0 \\ 0 & 0 \end{pmatrix} = \begin{pmatrix} 0 & 1 \\ 1 & 0 \end{pmatrix} = M_{\neg}.$$

9.3   Matrix Representation of Boolean Networks

The matrix representation of a Boolean function can be extended to that of a set of Boolean functions. In the following, we use x_i to denote both a Boolean variable and the corresponding column vector of size 2.

Let $N(V, F)$ be a BN with n nodes whose dynamics is given by

$$x_i(t+1) = f_i(x_1(t), \ldots, x_n(t)) \quad \text{for } i = 1, \ldots, n,$$

which can also be written as

$$\mathbf{x}(t+1) = F(\mathbf{x}(t)).$$

For an n-dimensional 0-1 vector $\mathbf{x} = [x_1, \ldots, x_n]$, $x = \delta(\mathbf{x})$ denotes the column vector defined by $\ltimes_{i=1}^{n} x_i$, that is, $x = \delta_{2^n}^z$ such that $z = 2^n - (2^{n-1}x_1 + 2^{n-2}x_2 + \cdots + 2x_{n-1} + x_n)$.

Proposition 9.4. *Let $N(V,F)$ be a BN with n nodes. Then there exists a unique matrix $L \in \mathcal{L}_{2^n \times 2^n}$ such that*

$$F(\mathbf{x}) = \mathbf{y} \quad \textit{iff} \quad L \ltimes x = y,$$

where $x = \delta(\mathbf{x})$ and $y = \delta(\mathbf{y})$.

Proof. Let $z = 2^n - (2^{n-1}x_1 + 2^{n-2}x_2 + \cdots + 2x_{n-1} + x_n)$ and $w = 2^n - (2^{n-1}y_1 + 2^{n-2}y_2 + \cdots + 2y_{n-1} + y_n)$. We define L by $L[-, z] = \delta_{2^n}^w$. Then, the required property holds because $L \ltimes x = L[-, z]$ holds. $\qquad\square$

Essentially, L represents a state transition table (equivalently, a state transition diagram).

Example 9.5. Consider a BN given by

$$x_1(t+1) = x_2(t) \wedge x_3(t),$$
$$x_2(t+1) = x_1(t),$$
$$x_3(t+1) = \overline{x_2(t)}.$$

Then, we have the state transition diagram given in Fig. 9.1 and

$$L = \begin{pmatrix} 0\,0\,0\,0\,0\,0\,0\,0 \\ 1\,0\,0\,0\,0\,0\,0\,0 \\ 0\,0\,0\,0\,0\,0\,0\,0 \\ 0\,0\,0\,0\,1\,0\,0\,0 \\ 0\,0\,1\,1\,0\,0\,0\,0 \\ 0\,1\,0\,0\,0\,0\,0\,0 \\ 0\,0\,0\,0\,0\,0\,1\,1 \\ 0\,0\,0\,0\,0\,1\,0\,0 \end{pmatrix}.$$

If $x(0) = \delta_8^1$, $x(1) = L \ltimes x(0) = \delta_8^2$. It corresponds to a transition from $\mathbf{x}(0) = [1,1,1]$ to $\mathbf{x}(1) = [1,1,0]$.

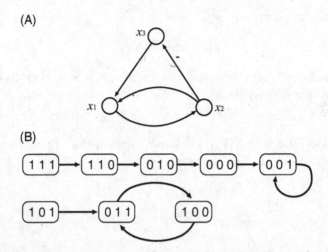

Fig. 9.1   Structure (A) and state transition diagram (B) of a BN in Example 9.5. An arrow with '-' corresponds to a negative input,

We can extend this proposition for a BN with internal nodes, control nodes, and output nodes, whose dynamics is described by

$$
\begin{aligned}
x_1(t+1) &= f_1(x_1(t), \ldots, x_n(t), u_1(t), \ldots, u_m(t)), \\
x_2(t+1) &= f_2(x_1(t), \ldots, x_n(t), u_1(t), \ldots, u_m(t)), \\
&\vdots \\
x_n(t+1) &= f_n(x_1(t), \ldots, x_n(t), u_1(t), \ldots, u_m(t)), \\
y_1(t) &= h_1(x_1(t), \ldots, x_n(t)), \\
y_2(t) &= h_2(x_1(t), \ldots, x_n(t)), \\
&\vdots \\
y_p(t) &= h_p(x_1(t), \ldots, x_n(t)).
\end{aligned}
\tag{9.1}
$$

The following proposition is obvious from Proposition 9.4.

Proposition 9.5. *The dynamics of a BN given by Eq. (9.2) can be expressed as*

$$
\begin{aligned}
x(t+1) &= L \ltimes (u(t) \ltimes x(t)), \\
y(t) &= H \ltimes x(t),
\end{aligned}
$$

where $L \in \mathcal{L}_{2^n \times 2^{m+n}}$ and $H \in \mathcal{L}_{2^p \times 2^n}$.

The matrix L in the above is called the *structure matrix*.

Example 9.6. Consider a BN given by

$$x_1(t+1) = x_2(t) \vee \overline{u_1(t)},$$
$$x_2(t+1) = x_1(t),$$
$$x_3(t+1) = x_1(t) \vee x_2(t),$$
$$y_1(t) = x_2(t),$$
$$y_2(t) = x_1(t) \wedge x_3(t),$$

Then, we have the state transition table given in Fig. 9.2 and

$$L = \delta_8[1, 1, 5, 5, 3, 3, 8, 8, 1, 1, 1, 1, 3, 3, 4, 4]$$

$$= \begin{pmatrix}
1 & 1 & 0 & 0 & 0 & 0 & 0 & 0 & 1 & 1 & 1 & 1 & 0 & 0 & 0 & 0 \\
0 & 0 & 0 & 0 & 0 & 0 & 0 & 0 & 0 & 0 & 0 & 0 & 0 & 0 & 0 & 0 \\
0 & 0 & 0 & 0 & 1 & 1 & 0 & 0 & 0 & 0 & 0 & 0 & 1 & 1 & 0 & 0 \\
0 & 0 & 0 & 0 & 0 & 0 & 0 & 0 & 0 & 0 & 0 & 0 & 0 & 0 & 1 & 1 \\
0 & 0 & 1 & 1 & 0 & 0 & 0 & 0 & 0 & 0 & 0 & 0 & 0 & 0 & 0 & 0 \\
0 & 0 & 0 & 0 & 0 & 0 & 0 & 0 & 0 & 0 & 0 & 0 & 0 & 0 & 0 & 0 \\
0 & 0 & 0 & 0 & 0 & 0 & 0 & 0 & 0 & 0 & 0 & 0 & 0 & 0 & 0 & 0 \\
0 & 0 & 0 & 0 & 0 & 0 & 1 & 1 & 0 & 0 & 0 & 0 & 0 & 0 & 0 & 0
\end{pmatrix},$$

$$H = \delta_4[1, 2, 3, 4, 2, 2, 4, 4]$$

$$= \begin{pmatrix}
1 & 0 & 0 & 0 & 0 & 0 & 0 & 0 \\
0 & 1 & 0 & 0 & 1 & 1 & 0 & 0 \\
0 & 0 & 1 & 0 & 0 & 0 & 0 & 0 \\
0 & 0 & 0 & 1 & 0 & 0 & 1 & 1
\end{pmatrix}.$$

If $x(0) = \delta_8^8$ and $u(0) = \delta_2^2$, then $x(1) = L \ltimes u(0) \ltimes x(0) = \delta_8^4$ and $y(1) = H \ltimes x(1) = H \ltimes \delta_8^4 = \delta_4^1$. If $x(0) = \delta_8^3$ and $u(0) = \delta_2^1$, then $x(1) = L \ltimes u(0) \ltimes x(0) = \delta_8^5$ and $y(1) = H \ltimes x(1) = H \ltimes \delta_8^5 = \delta_4^2$.

9.4 Number of Attractors

Detection/enumeration of attractors is one of the basic tasks for analyzing BNs. Once we have a matrix form L of a BN (given in Proposition 9.4), the number of attractors with period p can be calculated by using a simple recurrence using L.

Recall that $L \ltimes x$ is equal to the zth column of L where $x = \delta_{2^n}^z$ and $z = 2^n - (2^{n-1}x_1 + 2^{n-2}x_2 + \cdots + 2x_{n-1} + x_n)$. It implies that $x = L \ltimes x$ holds iff $L[-, z] = \delta_{2^n}^z$, This means that x is a singleton attractor iff $L[z, z] = 1$.

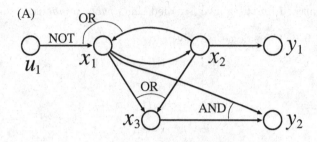

(A)

(B)

	t			$t+1$ $(u=1)$			$t+1$ $(u=0)$			t	
x_1	x_2	x_3	x_1	x_2	x_3	x_1	x_2	x_3	y_1	y_2
0	0	0	0	0	0	1	0	0	0	0
0	0	1	0	0	0	1	0	0	0	0
0	1	0	1	0	1	1	0	1	1	0
0	1	1	1	0	1	1	0	1	1	0
1	0	0	0	1	1	1	1	1	0	0
1	0	1	0	1	1	1	1	1	0	1
1	1	0	1	1	1	1	1	1	1	0
1	1	1	1	1	1	1	1	1	1	1

Fig. 9.2   Structure (A) and state transition table (B) of a BN in Example 9.6.

Therefore, the number of singleton attractors is given by $tr(L)$, where $tr(L)$ is the *trace* of L, that is, $tr(L) = \sum_{i=1}^{2^n} L[i,i]$.

This idea can be generalized for counting the number of attractors of period p. We denote $\overbrace{L \ltimes \cdots \ltimes L}^{i}$ by L^i. Since $x(t+p)$ is given by $L^p \ltimes x(t)$, $x(t+p) = L^p \ltimes x(t)$ holds iff $L^p[-,z] = \delta_{2^n}^z$ where $x(t) = \delta_{2^n}^z$. Therefore, $x(t)$ is a state in an attractor if $x(t+p) = L^p \ltimes x(t)$ holds for some p. However, we need to mind the following:

- An attractor of period p consists of p distinct states,
- $x(t+p) = L^p \ltimes x(t)$ holds if $x(t+q) = L^q \ltimes x(t)$ holds for some divisor q of p.

By taking these points into account, the following theorem holds.

Theorem 9.1. *Let $N(V,F)$ be an BN whose algebraic representation is L.*

The number of attractors of period p, N_p, is given by

$$N_p = \begin{cases} tr(L), & if\ p = 1, \\ \frac{tr(L^p) - \sum_{q \in \mathcal{P}(p)} qN_q}{p}, & otherwise, \end{cases}$$

where $p \leq 2^n$ and $\mathcal{P}(p)$ is the set of factors of p excluding p(e.g., $\mathcal{P}(6) = \{1, 2, 3\}$, $\mathcal{P}(12) = \{1, 2, 3, 4, 6\}$).

Example 9.7. Consider the BN given in Example 9.5. Since $tr(L) = 1$ and $tr(L^2) = 3$, the number of singleton attractors is $tr(L) = 1$ and the number of attractors of period 2 is $\frac{tr(L^2) - tr(L^1)}{2} = 1$.

9.5   Controllability and Observability

In this section, we consider two important properties of a BN, controllability and observability.

First, we consider the controllability. We consider a BN with internal nodes and control nodes, ignoring output nodes. This BN can be represented by Eq. (9.2) with ignoring y_is. As discussed in Section 9.3, the dynamics of a BN is given by

$$\tilde{x}(t+1) = (L \ltimes u(t)) \ltimes x(t),$$

where $L \in \mathcal{L}_{2^n \times 2^{m+n}}$.

For a $p \times q$ matrix A with $q = rp$ for some positive integer r, let $Blk_i(A)$ denote the submatrix of A given by the columns from $p(i-1)+1$ to ip. It means that A has the form:

$$A = (Blk_1(A)\ Blk_2(A)\ \cdots\ Blk_r(A)).$$

Note that each $Blk_i(A)$ is a $p \times p$ matrix.

For a given $L \in \mathcal{L}_{2^n \times 2^{m+n}}$, define M by

$$M = \sum_{i=1}^{2^m} Blk_i(L).$$

$M[i, j] > 0$ means that there exists some $u(t)$ which makes $x(t+1) = \delta_{2^n}^i$ when $x(t) = \delta_{2^n}^j$. Furthermore, $M[i, j] = c$ means that the number of such $u(t)$ is c. By repeatedly applying this discussion, it is seen that $M^s[i, j] = c$ means that there exist c control sequences which makes $x(t+s) = \delta_{2^n}^i$ when $x(t) = \delta_{2^n}^j$. Define M_c by

$$M_c = \sum_{i=1}^{2^n} M^i.$$

Note that M and M_c are defined via the conventional addition and multiplication operations for real matrices. Since there exist at most 2^n possible states of internal nodes, there exists a control sequence that drives a BN from $x(0) = \delta_{2^n}^j$ to $x(t) = \delta_{2^n}^i$ for some t if and only if $M_c[i,j] > 0$.

By summarizing the above discussions, we have the following theorem.

Theorem 9.2. *Let $L \in \mathcal{L}_{2^n \times 2^{m+n}}$ be the structure matrix of a BN with n internal nodes and m control nodes. Then, the followings hold.*

(1) There exists a control sequence that drives a BN from $x(0) = \delta_{2^n}^j$ to $x(t) = \delta_{2^n}^i$ iff $M^t[i,j] > 0$.

(2) There exists a control sequence that drives a BN from $x(0) = \delta_{2^n}^j$ to $x(t) = \delta_{2^n}^i$ for some $t > 0$ iff $M_c[i,j] > 0$.

(3) There exists a control sequence that drives a BN from $x(0) = \delta_{2^n}^j$ to an arbitrary state in finite time steps iff $M_c[i,j] > 0$ holds for all $i \in \{1, \ldots, 2^n\}$.

(4) There exists a control sequence that drives a BN from an arbitrary state to an arbitrary state in finite time steps iff $M_c[i,j] > 0$ holds for all $i, j \in \{1, \ldots, 2^n\}$.

Note that entries of M_c and M^s might be very large numbers since M is treated as a real matrix. However, we can treat matrices as binary matrices by replacing '+' and '×' with '∨' and '∧', respectively. It is straight-forward to verify that Theorem 9.2 holds using such a binary model.

Next, we consider the observability. Among several definitions of the observability, we adopt the following.

Definition 9.3. Consider a BN given by L in Eq. (9.2). $x(0)$ and $x'(0)$ are said to be distinguishable if there exists a control sequence $\langle u(0), u(1), \ldots, u(s) \rangle$ such that $y(s+1) \neq y'(s+1)$. A BN is observable, if any two initial states $x(0) \neq x'(0)$ are distinguishable.

As in the case of controllability analysis, we consider a partition of L into 2^m blocks:

$$L = (Blk_1(L) \; Blk_2(L) \; \cdots \; Blk_{2^m}(L)) = (B_1 \; B_2 \; \cdots \; B_{2^m}).$$

Recall that B_i corresponds to the state transition matrix when control $u(0) = \delta_{2^m}^i$ is applied.

We can discriminate $x(0)$ and $x'(0)$ ($x(0) \neq x'(0)$) if $y(0) \neq y'(0)$ where $y(0) = Hx(0)$ and $y'(0) = Hx'(0)$. Note that $y(0) \neq y'(0)$ is equivalent to that the jth column of H is not identical to the j'th column of H where $x(0) = \delta_{2^n}^j$ and $x'(0) = \delta_{2^n}^{j'}$.

Furthermore, we can discriminate $x(0)$ and $x'(0)$ $(x(0) \neq x'(0))$ if $y(0) \neq y'(0)$ holds or $y(1) \neq y'(1)$ holds for some $u(0)$. $y(1) \neq y'(1)$ is equivalent to that jth column of HB_k is not identical to the j'th column of HB_k for some k, which is also equivalent to that jth column of Γ_1 is not identical to the j'th column of Γ_1 where Γ_1 is defined by

$$\Gamma_1 = \begin{pmatrix} HB_1 \\ HB_2 \\ \vdots \\ HB_{2^m} \end{pmatrix}.$$

We can generalize this idea as follows.

Define a set of matrices $\Omega_i \subseteq \mathcal{L}_{2^p \times 2^n}$, $i = 0, 1, 2, \ldots$ by

$$\Omega_0 = \{H\},$$
$$\Omega_1 = \{HB_i | \ i \in \{1, 2, \ldots, 2^m\}\},$$
$$\Omega_2 = \{HB_i B_j | \ i, j \in \{1, 2, \ldots, 2^m\}\},$$
$$\vdots$$
$$\Omega_s = \{HB_{i_1} B_{i_2} \cdots B_{i_s} | \ i_1, i_2, \ldots, i_s \in \{1, 2, \ldots, 2^m\}\},$$
$$\vdots$$

Then we can see that there exists an integer $s \geq 0$ such that

$$\Omega_{s+1} \subseteq \cup_{k=0}^{s} \Omega_k.$$

Let s^* be the smallest integer satisfying this condition. Such an s^* must exist because the number of distinct $HB_{i_1} \cdots B_{i_k}$s is finite. Define Γ_i by arranging matrices appearing in Ω_i as

$$\Gamma_0 = H, \quad \Gamma_1 = \begin{pmatrix} HB_1 \\ HB_2 \\ \vdots \\ HB_{2^m} \end{pmatrix}, \quad \Gamma_2 = \begin{pmatrix} HB_1 B_1 \\ HB_1 B_2 \\ \vdots \\ HB_{2^m} B_{2^m} \end{pmatrix}, \quad \cdots$$

Define the observability matrix M_O as

$$M_O = \begin{pmatrix} \Gamma_0 \\ \Gamma_1 \\ \vdots \\ \Gamma_{s^*} \end{pmatrix}.$$

Then, it is easy to see that $x(0) = \delta_{2^m}^j \neq x'(0) = \delta_{2^m}^{j'}$ if $M_O[-,j] \neq M_O[-,j']$. It can also be seen that there does not exist a control sequence which makes $y(t) \neq y'(t)$ if $M_O[-,j] = M_O[-,j']$. Therefore, we have the following theorem.

Theorem 9.3. *A BN is observable if and only if* $rank(M_O) = 2^n$.

Example 9.8. Consider a BN given by

$$x_1(t+1) = \overline{x_1(t)} \vee x_2(t),$$
$$x_2(t+1) = \overline{x_1(t)} \vee u(t),$$
$$y_1(t+1) = x_1(t) \oplus x_2(t).$$

Then, L and H are given by

$$L = \delta_4[1,3,1,1,2,4,1,1] = \begin{pmatrix} 1\,0\,1\,1\,0\,0\,1\,1 \\ 0\,0\,0\,0\,1\,0\,0\,0 \\ 0\,1\,0\,0\,0\,0\,0\,0 \\ 0\,0\,0\,0\,0\,1\,0\,0 \end{pmatrix},$$

$$H = \delta_2[2,1,1,2] = \begin{pmatrix} 0\,1\,1\,0 \\ 1\,0\,0\,1 \end{pmatrix}.$$

Then, $B_1 = \delta_4[1,3,1,1]$, $B_2 = \delta_4[2,4,1,1]$, and the binary version of M_c is given by

$$M_c = \begin{pmatrix} 1\,1\,1\,1 \\ 1\,1\,1\,1 \\ 1\,1\,1\,1 \\ 1\,1\,1\,1 \end{pmatrix},$$

which means that the BN is controllable in the sense of Theorem 9.2 (4).

As for the observability, we have

$$H = \begin{pmatrix} 0\,1\,1\,0 \\ 1\,0\,0\,1 \end{pmatrix},$$

$$HB_1 = \begin{pmatrix} 0\,1\,0\,0 \\ 1\,0\,1\,1 \end{pmatrix},$$

$$HB_2 = \begin{pmatrix} 1\,0\,0\,0 \\ 0\,1\,1\,1 \end{pmatrix},$$

$$HB_1B_2 = \begin{pmatrix} 1\,0\,0\,0 \\ 0\,1\,1\,1 \end{pmatrix},$$

$$HB_2B_1 = \begin{pmatrix} 1\,0\,1\,1 \\ 0\,1\,0\,0 \end{pmatrix}.$$

Therefore, we have

$$M_O = \begin{pmatrix} 0\ 1\ 1\ 0 \\ 1\ 0\ 0\ 1 \\ 0\ 1\ 0\ 0 \\ 1\ 0\ 1\ 1 \\ 1\ 0\ 0\ 0 \\ 0\ 1\ 1\ 1 \\ 1\ 0\ 0\ 0 \\ 0\ 1\ 1\ 1 \\ 1\ 0\ 1\ 1 \\ 0\ 1\ 0\ 0 \\ \vdots\ \vdots\ \vdots\ \vdots \end{pmatrix}.$$

Since $rank(M_0) = 4$, the BN is observable.

9.6 Additional Remarks and Bibliographical Notes

The semi-tensor product approach to BNs was proposed and established by Cheng and his colleagues [Cheng (2009); Cheng *et al.* (2009, 2011, 2012)], from which a number of studies followed. This approach provides a unified and clear view on various problems on BNs although computational costs are high because matrices of $2^n \times 2^n$ size or more should be handled in most cases. This section is written based on [Cheng *et al.* (2011)]. Readers interested in more details on the semi-tensor product approach are referred to [Cheng *et al.* (2011, 2012)].

Chapter 10

Analysis of Metabolic Networks

BNs have been mainly used for modeling and analyzing genetic networks. However, BNs have also been used for modeling and analyzing other types of biological networks. In this chapter, we describe BN-based modeling and analysis of metabolic networks.

10.1 Boolean Model and Reaction Cut

A metabolic network consists of chemical compounds and chemical reactions. Chemical compounds are transformed to other compounds via chemical reactions, where chemical reactions in biological systems are often catalyzed by enzymes. In order to activate a chemical reaction, all of substates must be present. On the other hand, some amount of specific chemical compound can be generated if one of the chemical reactions generating the compound is active. These observations suggest that reactions and compounds correspond to AND and OR nodes, respectively. Based on this correspondence, a BN-based model of metabolic networks is defined as follows.

Let $V_c = \{v_{c_1}, \ldots, v_{c_m}\}$ and $V_r = \{v_{r_1}, \ldots, v_{r_n}\}$ be a set of *compound nodes* and a set of *reaction nodes*, respectively, where $V_c \cap V_r = \emptyset$. We reasonably assume that m and n are in the same order (i.e., m is $O(n)$ and n is $O(m)$). Let $V = V_c \cup V_r$. Let $V_s \subseteq V_c$ and $V_t \subseteq V_c$ be a set of *source nodes* and a set of *target nodes*, respectively, where $V_s \cap V_t = \emptyset$. Then, a metabolic network is defined as a directed graph $G(V, E)$ satisfying the following conditions:

- For each edge $(u, v) \in E$, either $(u \in V_c) \wedge (v \in V_r)$ or $(u \in V_r) \wedge (v \in V_c)$ holds,
- Each node $v \in V_s$ does not have an incoming edge,

- Each node $v \notin V_s$ has at least one incoming edge.

In general, metabolic networks contain cycles and bidirectional edges. However, existence of cycles and bidirectional edges makes it difficult to uniquely define an appropriate Boolean model. Therefore, we assume that $G(V, E)$ is *acyclic* until Section 10.4.

In this chapter, we focus on the minimum reaction cut problem (Reaction Cut, in short) in which it is required to find a minimum set of reactions knockout of which prevents production of a specified subset of the target compounds. Let $V_d \subseteq V_r$ be a set of reaction nodes that are to be knocked out. We assign 0-1 value to each node where 1 (resp., 0) means that the corresponding node is active (resp., inactive). Since we focus on stable states of metabolic networks, we do not consider time steps, and that we write $v = 1$ (resp., $v = 0$) if 1 (resp., 0) is assigned to a node $v \in V$. Let A be an assignment of 0-1 values to nodes in V. A is called a *valid assignment* if the following conditions are satisfied:

- For each $v \in V_s$, $v = 1$,
- For each $v \in V_c - V_s$, $v = 1$ iff there is u such that $(u.v) \in E$ and $u = 1$,
- For each $v \in V_r$, $v = 1$ iff $v \notin V_d$ holds and $u = 1$ holds for all a such that $(a, v) \in E$.

The first condition states that the source compounds are always available. The second condition states that compound nodes correspond to OR nodes. The third condition states that reaction nodes correspond to AND nodes, where the state of a node v is forced to be 0 if $v \in V_d$.

Proposition 10.1. *A valid assignment is uniquely determined if $G(V, E)$ is acyclic.*

Proof. The conditions of the valid assignment can be regarded as the rules to assign 0-1 values to nodes in V. Beginning from $v = 1$ for all $v \in V_s$, we can determine 0-1 valued of the other nodes by repeatedly applying the second and third rules. It is straightforward to see that there is no ambiguity to determine 0-1 values. $\square$

Reaction Cut is defined as follows.

Definition 10.1.   [Reaction Cut]
Instance: a BN-model of a metabolic network $G(V, E)$ with $V = V_c \cup V_r$ and $V_s \subseteq V_c$, and a set of target compounds $V_t \subseteq V_c$ such that $V_t \cap V_s = \emptyset$.

Problem: find a minimum cardinality set of reactions $V_d \subseteq V_r$ knockout of which prevents production of any compound of V_t (i.e., $v = 0$ for all $v \in V_t$).

V_d satisfying the above condition (without minimality) is called a *reaction cut*. Note that Reaction Cut always has a solution because $V_d = V_r$ is always a reaction cut.

Example 10.1. Consider a BN model of a metabolic network in Fig. 10.1 (A), where $V_c = \{v_1, v_2, v_3, v_4, v_5, v_6, v_7, v_8\}$, $V_r = \{v_a, v_b, v_c, v_d, v_e\}$, $V_s = \{v_1, v_2, v_3, v_4\}$, and $V_t = \{v_8\}$. If we select $V_d = \{v_a\}$ in BN (A), we have $v_1 = 1, v_2 = 1, v_3 = 1, v_4 = 1, v_a = 0, v_b = 1, v_5 = 0, v_6 = 1, v_7 = 1, v_c = 0, v_d = 0, v_e = 1, v_8 = 1$. Therefore, $\{v_a\}$ is not a reaction cut of BN (A). If we select $V_d = \{v_a, v_b\}$ in BN (A), we have $v_1 = 1, v_2 = 1, v_3 = 1, v_4 = 1, v_a = 0, v_b = 0, v_5 = 0, v_6 = 0, v_7 = 0, v_c = 0, v_d = 0, v_e = 0, v_8 = 0$. Therefore, $\{v_a, v_b\}$ is a reaction cut of BN (A). $\{v_a, v_e\}$ is also a reaction cut of BN (A). Furthermore, we can verify that these two are the minimum reaction cuts. If we select $V_d = \{v_a\}$ in BN (B), we have $v_1 = 1, v_2 = 1, v_3 = 1, v_4 = 1, v_a = 0, v_b = 1, v_5 = 0, v_6 = 1, v_7 = 0, v_8 = 1, v_c = 0, v_d = 0, v_9 = 0$. Therefore, $\{v_a\}$ is a reaction cut of BN (B). Since $v_9 = 1$ if $V_d = \emptyset$, $\{v_a\}$ is a minimum reaction cut of BN (B). $\{v_b\}$ is also a minimum reaction cut of BN (B).

10.2 Hardness of Reaction Cut

The minimum reaction cut problem [Klamt and Gilles (2004)] was originally proposed for the *flux balance analysis*-based model [Bordbar *et al.* (2014); David and Bockmayr (2014); Haus *et al.* (2008); Orth *et al.* (2010); Schuster and Hilgetag (1994); von Kamp *et al.* (2014)]. a widely used model of a metabolic network It is shown in [Acuña *et al.* (2009)] that the original problem is NP-hard. By adjusting that proof for the BN model, NP-hardness of Reaction Cut is shown as below.

Theorem 10.1. *Reaction Cut is NP-hard.*

Proof. We prove the theorem using a polynomial-time reduction from the Hitting Set problem, which is known to be NP-complete [Garey and Johnson (1979)]. Hitting Set is, given a set of elements $X = \{x_1, \ldots, x_N\}$, a collection of subsets $S = \{S_1, \ldots, S_M\}$ over X, and an integer z, to decide whether Y ($Y \subseteq X$) exists such that $S_i \cap Y \neq \emptyset$ for any $i = 1, \ldots, M$

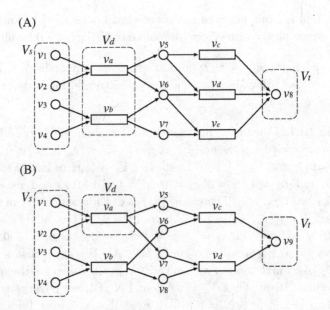

Fig. 10.1   Examples of BN models of metabolic networks. Circles represent compound nodes (i.e., OR nodes) and rectangles represent reaction nodes (i.e., AND nodes). $V_d = \{v_a, v_b\}$ is a minimum reaction cut in (A), whereas $V_d = \{v_a\}$ is a minimum reaction cut in (B).

and $|Y| \leq z$ hold. A set $Y \subseteq X$ with the minimum cardinality satisfying $S_i \cap Y \neq \emptyset$ for any $i = 1, \ldots, M$ is called a *minimum hitting set.*

For an instance of Hitting Set, we construct a metabolic network $G(V, E)$ as follows (see also Fig. 10.2 (A)). Define sets of nodes by

$$V_s = \{c_s\},$$
$$V_t = \{c_t\},$$
$$V_c = V_s \cup V_t \cup \{c_1, \ldots, c_N\},$$
$$V_r = \{r_1, \ldots, r_N\} \cup \{r_{s_1}, \ldots, r_{s_M}\}.$$

For each $S_i = \{x_{i_1}, \ldots, x_{i_{|S_i|}}\}$, a set of edges E_i is created by

$$E_i = \{(c_{i_j}, r_{s_i}) | \ j = 1, \ldots, |S_i|\}.$$

Then, the set of edges E is defined by

$$E = \{(c_s, r_i), (r_i, c_i) | \ i = 1, \ldots, N\} \ \cup \ \{(r_{s_i}, c_t) | \ i = 1, \ldots, M\}$$
$$\cup \ \bigcup_{i \in \{1, \ldots, M\}} E_i.$$

We show that Hitting Set has a solution if and only if there exists a reaction cut of size at most z.

Suppose that Hitting Set has a solution $Y = \{x_{i_1}, \ldots, x_{i_z}\}$. Then, $V_d = \{r_{i_1}, \ldots, r_{i_z}\}$ is a reaction cut because for each r_{s_j}, $S_j \cap Y$ is non-empty and $(c_k, r_{s_j}) \in E$ holds for any $k \in (S_j \cap Y)$.

Suppose that there exists a reaction cut V_d of size z. We can assume w.l.o.g. that V_d does not contain r_{s_i} because otherwise we can replace r_{s_i} with any r_j such that $(c_j, r_{s_i}) \in E$. Let $V_d = \{r_{i_1}, \ldots, r_{i_z}\}$. Then, it is straightforward to see that $Y = \{x_{i_1}, \ldots, x_{i_z}\}$ is a solution of Hitting Set.

Since the reduction can be clearly done in polynomial time, the theorem holds. $\qquad\square$

In the above, the indegree of a reaction node is not bounded. However, the indegree and outdegree are at most 3 in most chemical reactions. The proof can be modified so that the maximum indegree of each reaction node is bounded by 2, by encoding a reaction node with indegree more than 2 as in Fig. 10.2 (B).

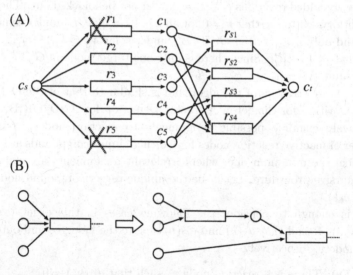

Fig. 10.2   Illustration for the hardness of Reaction Cut. (A) Reduction from an instance of Hitting Set such that $X = \{x_1, x_2, x_3, x_4, x_5\}$ and $\mathcal{S} = \{S_1, S_2, S_3, S_4\}$ with $S_1 = \{x_1, x_3\}$, $S_2 = \{x_2, x_5\}$, $S_3 = \{x_4, x_5\}$, $S_4 = \{x_1, x_2, x_4\}$. In this case, the minimum hitting set $Y = \{x_1, x_5\}$ corresponds to the minimum reaction cut $V_d = \{r_1, r_5\}$. (B) Encoding of a reaction node with indegree more than 2 by reaction nodes with indegree 2.

10.3   Algorithms for Reaction Cut

Reaction Cut can be solved in $O^*(2^n)$ time by examining all subsets of V_r as V_d since the number of such subsets is 2^n (recall that $|V_r| = n$). Therefore, it is reasonable to ask whether or not there exists an $o(2^n)$ time algorithm. This section shows that such an algorithm exists if the maximum outdegree of reaction nodes is bounded by a constant, which is a reasonable assumption as discussed in Section 10.2.

Here we present an $O(1.880^n)$ time algorithm for metabolic networks with the maximum outdegree 2. Before describing the algorithm, we show that we can assume $|V_t| = 1$. Suppose that $V_t = \{v_{t_1}, \ldots, v_{t_k}\}$ in a metabolic network $G(V, E)$, where $k > 2$. Then, we add new reaction nodes $r_{t_1}, \ldots, r_{t_k}$ and a new compound node v_{c_0} to V, and new edges E'' defined by

$$E'' = \{(v_{t_i}, r_{t_i}), (r_{t_i}, v_{c_0}) |\ i \in \{1, \ldots, k\}\}$$

to E. Let the resulting metabolic network be $G'(V', E')$ for which the target set of compound nodes is $\{v_{c_0}\}$. Furthermore, we add a constraint that newly added reactions $r_{t_1}, \ldots, r_{t_k}$ must not be knocked out. Then, it is straightforward to see that $v = 0$ for all $v \in V_t$ in $G(V, E)$ under some $V_d \subseteq V_r$ if and only if $v_{c_0} = 0$ in $G'(V', E')$ under some $V_d' \subseteq V_r \cup \{r_{t_1}, \ldots, r_{t_k}\}$ such that $|V_d| = |V_d'|$. Since there is only one target node in $G'(V', E')$, we can assume $|V_t| = 1$.

The basic strategy of the algorithm is similar to that of the $O(1.587^n)$ time algorithm for Singleton Attractor Detection for AND/OR BNs. We recursively examine possible assignments to reaction nodes, count the number of inactive reaction nodes for which all input compounds are active, and take the minimum one, where irrelevant assignments are skipped in the recursive procedure. Let v_t be the unique target compound node (i.e., $V_t = \{v_t\}$).

It is enough to consider the following cases in this order (see also Fig. 10.3). Recall that $d_I(v)$ and $d_O(v)$ denote the indegree and outdegree of a node v, respectively.

Case D0: There is a reaction node v_a such that $d_O(v_a) = 0$.

    Since v_a is not relevant, remove v_a.

Case D1: There is a reaction node v_a such that $d_O(v_a) = 1$.

    Let v_i be the successor of v_a (i.e., $(v_a, v_i) \in E$).

    Case D1-A; $d_I(v_i) \geq 2$.

        Let v_b is another predecessor of v_i (i.e., $(v_b, v_i) \in E$, $v_b \neq v_a$). We examine $v_b = 0$ and $v_b = 1$, If $v_b = 1$, we remove v_a since the value of v_a does not affect the states of the other nodes.

Case D1-B: $d_I(v_i) = 1$ and $v_i \neq v_t$.

If $d_O(v_i) = 0$, we remove v_a and v_i since v_a does not affect the states of the other nodes. Otherwise, there exists $v_b \in V_r$ such that $(v_i, v_b) \in E$. We examine $v_a = 0$ and $v_a = 1$. If $v_a = 0$, the state of v_b is unique determined as $v_b = 0$.

Case D1-C: $d_I(v_i) = 1$ and $v_i = v_t$.

We simply examine $v_a = 1$ and $v_a = 0$.

Case D2: $d_O(v_a) = 2$ for all remaining nodes v_a in V_r.

Let v_i and v_j be the successors of v_a.

Case D2-A: $d_I(v_i) \geq 2$ and $d_I(v_j) \geq 2$.

Let $v_b\ (\neq v_a)$ and $v_c\ (\neq v_a)$ be predecessors of v_i and v_j, respectively.

Case D2-A-(i): $v_b = v_c$.

We examine assignments of $v_b = 1$ and $v_b = 0$. If $v_b = 1$, we remove v_a since the value of v_a does not affect the states of the other nodes.

Case D2-A-(ii): $v_b \neq v_c$.

We examine four possible assignments on (v_b, v_c). If $(v_b, v_c) = (1, 1)$, we remove v_a since the value of v_a does not affect the states of the other nodes.

Case D2-B: $d_I(v_i) = 1$ or $d_I(v_j) = 1$.

We assume w.l.o.g. $d_I(v_i) = 1$. Then, this case is treated in the same way as in Cases D1-B and D1-C.

Theorem 10.2. *Reaction Cut can be solved in $O(1.880^n)$ time if the maximum outdegree of reaction nodes is bounded by 2.*

Proof. Since it is straightforward to see the correctness of the above algorithm, we analyze the time complexity.

Let $f(k)$ be the number of 0-1 assignments to V_r that are generated by the algorithm, where k is the number of unassigned and non-removed reaction nodes. Since the exponential factor depends only on $f(k)$, it is enough to analyze the order of $f(k)$.

Since **Case D0** does not add any assignment, we can ignore it.

Suppose that **Case D1-A** is executed. If $v_b = 1$ is examined, v_a is removed. Therefore, we have $f(k) \leq f(k-1) + f(k-2)$.

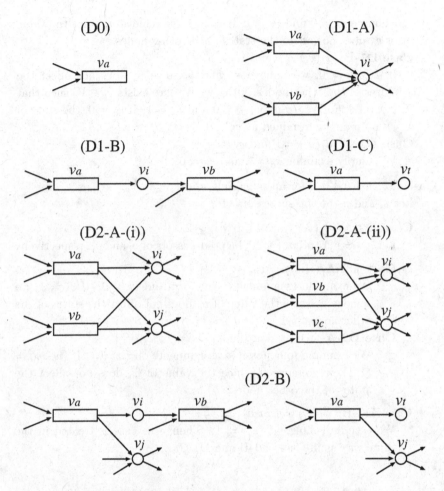

Fig. 10.3   Cases in the algorithm for Reaction Cut with the maximum outdegree 2. Circles represent compound nodes and rectangles represent reaction nodes.

Suppose that **Case D1-B** is executed. If $d_O(v_i) = 0$, we have $f(k) \leq f(k-1)$ because v_a is removed. Otherwise, we examine both $v_a = 0$ and $v_a = 1$. If $v_a = 0$ is examined, the state of v_b is uniquely determined. Therefore, we have $f(k) \leq f(k-1) + f(k-2)$.

Suppose that **Case D1-C** is executed. In this case, both $v_a = 0$ and $v_a = 1$ are examined. Although it doubles the number of assignments, it does not affect the order of $f(k)$ because it is executed for only one node.

Suppose that **Case D2-A-(i)** is executed. If $v_b = 1$ is examined, v_a is removed. Therefore, we have $f(k) \leq f(k-1) + f(k-2)$.

Suppose that **Case D2-A-(ii)** is executed. In this case, four assignments on (v_b, v_c) are examined. If $(v_b, v_c) = (1, 1)$ is examined, v_a is removed. Therefore, we have $f(k) \leq 3f(k-2) + f(k-3)$.

Suppose that **Case D2-B** is executed. This case can be analyzed analogously as in the cases of **D1-1** and **D1-C**.

Summarizing the above, it is seen that $f(k)$ is bounded by

$$f(k) \leq \max \begin{cases} f(k-1) + f(k-2), \\ 3f(k-2) + f(k-3). \end{cases}$$

$f(k) = f(k-1) + f(k-2)$ leads to the complexity of $O(1.619^k)$, which is obtained by solving $x^2 = x + 1$. $f(k) = 3f(k-2) + f(k-3)$ leads to the complexity of $O(1.880^k)$, which is obtained by solving $x^3 = 3x + 1$. Taking the maximum of these two, it is seen that the worst case complexity is $O(1.880^n)$. Note that an $O(poly(n, m))$ factor can be ignored because the solution of $x^3 = 3x + 1$ is slightly smaller than 1.880 and we assume that m is $O(n)$. $\qquad \square$

The time complexity of Theorem 10.2 was improved to $O(1.822^n)$ [Tamura and Akutsu (2010)] by considering more detailed classification of cases. Furthermore, it is also shown that Reaction Cut can be solved in $O((2 - \epsilon)^n)$ time if the maximum outdegree is bounded by a constant d where ϵ is a positive constant depending on d [Tamura and Akutsu (2010)].

10.4 ILP-based Method for Reaction Cut

We have seen Integer Linear Programming (ILP)-based methods for Singleton Attractor Detection and BN Control in Chapters 4 and 7. ILP can also be applied to development of practical methods for solving Reaction Cut. However, many cycles appear in BN models of practical metabolic networks, which causes a problem as discussed below.

Consider a BN model given in Fig. 10.4. For this BN, there exist two valid assignments: $[v_1, v_2, v_3, v_4, v_a, v_b] = [1, 1, 1, 1, 1, 1]$ and $[v_1, v_2, v_3, v_4, v_a, v_b] = [1, 0, 0, 0, 0, 0]$. If we adopt the latter, $V_d = \emptyset$ becomes a solution for Reaction Cut. However, it is not a solution if we adopt the former.

In order to avoid such an ambiguity, the concept of a *maximal valid assignment* has been introduced [Tamura *et al.* (2010)]. An assignment A is called *maximal* if $A[v] \geq A'[v]$ holds for all nodes $v \in (V_c \cup V_r)$ for any valid assignment A', where $A[v]$ denotes the 0-1 value of node v under A. Since

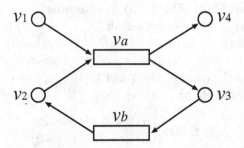

Fig. 10.4   Example of a BN model of a metabolic network with a loop, where $V_c = \{v_1, v_2, v_3, v_4\}$, $V_s = \{v_1\}$, $V_t = \{v_4\}$, and $V_r = \{v_a, v_b\}$. In this case, there are two valid assignments: $[v_1, v_2, v_3, v_4, v_a, v_b] = [1, 1, 1, 1, 1, 1]$ and $[v_1, v_2, v_3, v_4, v_a, v_b] = [1, 0, 0, 0, 0, 0]$. where the former is the maximal one.

each BN model of a metabolic network consists of AND and OR nodes only, the maximal valid assignment always exists and is uniquely determined. For the BN model given in Fig. 10.4, $[v_1, v_2, v_3, v_4, v_a, v_b] = [1, 1, 1, 1, 1, 1]$ is the maximal valid assignment. In order to prevent production of compound v_4, it is enough to let $V_d = \{v_a\}$ or $V_d = \{v_b\}$, for each of which $[v_1, v_2, v_3, v_4, v_a, v_b] = [1, 0, 0, 0, 0, 0]$ is the maximal valid assignment.

Computation of a valid assignment can be done by beginning with setting $v = 1$ for all $v \in (V_c \cup V_r) - V_d$ and $v = 0$ for all $v \in V_d$ and updating the states of all nodes synchronously according to AND/OR functions assigned to the nodes. Then, the number of nodes with state 1 is monotonically decreasing and the state of the BN eventually falls into a steady one, which is equal to the maximal valid assignment. In order to simulate this procedure by using ILP, a variable $v_{i,t}$ is associated with each node v_i, where $v_{i,t}$ denotes the state of v_i at time t, as in the ILP-based method for BN Control. However, this would cause creation of too many variables. In order to reduce the number of variables, the feedback vertex set has been utilized. The details of the ILP-based method for Reaction Cut are given in [Tamura *et al.* (2010)].

Another interesting topic on BN-models of metabolic networks is the *impact degree* [Jiang *et al.* (2009); Tamura *et al.* (2011)]. For example, consider the BN given in Fig. 10.1 (A). If v_a is knocked out (i.e., $v_a = 0$), the states of $v_a, v_c.v_d$ change from 1 to 0. On the other hand, if v_b is knocked out (i.e., $v_b = 0$), the states of v_b, v_e change from 1 to 0. In this case, the impact of knockout of v_a is considered to be stronger than that of knockout of v_b. Based on this idea, the *impact degree* has been defined as the number of reactions that are affected by knockout of a specific reaction or a specific set of reactions. Algorithms for computing the impact degree have been developed [Tamura *et al.* (2011)] and the distribution of the impact degree has been analyzed [Takemoto *et al.* (2012, 2013)] using BN models of metabolic networks.

10.5 Additional Remarks and Bibliographical Notes

The results in Sections 10.1, 10.2, and 10.3 are based on [Tamura and Akutsu (2010)]. As mentioned in Section 10.1, a number of studies have been done on analyses of metabolic networks under the flux balance analysis (FBA) framework [Acuña *et al.* (2009); Bordbar *et al.* (2014); Burgard *et al.* (2003); David and Bockmayr (2014); Haus *et al.* (2008); Orth *et al.* (2010); Schuster and Hilgetag (1994); von Kamp *et al.* (2014)]. In mathematical and computational analysis of FBA, elementary modes (EMs) play an important role, which are minimal sets of reactions that can operate at the steady state [Schuster and Hilgetag (1994)]. Although it is known that the number of EMs grows exponentially with the network size [Acuña *et al.* (2009); Haus *et al.* (2008)] and counting the number of EMs is #P-complete [Acuña *et al.* (2009)], some practically efficient methods have been proposed for enumerating EMs [Haus *et al.* (2008)]. The minimum cut set was defined based on FBA and EMs [Klamt and Gilles (2004)], which correspond to Reaction Cut in Section 10.1. Some practical algorithms have been proposed for computing this FBA-based minimum cut set [Klamt and Gilles (2004); Ballerstein *et al.* (2012)]. Bilevel programming-approach has also been proposed for finding an optimal knockout strategy under an FBA-based model [Burgard *et al.* (2003)].

The ILP-based method for Reaction Cut described in Section 10.4 was proposed in [Tamura *et al.* (2010)], where a branch-and-bound algorithm [Sridhar *et al.* (2008)] and another ILP-based method [Li *et al.* (2009)] were proposed using similar Boolean models. Furthermore, Reaction Cut was extended for handling multiple metabolic networks [Tamura *et al.* (2015)]. The concept of the impact degree was originally proposed in [Jiang *et al.* (2009)], where it was extended for dealing with cycles in [Tamura *et al.* (2010)]. Similar concepts have also been proposed and studied, which include *damage* [Lemke *et al.* (2004); Smart *et al.* (2008)], *scope* [Handorf *et al.* (2008)], and *FBID* (Flux Balance Impact Degree) [Zhao *et al.* (2013)].

Chapter 11

Probabilistic Boolean Networks

The Boolean network (with synchronous update) is a deterministic model: one regulation rule (one Boolean function) is assigned to each node and thus the next state of the network is uniquely determined from the current state. However, real biological networks do not necessarily work deterministically due to factors such as environment noise, intrinsic stochasticity of biological systems, and unknown mechanisms. Therefore, various stochastic extensions of the BN have been proposed. Among them, the Probabilistic Boolean Network (PBN) is the most extensively studied model [Shmulevich *et al.* (2002); Shmulevich and Dougherty (2010)]. In this chapter, we describe the definition of PBN and its basic properties.

11.1 Definition of PBN

As mentioned above, PBN is an extension of BN. The difference between BN and PBN lies in that exactly one Boolean function is assigned to each node in a BN whereas multiple Boolean functions can be assigned to each node in a PBN and one Boolean function is randomly selected for each node at each time step independently of other nodes and other time steps, according to the prescribed probability distribution.

Let $f_j^{(i)}$ denote the jth Boolean function assigned to node x_i, where l_i Boolean functions are assigned to x_i (i.e., $j = 1, \ldots, l_i$). Let $F_i = (f_1^{(i)}, \ldots, f_{l_i}^{(i)})$. For each node x_i and each time step t, $f_j^{(i)}$ $(j = 1, \ldots, l_i)$ is chosen with probability $c_j^{(i)}$, where $c_j^{(i)}$ should satisfy the following constraints:

$$0 \le c_j^{(i)} \le 1 \quad \text{and} \quad \sum_{j=1}^{l_i} c_j^{(i)} = 1 \quad \text{for} \quad i = 1, 2, \ldots, n.$$

Therefore, a PBN is defined by a set of nodes $V = \{x_1, \ldots, x_n\}$, and a list of lists of functions $(F_1, \ldots, F_n)$ along with their probability distributions $c_j^{(i)}$.

Once a Boolean function is chosen for each node, it corresponds to one BN, which is called a *realization* of a BN. Since l_i Boolean functions are assigned to each node, there exist $N = \prod_{i=1}^n l_i$ realizations. Let $\mathbf{f}_j$ be the jth possible realization:

$$\mathbf{f}_j = (f_{j_1}^{(1)}, \ldots, f_{j_n}^{(n)}), \ 1 \le j_i \le l_i, \ i = 1, 2, \ldots, n,$$

where $j = 1, \ldots, N$. The probability of choosing such a realization is given by

$$p_j = \prod_{i=1}^n c_{j_i}^{(i)}, \quad j = 1, 2, \ldots, N.$$

Example 11.1. Consider a PBN given in Fig. 11.1, where $l_1 = 2$, $l_2 = 1$ and $l_3 = 2$. This PBN has $N = \prod_{i=1}^3 l_i = 4$ realizations of BNs. Suppose that the state of the PBN at time t is $[0, 0, 0]$. If $(f_1^{(1)}, f_1^{(2)}, f_1^{(3)})$ is selected with probability $0.8 \times 0.7 = 0.56$, the state at time $t + 1$ is still $[0, 0, 0]$. Similarly, if $(f_1^{(1)}, f_1^{(2)}, f_2^{(3)})$ is selected with probability $0.8 \times 0.3 = 0.24$, the state at time $t + 1$ is still $[0, 0, 0]$. On the other hand, if $(f_2^{(1)}, f_1^{(2)}, f_1^{(3)})$ is selected with probability $0.2 \times 0.7 = 0.14$ or $(f_2^{(1)}, f_1^{(2)}, f_2^{(3)})$ is selected with probability $0.2 \times 0.3 = 0.06$, the state at time $t + 1$ becomes $[1, 0, 0]$. Therefore, we have the following state transition probabilities:

$$Prob(\mathbf{x}(t + 1) = [0, 0, 0] \mid \mathbf{x}(t) = [0, 0, 0]) = 0.8,$$
$$Prob(\mathbf{x}(t + 1) = [1, 0, 0] \mid \mathbf{x}(t) = [0, 0, 0]) = 0.2,$$

where the probabilities of the other transitions from $[0, 0, 0]$ are all 0.

For another example, the (non-zero) transition probabilities from $[0, 1, 0]$ are as follows:

$$Prob(\mathbf{x}(t + 1) = [0, 0, 0] \mid \mathbf{x}(t) = [0, 1, 0]) = 0.56,$$
$$Prob(\mathbf{x}(t + 1) = [0, 0, 1] \mid \mathbf{x}(t) = [0, 1, 0]) = 0.24,$$
$$Prob(\mathbf{x}(t + 1) = [1, 0, 0] \mid \mathbf{x}(t) = [0, 1, 0]) = 0.14,$$
$$Prob(\mathbf{x}(t + 1) = [1, 0, 1] \mid \mathbf{x}(t) = [0, 1, 0]) = 0.06.$$

The transition probabilities of an PBN can be represented by using a *transition matrix* A of size $2^n \times 2^n$. For each $\mathbf{a} = [a_1, \ldots, a_n] \in \{0, 1\}^n$, let

$$id(\mathbf{a}) = 2^{n-1}a_1 + 2^{n-2}a_2 + \cdots + 2a_{n-1} + a_n + 1.$$

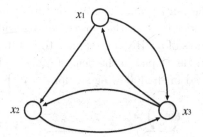

	Boolean Function	$c_j^{(i)}$
$f_1^{(1)}$	$x_1(t{+}1) = x_3(t)$	0.8
$f_2^{(1)}$	$x_1(t{+}1) = \overline{x_3(t)}$	0.2
$f_1^{(2)}$	$x_2(t{+}1) = x_1(t) \wedge \overline{x_3(t)}$	1.0
$f_1^{(3)}$	$x_3(t{+}1) = x_1(t) \wedge \overline{x_2(t)}$	0.7
$f_2^{(3)}$	$x_3(t{+}1) = x_2(t)$	0.3

Fig. 11.1   Example of an PBN.

Clearly, $id(\mathbf{a})$ is an integer between 1 and 2^n. Then, A is defined by

$$A_{ij} = Prob(\mathbf{x}(t+1) = \mathbf{b} \mid \mathbf{x}(t) = \mathbf{a}),$$

where $i = id(\mathbf{b})$ and $j = id(\mathbf{a})$. As in the BN, a state transition diagram can be associated to each PBN, in which each vertex corresponds to a state (among 2^n possible states) of a PBN and there exists a directed edge from state $\mathbf{a}$ to state $\mathbf{b}$ if the probability of a transition from $\mathbf{a}$ to $\mathbf{b}$ is not 0.

Example 11.2. Consider the PBN given in Example 11.1. Then, the transition matrix of this PBN is given by

$$
\begin{pmatrix}
0.8 & 0.2 & 0.56 & 0.14 & 0 & 0.06 & 0 & 0.14 \\
0 & 0 & 0.24 & 0.06 & 0 & 0.14 & 0 & 0.06 \\
0 & 0 & 0 & 0 & 0.24 & 0 & 0.56 & 0 \\
0 & 0 & 0 & 0 & 0.56 & 0 & 0.24 & 0 \\
0.2 & 0.8 & 0.14 & 0.56 & 0 & 0.24 & 0 & 0.56 \\
0 & 0 & 0.06 & 0.24 & 0 & 0.56 & 0 & 0.24 \\
0 & 0 & 0 & 0 & 0.06 & 0 & 0.14 & 0 \\
0 & 0 & 0 & 0 & 0.14 & 0 & 0.06 & 0
\end{pmatrix}.
$$

For example, the first column of this matrix represents the transition probabilities from $[0,0,0]$. The second, third, and fourth columns represent the transition probabilities from $[0,0,1]$, $[0,1,0]$, and $[0,1,1]$, respectively. The corresponding state transition diagram is given in Fig. 11.2.

As seen from the matrix and diagram in this example, the dynamics of a PBN can be understood in the context of a standard Markov chain, where each of 2^n states of a PBN corresponds to a state in a Markov chain. Thus, the techniques developed in the field of Markov chain can be applied to PBNs, as explained in the following section.

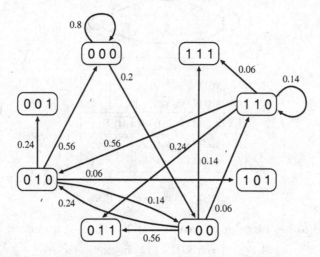

Fig. 11.2 State transition diagram corresponding to the PBN given in Fig. 11.1. In order to avoid making the figure complicated, only edges from states $[0,0,0]$, $[0,1,0]$, $[1,0,0]$, and $[1,1,0]$ are shown here.

11.2   Steady State Distributions

One of the important properties of the PBN is the steady-state distribution [Shmulevich *et al.* (2003)]. Recall that a PBN can be represented by a $2^n \times 2^n$ matrix A. Let π be a $2^n \times 1$ column vector such that $\sum_{i=1}^{2^n} \pi_i = 1$ is satisfied, where π_i denotes the ith row of π. π is called a *steady-state distribution* if the following holds

$$\pi = A\pi.$$

It is known that there always exists a steady-state distribution for any finite state Markov chain. Therefore, for any PBN, there always exists a steady-state distribution. However, a steady-state distribution is not necessarily unique.

Example 11.3.

(i) Consider a PBN defined by

$$f_1^{(1)} : x_1(t+1) = x_1(t) \wedge x_2(t), \quad c_1^{(1)} = \frac{1}{3},$$

$$f_2^{(1)} : x_1(t+1) = \overline{x_1(t)} \vee \overline{x_2(t)}, \quad c_2^{(1)} = \frac{2}{3},$$

$$f_1^{(2)} : x_2(t+1) = x_2(t), \quad c_1^{(2)} = \frac{1}{2},$$

$$f_2^{(2)} : x_2(t+1) = \overline{x_2(t)}, \quad c_2^{(2)} = \frac{1}{2}.$$

Then, the transition diagram is as shown in Fig. 11.3 (A) and the transition matrix is given by

$$A = \begin{pmatrix} \frac{1}{6} & \frac{1}{6} & \frac{1}{6} & \frac{1}{3} \\ \frac{1}{6} & \frac{1}{6} & \frac{1}{6} & \frac{1}{3} \\ \frac{1}{3} & \frac{1}{3} & \frac{1}{3} & \frac{1}{6} \\ \frac{1}{3} & \frac{1}{3} & \frac{1}{3} & \frac{1}{6} \end{pmatrix}.$$

The steady-state distribution is uniquely determined as $[\frac{3}{14}, \frac{3}{14}, \frac{2}{7}, \frac{2}{7}]^{\top}$. Furthermore,
starting from any probability distribution π', $P^k \pi'$ converges to the unique steady state distribution π (i.e., $\lim_{k \to +\infty} A^k \pi' = \pi$).

(ii) Consider a PBN defined by

$$f_1^{(1)} : x_1(t+1) = x_1(t), \quad c_1^{(1)} = 1,$$

$$f_1^{(2)} : x_2(t+1) = x_1(t), \quad c_1^{(2)} = \frac{1}{2},$$

$$f_2^{(2)} : x_2(t+1) = x_2(t), \quad c_2^{(2)} = \frac{1}{2}.$$

Then, the transition diagram is as shown in Fig. 11.3 (B) and the transition matrix is given by

$$A = \begin{pmatrix} 1 & \frac{1}{2} & 0 & 0 \\ 0 & \frac{1}{2} & 0 & 0 \\ 0 & 0 & \frac{1}{2} & 0 \\ 0 & 0 & \frac{1}{2} & 1 \end{pmatrix}.$$

There are infinitely many steady-state distributions: for any $0 \leq x \leq 1$, $[x, 0, 0, 1 - x]^{\top}$ is a steady-state distribution.

(iii) Consider a PBN defined by

$$f_1^{(1)} : x_1(t+1) = \overline{x_1(t)}, \quad c_1^{(1)} = 1,$$
$$f_1^{(2)} : x_2(t+1) = x_2(t), \quad c_1^{(2)} = \frac{1}{2},$$
$$f_2^{(2)} : x_2(t+1) = \overline{x_2(t)}, \quad c_2^{(2)} = \frac{1}{2}.$$

Then, the transition diagram is as shown in Fig. 11.3 (C) and the transition matrix is given by

$$A = \begin{pmatrix} 0 & 0 & \frac{1}{2} & \frac{1}{2} \\ 0 & 0 & \frac{1}{2} & \frac{1}{2} \\ \frac{1}{2} & \frac{1}{2} & 0 & 0 \\ \frac{1}{2} & \frac{1}{2} & 0 & 0 \end{pmatrix}.$$

The steady-state distribution is uniquely determined as $[\frac{1}{2}, \frac{1}{2}, \frac{1}{2}, \frac{1}{2}]^\mathsf{T}$. However, $P^k\pi'$ does not necessarily converge to this distribution. For example, let $\pi' = [1/6, 1/6, 1/3, 1/3]^\mathsf{T}$. Then, $\pi' = P^2\pi' = P^4\pi' = \cdots = [1/6, 1/6, 1/3, 1/3]^\mathsf{T}$ and $P\pi' = P^3\pi' = P^5\pi' = \cdots = [1/3, 1/3, 1/6, 1/6]^\mathsf{T}$.

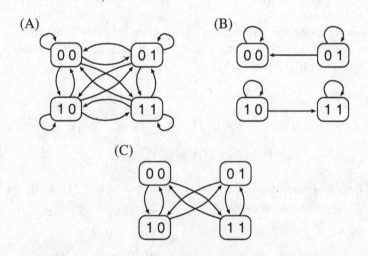

Fig. 11.3   State transition diagrams for Example 11.3.

In order to compute a steady-state distribution, we may apply various methods of computation of eigenvectors. However, usually A is very large (recall that its size is $2^n \times 2^n$) and thus many of existing methods are not practical. If $l_i = 1$ holds for most i, we may use the *power method* effectively. The power method is a simple method used for computing the largest eigenvalue in modulus (the dominant eigenvalue) and its corresponding eigenvector of a square matrix. Starting from any probability distribution $\pi^{(0)}$, it repeatedly computes

$$\pi^{(k)} = A\pi^{(k-1)}$$

until $\|\pi^{(k)} - \pi^{(k-1)}\|_\infty < \varepsilon$ holds for some given tolerance ε, where $\|\pi\|_\infty$ denotes the L_∞ norm of vector π (i.e., the maximum absolute value of the elements of π). It is known that if the underlying Markov chain of the PBN is *irreducible*, the maximum eigenvalue of the transition probability matrix is one and the modulus of the other eigenvalues are less than one, and the eigenvector corresponding to the maximum eigenvalue is the steady-state distribution vector. It is also known that the convergence rate of the power method depends on the ratio of $|\lambda_2/\lambda_1|$, where λ_1 and λ_2 are respectively the largest and the second largest eigenvalues of A.

Recall that the number of realizations of BNs is given by $N = \prod_{i=1}^{n} l_i$. Then, A is represented as

$$A = p_1 A_1 + p_2 A_2 + \cdots + p_N A_N,$$

where each A_i is to a realization of a BN and has 2^n non-zero entries, and p_i is the probability that the transition corresponding to A_i is used.

Suppose that each A_i is given as a table of size $O(2^n)$. Then, $A_i\pi^{(k-1)}$ can be computed in $O(2^n)$ time, and thus $A\pi^{(k-1)}$ can be computed in $O(N2^n)$ time. If $l_i = 1$ holds for many i (i.e., many nodes work deterministically), then N would be small. In such a case, $N2^n$ would be much smaller than the size of A and each iteration would be done much faster than in the case of naive calculation of $A\pi^{(k-1)}$.

11.3 Influences of Nodes in a PBN

In biological networks, some nodes may play important roles. For example, mutations of some genes may lead to some type of cancer. Therefore, it is important to measure the influence of each node in a PBN. For example, consider a Boolean function $f(x_1, x_2, x_3, x_4) = x_1 \vee (x_2 \wedge x_3 \wedge x_4)$. If we let $x_1 = 1$, $f = 1$ holds regardless of the other variables. However, there is no such property for x_2, x_3, or x_4. Therefore, it is considered to be that x_1 is more influential than the other variables.

In order to define the notion of influence, we introduce the *partial derivative* of a Boolean function with respect to variable x_i as

$$\frac{\partial f(\mathbf{x})}{\partial x_j} = |f(\mathbf{x}) - f(\mathbf{x}_{(j)})| = f(\mathbf{x}) \oplus f(\mathbf{x}_{(j)}).$$

Recall that $\mathbf{x}_{(j)}$ denotes the vector obtained by flipping jth element of $\mathbf{x}$. For example, consider $f(x_1, x_2, x_3, x_4) = x_1 \vee (x_2 \wedge x_3 \wedge x_4)$ and $\mathbf{x} = [0, 1, 1, 0]$. Then, $\frac{\partial f(\mathbf{x})}{\partial x_1} = 1$, $\frac{\partial f(\mathbf{x})}{\partial x_2} = 0$, $\frac{\partial f(\mathbf{x})}{\partial x_3} = 0$, and $\frac{\partial f(\mathbf{x})}{\partial x_4} = 1$ hold.

The *influence* of a variable x_i on a Boolean function f is defined to be the expectation of the partial derivative with the probability distribution $D(\mathbf{x})$ on $\mathbf{x}$:

$$I_j(f) = E_D\left[\frac{\partial f(\mathbf{x})}{\partial x_j}\right] = Prob\left(\frac{\partial f(\mathbf{x})}{\partial x_j} = 1\right) = Prob(f(\mathbf{x}) \neq f(\mathbf{x}^{(j)})).$$

The concept of influence can be extended for PBNs by taking the weighted average of influences. Recall that $f_1^{(i)}, \ldots, f_{l_i}^{(i)}$ functions are assigned to node x_i along with their selection probabilities $c_1^{(i)}, \ldots, c_{l_i}^{(i)}$. Then, the *influence* of node x_k on x_i is defined as

$$I_k(x_i) = \sum_{j=1}^{l_i} c_j^{(i)} \cdot I_k(f_j^{(i)}).$$

Since $I_k(x_i)$ can be defined for all $i = 1, \ldots, n$ and all $k = 1, \ldots, n$, $I_k(x_i)$s constitute an $n \times n$ matrix Γ, which is defined by $\Gamma_{ij} = I_i(x_j)$.

Furthermore, the *average sensitivity* $s(x_i)$ and the *average influence* $r(x_i)$ of node x_i are defined as below.

$$s(x_i) = \sum_{k=1}^{n} \Gamma_{ki},$$

$$r(x_i) = \sum_{k=1}^{n} \Gamma_{ik}.$$

Intuitively, the sensitivity of a gene represents the instability of the gene, and the influence of a gene represents its collective impact on the other genes.

Example 11.4. Consider the following PBN with two nodes x_1 and x_2.

	Boolean function	$c_j^{(i)}$
$f_1^{(1)}$	$x_1(t+1) = x_1(t) \wedge x_2(t)$	0.4
$f_2^{(1)}$	$x_1(t+1) = x_2(t)$	0.6
$f_1^{(2)}$	$x_2(t+1) = x_1(t) \oplus x_2(t)$	0.7
$f_2^{(2)}$	$x_2(t+1) = \overline{x_1(t)}$	0.3

Suppose that D is the uniform distribution, that is, $D(\mathbf{x}) = \frac{1}{4}$ for all $\mathbf{x} \in \{0, 1\}^2$.

Since $f_1^{(1)}(\mathbf{x}) \neq f_1^{(1)}(\mathbf{x}_{(1)})$ holds for $\mathbf{x} = [0, 1]$ and $\mathbf{x} = [1, 1]$, $I_1(f_1^{(1)}) = \frac{1}{4} \cdot 2 = 0.5$. By doing similar calculations, $I_k(f_j^{(i)})$s are determined as follows.

k	$f_1^{(1)}$	$f_2^{(1)}$	$f_1^{(2)}$	$f_2^{(2)}$
1	0.5	0.0	1.0	1.0
2	0.5	1.0	1.0	0.0

Then, $I_1(x_1)$ is determined as

$$I_1(x_1) = \sum_{j=1}^{2} c_j^{(1)} \cdot I_1(f_j^{(1)}) = 0.4 \cdot 0.5 + 0.6 \cdot 0.0 = 0.2.$$

By doing similar calculations, Γ is determined as

$$\Gamma = \begin{pmatrix} I_1(x_1) & I_1(x_2) \\ I_2(x_1) & I_2(x_2) \end{pmatrix} = \begin{pmatrix} 0.2 & 0.8 \\ 1.0 & 0.4 \end{pmatrix}.$$

Then, we have $s(x_1) = 1.2$, $s(x_2) = 1.2$, $r(x_1) = 1.0$, and $r(x_2) = 1.4$.

11.4 Additional Remarks and Bibliographical Notes

The PBN was introduced in [Shmulevich *et al.* (2002)]. After that, a lot of studies have been on the PBN and its variants, See a book [Shmulevich and Dougherty (2010)] and and review articles [Datta *et al.* (2007); Trairatphisan *et al.* (2013)] for details of such studies. Most contents of this chapter are based on [Shmulevich *et al.* (2002)]. An application of the power method described in Section 11.2 was proposed in [Zhang *et al.* (2007b)]. In order to improve the efficiency of that approach, a method for approximately computing the steady-state distribution of a PBN by ignoring realizations with very small probabilities was proposed and analyzed in [Ching *et al.* (2007)]. PBNs have a close relationship with dynamic Bayesian networks, details of which are discussed in [Lähdesmäki *et al.* (2006)]. PBN-based bipartite modeling of signaling networks has been studied in [Mori *et al.* (2015)].

Chapter 12

Identification of Probabilistic Boolean Networks

In Chapter 6, we have seen that a BN with bounded indegree can always be identified if enough number of samples are given. It is reasonable to try to get similar results for a PBN. However, it is much harder to uniquely determine a PBN from samples because PBN is a probabilistic system. In this Chapter, we describe a practical method for inference of a PBN and theoretical methods for identification of a PBN and its variant. Furthermore, it will be shown that there are cases in which it is impossible to uniquely determine a PBN that is consistent with given samples even if all possible samples are given.

12.1 Inference of a PBN by Coefficient of Determination

In this section, we present a practical heuristic method for inference of a PBN from samples that is based on the *Coefficient Of Determination* (COD) [Shmulevich *et al.* (2002)].

The COD measures the degree to which the input node set can be used to improve the prediction accuracy for a target node relative to the best possible prediction in the absence of the input node set. Let x_i be a target node, and $\mathbf{u}(t) = [x_{i_1}(t), \ldots, x_{i_k}(t)]$ denote the state vector of input nodes. Let ε_i be the error for the best prediction in the absence of observations and ε_{opt} be the error for the best prediction with observations on the input node set. Then, the COD is defined by

$$\theta = \frac{\varepsilon_i - \varepsilon_{opt}}{\varepsilon_i}.$$

Since $\varepsilon_{opt} \leq \varepsilon_i$, the COD must be between 0 and 1.

Although various error functions can be considered, one of the simplest error functions is the *Mean-Square Error* (MSE) given by

$$E[(x_i^{pred} - x_i)^2],$$

where $E[\cdots]$ denotes the expectation. Then, the best prediction x_i^{pred} in the absence of observations is the mean of the observed values of x_i, and the error is its variance. The optimal prediction function with the observation of input nodes would be given by

$$f_i^{opt}(\mathbf{a}) = E[x_i(t+1) = 1 | \mathbf{u}(t) = \mathbf{a}].$$

However, this f_i^{opt} is not a Boolean function. Therefore, some heuristic method has been proposed for finding a Boolean function that approximates the optimal one.

Suppose that a set of Boolean functions $f_1^{(i)}, \ldots, f_{l_i}^{(i)}$ is found for each node x_i along with their COD values $\theta_1^i, \ldots, \theta_{l_i}^i$. Then, the probability of $f_j^{(i)}$ being chosen is given by

$$c_j^{(i)} = \frac{\theta_j^i}{\sum_{k=1}^{l_i} \theta_k^i}.$$

This method may be practically useful. However, there is no theoretical guarantee on the quality of the resulting PBNs. Therefore, we will discuss more rigorous combinatorial methods in the following sections. In particular, we focus on how to exactly identify Boolean functions from samples, without paying attentions to estimation of $c_j^{(i)}$s.

12.2   Identification of a Noisy Boolean Network

Before discussing identification of a PBN, we consider identification of a simpler model, a *noisy Boolean network* (noisy BN), which was proposed in order to cope with noisy gene expression data [Akutsu *et al.* (2000a)] before the proposal of a PBN [Shmulevich *et al.* (2002)]. Let $N(V, F)$ be a BN. Then, a noisy BN consists of $N(V, F)$ and p, where p is a constant with $0 \leq p \leq 1$. Let $(\mathbf{a}^j, \mathbf{b}^j)$ $(j = 1, \ldots, m)$ be samples. In a usual BN, it is assumed that $\mathbf{b}^j[i] = f_i(\mathbf{a}^j)$ holds for all $i = 1, \ldots, n$ and for all $j = 1, \ldots, m$. In a noisy BN, for each i, j, $\mathbf{b}^j[i] \neq f_i(\mathbf{a}^j)$ occurs with probability not greater than p. That is, a noisy output is given with probability not greater than p.

The identification algorithm for noisy BNs can be obtained by slightly modifying the algorithm in Section 6.1.3. In the original algorithm, f_i is discarded as soon as one inconsistent sample is found. In the modified algorithm, f_i is discarded only if a certain number of inconsistent samples are found. The following is a pseudo-code of the resulting algorithm, where θ is a constant to be determined.

Procedure IdentNoisyBN(S)
for all nodes x_i **do**
  let $F_i \leftarrow \emptyset$;
  for all Boolean functions f_i with at most K input nodes **do**
    mismatch $\leftarrow 0$;
    for all $j = 1, \ldots, m$ **do**
      if $\mathbf{b}^j[i] \neq f_i(\mathbf{a}^j)$ **then** *mismatch* $\leftarrow$ *mismatch* $+ 1$;
    if *mismatch* $< \theta \cdot m$ **then**
      $F \leftarrow F \cup \{f_i\}$;
  if $|F_i| \neq 1$ **then return** FALSE;
return TRUE.

It is straightforward to see that **IdentNoisyBN** works in $O(2^{2^K} \cdot n^K \cdot poly(n, m))$ time. We can show that **IdentNoisyBN** correctly identifies a noisy BN with high probability if p is small, by modifying the proof for Theorem 6.1.

Theorem 12.1. *Suppose that* $p < \frac{1}{e \cdot 2^{2K+2}}$. *Let* $\theta = \frac{1}{2^{2K+1}}$. *If* $O\left(2^{2K} \cdot (\alpha + K + 1) \cdot \left(1 + \frac{1}{\log \frac{1}{p} - \log e - (2K+2)}\right) \cdot \log n\right)$ *samples are given uniformly at random,* **IdentNoisyBN** *correctly identifies the structure of the underlying noisy BN (i.e., noisy BN without p) with maximum indegree* K *with probability at least* $1 - \frac{1}{n^\alpha}$, *where* $\alpha > 1$ *is any fixed constant.*

Proof. Since the output value of each node is determined independently of those of the other nodes, we consider the probability that **IdentNoisyBN** does not output the correct Boolean function for a fixed node x_i. There are two cases in which the algorithm makes an error: (A) the correct Boolean function is discarded, (B) an incorrect Boolean function is not discarded.

We begin with Case (A). Let f_i be the correct Boolean function assigned to x_i. Let M be the number of samples inconsistent with f_i. Since an incorrect output value is obtained with probability at most p, the expected value μ of M satisfies $\mu \leq pm$. Recall that the Chernoff bound states that $Prob(M > (1 + \delta)\mu) < \left(\frac{e^\delta}{(1+\delta)^{(1+\delta)}}\right)^\mu$ holds for $\delta > 0$. By letting $\delta = \frac{1}{p \cdot 2^{2K+1}} - 1$ and using $e^\delta < e^{1+\delta}$, the probability that Case (A) occurs is bounded by

$$Prob\left(M > \frac{m}{2^{2K+1}}\right) < \left(e \cdot p \cdot 2^{2K+1}\right)^{\frac{m}{2^{2K+1}}}.$$

Next we consider Case (B). For any Boolean function g_i different from f_i, we estimate the probability that g_i is not discarded. From

Lemma 6.1, we see that the expected value of *mismatch* is at least $\frac{m}{2^{2K}}$ in the noiseless model. Then, the required probability is at most the sum of the probabilities of two cases: (B1) the number of samples for which $g_i(\mathbf{a}) \neq f_i(\mathbf{a})$ holds is less than $\frac{3}{4} \cdot \frac{m}{2^{2K}}$; (B2) the number of samples for which $\mathbf{b}^j[i] \neq f_i(\mathbf{a}^j)$ holds is greater than $\frac{1}{4} \cdot \frac{m}{2^{2K}} = \frac{m}{2^{2K+2}}$.

As in Case (A) but letting $\delta = \frac{1}{p \cdot 2^{2K+2}} - 1$, the probability that (B2) occurs is bounded above by $\left(e \cdot p \cdot 2^{2K+2}\right)^{\frac{m}{2^{2K+2}}}$ for $p < \frac{1}{e \cdot 2^{2K+2}}$. Let X be the number of samples corresponding to Case (B1). From the Chernoff bound $Prob(X < (1 - \delta)\mu) < e^{-\frac{\mu\delta^2}{2}}$ $(0 < \delta < 1)$ and the fact $\mu \geq \frac{m}{2^{2K}}$, the probability that (B2) occurs is bounded above by

$$Prob\left(X < \frac{3}{4} \cdot \frac{m}{2^{2K}}\right) < e^{-\frac{1}{32} \cdot \frac{m}{2^{2K}}},$$

where we let $\delta = \frac{1}{4}$.

Since there are at most $2^{2^K} \cdot n^K$ Boolean functions $g_i \neq f_i$ and Case (A) is included in Case (B2), the probability that the correct Boolean function is not identified for x_i is bounded above by

$$\left(e \cdot p \cdot 2^{2K+2}\right)^{\frac{m}{2^{2K+2}}} + 2^{2^K} \cdot n^K \cdot e^{-\frac{1}{32} \cdot \frac{m}{2^{2K}}}.$$

Since there are n nodes, the probability that the correct Boolean functions are not identified for at least one node is bounded above by n times this value. Accordingly, we have the following inequality:

$$n\left[\left(e \cdot p \cdot 2^{2K+2}\right)^{\frac{m}{2^{2K+2}}} + 2^{2^K} \cdot n^K \cdot e^{-\frac{1}{32} \cdot \frac{m}{2^{2K}}}\right] < \frac{1}{n^\alpha}.$$

Since it is difficult to directly solve it, we solve the following two inequalities:

$$n\left[\left(e \cdot p \cdot 2^{2K+2}\right)^{\frac{m}{2^{2K+2}}}\right] < \frac{1}{2n^\alpha},$$

$$n\left[2^{2^K} \cdot n^K \cdot e^{-\frac{1}{32} \cdot \frac{m}{2^{2K}}}\right] < \frac{1}{2n^\alpha}.$$

Then, we have the following bounds, respectively:

$$m > \frac{2^{2K+2}(1 + (\alpha + 1)\log n)}{\log \frac{1}{p} - \log e - (2K + 2)},$$

$$m > \frac{32 \cdot 2^{2K}}{\log e}\left((K + \alpha + 1)\log n + 2^K + 1\right).$$

Combining these two conditions, we have the theorem.

$\square$

12.3   Identification of the Structure of a PBN

In Section 12.2, we have seen that a noisy BN can be identified if the probability of generating a noisy sample is low. However, if the probability is $1/2$, each output bit can be regarded as a random bit and thus we cannot get any information from samples. Therefore, it is impossible to identify a noisy BN if there is no restriction on the error probability. A noisy BN can be considered as a special case of a PBN in which the following Boolean functions are assigned to each node x_i, where f_i is a Boolean function assigned to x_i in the original noisy BN:

$$x_i(t+1) = f_i(\mathbf{x}(t)) \qquad \text{with probability } 1-p,$$
$$x_i(t+1) = \overline{f_i(\mathbf{x}(t))} \qquad \text{with probability } p.$$

This means that it is impossible to identify a PBN if there is no restriction. However, it may be possible to identify the structure a PBN (i.e., a PBN without $c_j^{(i)}$s) if there are some restrictions on the structure of a PBN, regardless of the selection probabilities of Boolean functions. This section provides several results for clarifying which classes of PBNs can (resp., cannot) be identified from samples.

12.3.1   *Two Models*

As in Chapter 6, we focus on one output node until considering the sample complexity. In the following, the target output node is denoted as y (i.e., $y = x_i$ for some i). A *sample* is defined by a pair of an assignment of 0-1 values to $x_1, \ldots, x_n$ and the value of output y, and is represented by a pair $(\mathbf{a}, b)$ of n-dimensional 0-1 input vector $\mathbf{a}$ and 0-1 (output) value b, where $\mathbf{a}$ and b correspond to the global state at time t and the state of node y at time $t+1$, respectively.

We assume that a class $\mathcal{C}$ of PBNs is given, and that a set of samples S is generated using some $F \in \mathcal{C}$. Since we are focusing on only one output node y, F is a set of Boolean functions assigned to y. For simplicity, we use f_i to denote an element of F, and that F is given as $F = \{f_1, \ldots, f_s\}$, where s is the number of Boolean functions assigned to y. Note that f_i is used in a way different from that for BNs. Although f_i is randomly selected according to the underlying probability in each sample, we ignore the selection probability in this section because we consider the identifiability of a PBN regardless of the selection probability. Then, for each sample $(\mathbf{a}, b) \in S$, $b \in F(\mathbf{a}) = \{f_1(\mathbf{a}), \ldots, f_s(\mathbf{a})\}$ holds.

Definition 12.1. A PBN $F = \{f_1, \ldots, f_s\}$ is *consistent* with a sample $(\mathbf{a}, b)$ if $b \in F(\mathbf{a}) = \{f_1(\mathbf{a}), \ldots, f_s(\mathbf{a})\}$ holds. Furthermore, F is *consistent* with a set of samples S if F is consistent with every sample in S.

The purpose of this section is to describe classes $\mathcal{C}$ of PBNs having the property that there is a unique $F \in \mathcal{C}$ that is consistent with S provided the set of samples S is sufficiently large.

We consider two models, the *Partial Information Model* (PIM), and the *Full Information Model* (FIM). Intuitively, it is required under PIM that all samples are consistent with the underlying PBN, and no other PBN in the class under consideration could have generated these samples. On the other hand, under FIM, this requirement is relaxed to that the property holds under the assumption that the current set of samples contain all relevant samples.

Definition 12.2. S identifies F from among $\mathcal{C}$ under PIM if F is the only PBN in $\mathcal{C}$ that is consistent with all samples in S.

Definition 12.3. S identifies F from among $\mathcal{C}$ under FIM if

(1) F is the only PBN in $\mathcal{C}$ that is consistent with all samples in S, and
(2) if $(\mathbf{a}, b) \in S$ then $\mathbf{a} \times F(\mathbf{a}) \subseteq S$, i.e. all possible samples $(\mathbf{a}, f(\mathbf{a})), f \in F$ were generated.

Under each model, when the class is clear from the context, we say that S PIM-identifies (resp., FIM-identifies) F. If F is consistent with S and S satisfies the second condition (i.e., if $(\mathbf{a}, b) \in S$ then $\mathbf{a} \times F(\mathbf{a}) \subseteq S$), we say that F is *strongly consistent* with S.

Example 12.1. Let $F = \{\{x_1 \wedge x_2\}, \{x_1 \vee x_2\}\}$. Suppose that the following S_1, S_2, and S_3 are given.

$$S_1 = \{([0,0], 0), ([0,1], 1), ([1,1], 1)\},$$
$$S_2 = \{([0,0], 0), ([0,1], 0), ([0,1], 1), ([1,1], 1)\},$$
$$S_3 = \{([0,0], 0), ([0,0], 1), ([0,1], 1), ([1,1], 1)\}.$$

Then, F is consistent with each of S_1 and S_2, and is strongly consistent with S_2, but is not consistent with S_3.

Definition 12.4. A class $\mathcal{C}$ is identifiable from samples under PIM (resp., under FIM) if for every $F \in \mathcal{C}$ there is a set of samples that PIM-identifies (resp., FIM-identifies) F.

We also say for short that $\mathcal{C}$ is PIM-identifiable (resp., FIM-identifiable).

The following theorem gives the condition to characterize the identifiability under each model, where $S_1 \setminus S_2$ denotes the set $\{x | x \in S_1, x \notin S_2\}$.

Theorem 12.2. *A class $\mathcal{C}$ of PBNs is PIM-identifiable if and only if for every $F, G \in \mathcal{C}$ there is an assignment* **a** *such that*

$$F(\mathbf{a}) \setminus G(\mathbf{a}) \neq \emptyset.$$

$\mathcal{C}$ is FIM-identifiable if and only if for every $F, G \in \mathcal{C}$ there is an assignment **a** *such that*

$$F(\mathbf{a}) \neq G(\mathbf{a}).$$

Proof. First we prove the theorem for PIM. Suppose that the condition holds. Then, for each $G \in \mathcal{C}$, $G \neq F$, there is an $\mathbf{a}_G$ such that $b_G \in F(\mathbf{a}_G) \setminus G(\mathbf{a}_G)$. Let $S_F = \{(\mathbf{a}_G, b_G) | G \in \mathcal{C}, G \neq F\}$. Clearly F is consistent with S_F whereas every $G \in \mathcal{C}$, $G \neq F$, is inconsistent with S_F. Conversely, suppose that $\mathcal{C}$ is PIM-identifiable. Let S be a set of samples that PIM-identifies $F \in \mathcal{C}$. Let $G \in \mathcal{C}$ such that $G \neq F$. Then, there exists a sample $(\mathbf{a}, b)$ with which F is consistent but G is inconsistent, that is, $b \in F(\mathbf{a})$ but $b \notin G(\mathbf{a})$. Hence $F(\mathbf{a}) \setminus G(\mathbf{a}) \neq \emptyset$.

Next we prove the theorem for FIM. Suppose that the condition holds. Then, for each $G \in \mathcal{C}$, $G \neq F$, there is an $\mathbf{a}_G$ such that $F(\mathbf{a}_G) \neq G(\mathbf{a}_G)$. Let $S_F = \{(\mathbf{a}_G, b) | G \in \mathcal{C}, G \neq F, b \in F(\mathbf{a}_G)\}$. Clearly, F is consistent with S_F and that for all $(\mathbf{a}, b) \in S_F$, $\mathbf{a} \times F(\mathbf{a}) \subseteq S_F$ holds. Furthermore, there exists b such that $b \in F(\mathbf{a}_G) \setminus G(\mathbf{a}_G)$ or $b \in G(\mathbf{a}_G) \setminus F(\mathbf{a}_G)$. In the former case G is not consistent with $(\mathbf{a}_G, b)$, and in the latter case $(\mathbf{a}_G, b) \notin S_F$ holds and thus G is not strongly consistent with S_F. Conversely, suppose that $\mathcal{C}$ is FIM-identifiable. Let S be a set of samples that FIM-identifies $F \in \mathcal{C}$. Let $G \in \mathcal{C}$ such that $G \neq F$. Then, either G is inconsistent with S (i.e., there exists $(\mathbf{a}, b)$ such that $b \in F(\mathbf{a}) \setminus G(\mathbf{a}))$, or there exists a sample which is generated by G but is not in S (i.e., there exists $(\mathbf{a}, b)$ such that $b \in G(\mathbf{a}) \setminus F(\mathbf{a}))$. In both cases, $F(\mathbf{a}) \neq G(\mathbf{a})$ holds. $\qquad\square$

From this theorem, we immediately have the following.

Corollary 12.1. *If C is PIM-identifiable, C is FIM-identifiable.*

The following example shows that there exists a class $\mathcal{C}$ that is not PIM-identifiable or FIM-identifiable.

Example 12.2. Let $\mathcal{C} = \{\{x_i, \overline{x_i}\}| \ i \in \{1, \ldots, n\}\}$. Then, $\mathcal{C}$ is not identifiable under PIM or FIM since for any $(F, G) = (\{x_i, \overline{x_i}\}, \{x_j, \overline{x_j}\})$ with $i \neq j$, $F(\mathbf{a}) = G(\mathbf{a}) = \{0, 1\}$ holds for all $\mathbf{a}$.

This example can be generalized as follows.

Proposition 12.1. *The class of pairs of AND functions (resp., OR functions) of degree 2 is not identifiable from samples under PIM or FIM.*

Proof. Let $n = 3$. Consider two pairs of Boolean functions $\{f_1, f_2\} = \{x_1 \wedge x_2, x_1 \wedge \overline{x_2}\}$ and $\{g_1, g_2\} = \{x_1 \wedge x_3, x_1 \wedge \overline{x_3}\}$. Then, $F(\mathbf{a}) = \{f_1(\mathbf{a}), f_2(\mathbf{a})\} = \{g_1(\mathbf{a}), g_2(\mathbf{a})\} = G(\mathbf{a})$ holds for all $\mathbf{a} \in \{0, 1\}^3$ as shown below, where "0/1" means that we have both outputs.

x_1	0	0	0	0	1	1	1	1
x_2	0	0	1	1	0	0	1	1
x_3	0	1	0	1	0	1	0	1
f_1	0	0	0	0	0	0	1	1
f_2	0	0	0	0	1	1	0	0
Output	0	0	0	0	0/1	0/1	0/1	0/1
g_1	0	0	0	0	0	1	0	1
g_1	0	0	0	0	1	0	1	0

Therefore, the proposition follows from Theorem 12.2.   □

It can also be shown that there exists a class $\mathcal{C}$ of PBNs that is FIM-identifiable but is not PIM-identifiable.

Example 12.3. Let $F = \{x_1, x_1 \vee x_2\}$, $G = \{x_1 \wedge x_2, x_1 \vee x_2\}$. and $\mathcal{C} = \{F, G\}$. Consider the following two sample sets S_1 and S_2, where "0/1" means that we have both outputs.

x_1	0	0	1	1
x_2	0	1	0	1
Output in S_1	0	0/1	1	1
Output in S_2	0	0/1	0/1	1

Then, F is strongly consistent with S_1, but is not consistent with S_2. G is strongly consistent with S_2 and is consistent with but is not strongly consistent with S_1. Therefore, from the definition of FIM, the class $\mathcal{C}$ is

FIM-identifiable. However, the class $\mathcal{C}$ is not PIM-identifiable because for any set of samples S' with which F is consistent, G is also consistent with S'.

The above example shows that there exists a class of PBNs which is FIM-identifiable but not PIM-identifiable. It also shows another difference between PIM and FIM. When S_1 is given, only F is strongly consistent. After a sample $([1,0],0)$ is added and thus the set of samples becomes S_2, F is no more strongly consistent but G newly becomes strongly consistent. Therefore, the existence of only one $H \in \mathcal{C}$ that is strongly consistent with the current set of samples does not necessarily mean that H is strongly consistent with future samples. Hence, under FIM, we may not be able to decide whether the current set of samples is enough. On the other hand, under PIM, the existence of only one $H \in \mathcal{C}$ that is consistent with the current set of samples means that only H is consistent with a sample set including future samples. That is, once only one H becomes consistent, no other H' can be consistent forever. Therefore, under PIM, we can decide whether the current set of samples is enough to uniquely identify a PBN.

12.3.2 *Identification of an AND/OR PBN*

In the above, we have shown that there are PBN classes not identifiable from samples, different from the case of BNs. However, several interesting classes of PBNs are identifiable. In this subsection, we show that a subclass of PBNs consisting of AND/OR functions is PIM-identifiable, which also means that this subclass is FIM-identifiable.

Recall that a Boolean function is an AND/OR function if it is either a conjunction or a disjunction of literals. Proposition 12.1 shows that PBNs are not identifiable under PIM or FIM even if Boolean functions are limited to AND/OR functions. By looking at the proof of Proposition 12.1, we can see that the appearance of a variable and its negation plays an important role in the counter example. This observation leads to an introduction of admissible pairs.

Definition 12.5. A pair of AND/OR functions $\{f_1, f_2\}$ is called *admissible* if both a variable and its negation do not appear in the pair (i.e., if x appears in f_1, then $\overline{x}$ does not appear in f_2).

We show that the class of admissible AND/OR pairs of fixed degree K ($K > 1$) is PIM-identifiable. From Theorem 12.2, it is enough to show that for any $G = \{g_1, g_2\} \neq F = \{f_1, f_2\}$, there exists $\mathbf{a}$ such that $F(\mathbf{a}) \setminus G(\mathbf{a}) \neq \emptyset$.

Theorem 12.3. *The class of PBNs consisting of admissible AND/OR pairs of degree K is PIM-identifiable.*

Proof. We prove the theorem by considering five possibles AND/OR combinations of (F, G), excluding symmetric cases. For each case, we show that there exists $\mathbf{a}$ such that $F(\mathbf{a}) \setminus G(\mathbf{a}) \neq \emptyset$.

Case 1: f_1, f_2, g_1, and g_2 are AND. It is enough two consider the following two subcases (see also Fig. 12.1).

Case 1-A: $IN(f_1) = IN(g_1)$ and $IN(f_2) = IN(g_2)$.
We assume w.l.o.g. that there exists a variable x_i such that x_i appears negatively in f_1 but positively in g_1. Since $\{g_1, g_2\}$ is an admissible pair, there exists $\mathbf{a}$ such that $g_1(\mathbf{a}) = g_2(\mathbf{a}) = 1$. On the other hand, $f_1(\mathbf{a}) = 0$ holds for any such $\mathbf{a}$ because $x_i = \mathbf{a}[i] = 0$.

Case 1-B: $IN(f_1) \neq IN(g_1)$ and $IN(f_1) \neq IN(g_2)$.
We assume w.l.o.g. from the symmetry and the discussion in Case 1-A that all variables appear positively in f_1, f_2, g_1, and g_2. Let $x_i \in IN(g_1) \setminus IN(f_1)$ and $x_j \in IN(g_2) \setminus IN(f_1)$, where $x_i = x_j$ is allowed. Consider an assignment $\mathbf{a}$ such that 0 is assigned to x_i and x_j and 1 is assigned to the other variables. Then, $g_1(\mathbf{a}) = g_2(\mathbf{a}) = 0$ whereas $f_1(\mathbf{a}) = 1$.

Case 2: f_1, f_2, g_1 are AND, g_2 is OR.
We assume w.l.o.g. that $IN(f_2) \neq IN(g_1)$. We further assume w.l.o.g. that all variables appear positively in each function. Let $x_i \in IN(f_2) \setminus IN(g_1)$. Consider an assignment $\mathbf{a}$ such that 0 is assigned to x_i and 1 is assigned to the other variables. Then, $g_1(\mathbf{a}) = g_2(\mathbf{a}) = 1$ whereas $f_2(\mathbf{a}) = 0$.

Case 3: f_1, g_1, g_2 are AND, f_2 is OR.
We assume w.l.o.g. that $IN(f_2) \neq IN(g_1)$. We further assume w.l.o.g. that all variables appear positively. Let $x_i \in IN(f_2) \setminus IN(g_1)$. Consider an assignment $\mathbf{a}$ such that 1 is assigned to x_i and 0 is assigned to the other variables. Then, $g_1(\mathbf{a}) = g_2(\mathbf{a}) = 0$, whereas $f_2(\mathbf{a}) = 1$.

Case 4: f_1 and f_2 are AND, g_1 and g_2 are OR.
We assume w.l.o.g. that all variables appear positively. Choose an arbitrary variable $x_i \in IN(f_1)$. Consider an assignment $\mathbf{a}$ such that 0 is assigned to x_i and 1 is assigned to the other variables. Then, $g_1(\mathbf{a}) = g_2(\mathbf{a}) = 1$, whereas $f_1(\mathbf{a}) = 0$.

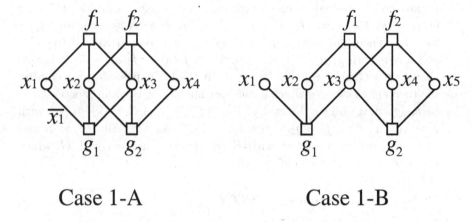

Case 1-A   Case 1-B

Fig. 12.1   Illustration of two subcases of Case 1 in the proof of Theorem 12.3. In these figures, an edge between function f_j (resp., g_j) and variable x_i means that x_i appears positively in f_j (resp., g_j) unless otherwise shown by $\overline{x_i}$, which means that x_i appears negatively in f_j (resp., g_j). In Case 1-A, x_1 corresponds to x_i in the proof, and $g_1(\mathbf{a}) = g_2(\mathbf{a}) = 1$ but $f_1(\mathbf{a}) = 0$ hold for $\mathbf{a} = [0, 1, 1, 1]$. In Case 1-B, x_1 and x_5 correspond to x_i and x_j in the proof, respectively, and $g_1(\mathbf{a}) = g_2(\mathbf{a}) = 0$ but $f_1(\mathbf{a}) = 1$ hold $\mathbf{a} = [0, 1, 1, 1, 0]$.

Case 5: f_1 and g_1 are AND, f_2 and g_2 are OR.
It is enough to consider the following cases.

Case 5-A: $IN(f_1) = IN(g_1)$ and $IN(f_2) = IN(g_2)$.
Since $\{f_1, f_2\} \neq \{g_1, g_2\}$, we assume w.l.o.g. that there exists x_i such that x_i appears negatively in f_1 or f_2 and all variables in $IN(g_1) \cup IN(g_2)$ appear positively in g_1 and g_2. Suppose that x_i appears negatively in f_1, where the other case can be proved in an analogous manner. Consider an assignment $\mathbf{a}$ such that 1 is assigned to all variables. Then, $g_1(\mathbf{a}) = g_2(\mathbf{a}) = 1$, whereas $f_1(\mathbf{a}) = 0$.

Case 5-B: $IN(f_1) \neq IN(g_1)$ (resp., $IN(f_2) \neq IN(g_2)$).
We consider only the case of $IN(f_1) \neq IN(g_1)$, where the other case can be proved in an analogous manner. We assume w.l.o.g. that all variables appear positively in each f_i.
Let $x_i \in IN(f_1) \setminus IN(g_1)$. Consider an assignment $\mathbf{a}$ such that 0 is assigned to x_i and 1 is assigned to the other variables. Then, $g_1(\mathbf{a}) = g_2(\mathbf{a}) = 1$, whereas $f_1(\mathbf{a}) = 0$. $\qquad\square$

The degree constraint is crucial in this theorem. In fact, the theorem cannot be generalized to cases with different degrees. Consider tha case of $f_1 = x_1 \wedge x_2 \wedge x_3$, $f_2 = x_2 \wedge x_3 \wedge x_4$, $g_1 = x_1 \wedge x_2 \wedge x_3$, and $g_2 = x_3 \wedge x_4$. Then, any **a** with $g_1(\mathbf{a}) = g_2(\mathbf{a}) = 1$ makes $f_1(\mathbf{a}) = f_2(\mathbf{a}) = 1$, and any **a** with $g_1(\mathbf{a}) = g_2(\mathbf{a}) = 0$ makes $f_1(\mathbf{a}) = f_2(\mathbf{a}) = 0$. It means that $F(\mathbf{a}) \setminus G(\mathbf{a}) = \emptyset$ holds for all **a**. It is also impossible to generalize the theorem to cases in which a different number of Boolean functions can be assigned. Consider the case of $F = \{f_1, f_2\}$ and $G = \{g_1, g_2, g_3\}$ with $f_1 = g_1 = x_1 \wedge x_2$, $f_2 = g_2 = x_1 \wedge x_3$, and $g_3 = x_3 \wedge x_4$. Since $f_1 = g_1$ and $f_2 = g_2$, samples consistent with F are always consistent with G, which means $F(\mathbf{a}) \setminus G(\mathbf{a}) = \emptyset$ holds for all **a**.

12.3.3   *Identification of a PBTN*

In the previous subsection, we focused on identification of a PBN consisting of AND/OR functions. In this subsection, we consider more general function, Boolean threshold functions.

Here we define a Boolean threshold function in a slightly different but essentially same way as in Section 1.1. A Boolean function $f(x_1, \ldots, x_n)$ is a *Boolean threshold function* if there exist some integers $w_1, \ldots, w_n, \theta$ such that

$$f(x_1, \ldots, x_n) = \begin{cases} 1, & \text{if } w_1 \ell_1 + w_2 \ell_2 + \cdots + w_n \ell_n \geq \theta, \\ 0, & \text{otherwise,} \end{cases}$$

holds for all $[x_1, \ldots, x_n] \in \{0, 1\}^n$, where ℓ_i is either x_i or $\overline{x_i}$. Recall that Boolean threshold functions cover various Boolean functions, including AND and OR functions, majority functions, and decision lists [Anthony (2001)]. For example, an AND function (resp., an OR function) is represented as $x_1 + x_2 + \cdots + x_n \geq n$ (resp., $x_1 + x_2 + \cdots + x_n \geq 1$).

A PBN consisting of threshold functions is called a *probabilistic Boolean threshold network* (PBTN, for short). If threshold functions are restricted to those with *unary weights* (i.e., w_i is either 0 or 1), the concept of admissibility can be extended for threshold functions. Note that AND functions and OR functions can be represented as threshold functions with unary weights. Let $LIT(f) = \{\ell_i | w_i = 1\}$ and $LIT(F) = \cup_{f \in F} LIT(F)$. Then, a PBTN F is *admissible* if at most one of $\ell, \overline{\ell}$ appears in $LIT(F)$ for all ℓ.

Example 12.4. Let $f_1 = x_1 + x_2 + x_3 \geq 2$, $f_2 = x_1 + \overline{x_3} \geq 1$, $f_3 = x_1 + x_2 + x_3 \geq 3$, and $f_4 = x_1 \geq 1$. Let $F = \{f_1, f_2\}$, $G = \{f_1, f_3\}$, $H = \{f_1, f_4\}$, $\mathcal{C}_1 = \{F, H\}$ and $\mathcal{C}_2 = \{G, H\}$. Then, $LIT(f_1) = \{x_1, x_2, x_3\}$, $LIT(f_2) =$

$\{x_1, \overline{x_3}\}$, and $LIT(F) = \{x_1, x_2, x_3, \overline{x_3}\}$. G and H are admissible, but F is not.

$F(\mathbf{a})$, $G(\mathbf{a})$, and $H(\mathbf{a})$ are determined as below, where "0/1" means that we have both outputs.

x_1	0	0	0	0	1	1	1	1
x_2	0	0	1	1	0	0	1	1
x_3	0	1	0	1	0	1	0	1
f_1	0	0	0	1	0	1	1	1
f_2	1	0	1	0	1	1	1	1
f_3	0	0	0	0	0	0	0	1
f_4	0	0	0	0	1	1	1	1
$F = \{f_1, f_2\}$	0/1	0	0/1	0/1	0/1	1	1	1
$G = \{f_1, f_3\}$	0	0	0	0/1	0	0/1	0/1	1
$H = \{f_1, f_4\}$	0	0	0	0/1	0/1	1	1	1

It is seen from Theorem 12.2 that C_1 is identifiable from samples under FIM but not under PIM because $H(\mathbf{a}) \subseteq F(\mathbf{a})$ for all $\mathbf{a}$, whereas C_2 is identifiable from samples under both PIM and FIM because $G(\mathbf{a}') \setminus H(\mathbf{a}') = \{0\}$ for $\mathbf{a}' = [1, 0, 1]$ and $H(\mathbf{a}'') \setminus G(\mathbf{a}'') = \{1\}$ for $\mathbf{a}'' = [1, 0, 0]$.

The following lemma gives a necessary condition for PIM-identifiability.

Lemma 12.1. *A class C of admissible PBTNs is PIM-identifiable only if it does not contain F and G, such that $F \subseteq G$.*

Proof. If $F \subseteq G$, $F(\mathbf{a}) \setminus G(\mathbf{a}) = \emptyset$ holds for all $\mathbf{a}$. Therefore, the lemma follows from Theorem 12.2. □

Recall that Boolean threshold functions include AND/OR functions. Theorem 12.3 is extended as below [Melkman *et al.* (2017)].

Theorem 12.4. *Let $1 \leq \theta_1 < \theta_2 \leq K$ be two fixed thresholds, and let C be a class of admissible PBTNs satisfying the necessary condition of Lemma 12.1, such that each $F \in C$ consists of two (not necessarily different) threshold functions with the following properties: every $f \in F$ depends on exactly K variables, has unit coefficients, and has a threshold that is either θ_1 or θ_2. Then C is PIM-identifiable.*

Furthermore, this theorem can be partially extended for multiple functions [Melkman *et al.* (2017)].

Theorem 12.5. *Let $1 \leq \theta_1 < \theta_m \leq K$ be two fixed thresholds, and let C be* a class of admissible PBTNs satisfying necessary condition of Lemma 12.1, such that each $F \in C$ consists of m threshold functions with the following properties: every $f \in F$ depends on exactly K variables and has unit coefficients, and the thresholds of F are $\theta(f_1) = \theta_1$, $\theta(f_m) = \theta_m$ and $\theta_1 < \theta(f) < \theta_m$, $f \neq f_1, f_m$. Then C is PIM-identifiable if $f_1 \neq g_1$ or $f_m \neq g_m$ for all pairs $F, G \in C$.

Next, we consider FIM-identifiability. The following lemma gives a necessary condition for FIM-identifiability

Lemma 12.2. *Let C be a class of admissible PBTNs each of which consists of one or two threshold functions that have unit coefficients. If C is FIM-identifiable then it does not contain $F = \{f_1, f_2\}$ and $G = \{g_1, g_2\}$ such that $f_1 = \ell_1 \geq 1$ $f_2 = \ell_2 \geq 1$, $g_1 = \ell_1 + \ell_2 \geq 1$, $g_2 = \ell_1 + \ell_2 \geq 2$, with ℓ_1, ℓ_2 literals.*

Proof. It is enough to consider the case of $C = \{F, G\}$ such that $F = \{x_1 \geq 1, x_2 \geq 1\}$, $G = \{x_1 + x_2 \geq 1, x_1 + x_2 \geq 2\}$. In this case, $F(\mathbf{a}) = G(\mathbf{a})$ holds for all $\mathbf{a}$. Therefore, the lemma follows from Theorem 12.2.   □

Interestingly, the necessary condition of this lemma also gives a sufficient condition for a certain class of PBTNs as states below [Melkman *et al.* (2017)].

Theorem 12.6. *Let C be a class of admissible PBTNs each of which consists of one or two threshold functions that have unit coefficients. Then C is FIM-identifiable if and only if the condition of Lemma 12.2 holds.*

The following example shows that the class given by Theorem 12.6 is broader than that given by Theorem 12.4.

Example 12.5. Consider $F = \{x_1 + x_2 + x_3 \geq 1, x_1 + x_2 + x_4 \geq 2\}$ and $G = \{x_1 + x_2 + x_3 \geq 1, x_1 + x_2 + x_4 \geq 3\}$. Then, $F(\mathbf{a}) \subseteq G(\mathbf{a})$ holds for all $\mathbf{a}$, whereas $F(\mathbf{b}) \neq G(\mathbf{b})$ holds for $\mathbf{b} = [1, 1, 0, 0]$. Besides, $C = \{F, G\}$ satisfies the condition of Theorem 12.6 but does not satisfy that of Theorem 12.4. Indeed, C is identifiable under FIM, but is not identifiable under PIM.

In the above, we have focused on unit coefficient cases. It is difficult to generalize these results to general coefficients. One reason is that a pair can take on many forms that are hard to catalog. For example, consider $F = \{x_1 + 2x_2 \geq 2, 2x_1 + x_2 \geq 2\}$ and $G = \{x_1 + x_2 \geq 1, x_1 + x_2 \geq 2\}$. Then, these two represent essentially the same pair since $F(\mathbf{a}) = G(\mathbf{a})$ holds for all $\mathbf{a}$. Nevertheless, this example leads to a positive result as below.

Theorem 12.7. *Let $\mathcal{C}$ be a class of PBTNs each consisting of a pair of threshold functions. Suppose that for any non-identical pair $F = \{f_1, f_2\} \in \mathcal{C}, G = \{g_1, g_2\} \in \mathcal{C}$, there does not exist a pair of assignments $(\mathbf{a}, \mathbf{a}')$ such that $f_1(\mathbf{a}) = g_1(\mathbf{a}) \neq f_2(\mathbf{a}) = g_2(\mathbf{a})$ and $f_1(\mathbf{a}') = g_2(\mathbf{a}') \neq f_2(\mathbf{a}') = g_1(\mathbf{a}')$. Then, $\mathcal{C}$ is FIM-identifiable.*

Proof. We prove the theorem by contrapositive. Suppose that $\mathcal{C}$ is not FIM-identifiable. Then, there must exist a non-identical pair (F, G) for which $F(\mathbf{a}) = G(\mathbf{a})$ holds for all $\mathbf{a}$. Note that for each $\mathbf{a}$, $F(\mathbf{a}) = G(\mathbf{a})$ means that one of the following holds:

$$f_1(\mathbf{a}) = g_1(\mathbf{a}) = f_2(\mathbf{a}) = g_2(\mathbf{a}), \qquad (\#1)$$
$$f_1(\mathbf{a}) = g_2(\mathbf{a}) \neq f_2(\mathbf{a}) = g_1(\mathbf{a}), \qquad (\#2)$$
$$f_1(\mathbf{a}) = g_1(\mathbf{a}) \neq f_2(\mathbf{a}) = g_2(\mathbf{a}). \qquad (\#3)$$

If (#1) or (#2) always holds, $\{f_1, f_2\}$ is identical to $\{g_2, g_1\}$. Similarly, if (#1) or (#3) always holds, $\{f_1, f_2\}$ is identical to $\{g_1, g_2\}$. Each case contradicts the assumption that F and G are not identical. Therefore, $F(\mathbf{a}) = G(\mathbf{a})$ holds only if (#2) holds for some assignment $\mathbf{a}$ and (#3) holds for another assignment $\mathbf{a}$, where the former one corresponds to $\mathbf{a}'$ in the statement of the theorem. $\qquad\square$

Here we consider the normalized form of a threshold function, where normalization is done by multiplicating a constant to both sides of the inequality so that $\theta = 1$ holds. Although we assumed that weights are integers, we allow here that rational numbers are used as weights. For example, "$4x_1 + x_2 \geq 2$" is normalized to "$2x_1 + 0.5x_2 \geq 1$". For a threshold function f, let $\hat{f}$ denote the left hand side of its normalized function and $\hat{w}_i^f$ denote the coefficient of x_i in $\hat{f}$. For example, for $f = x_1 + 2x_2 \geq 2$, $\hat{f} = 0.5x_1 + x_2$, $\hat{w}_1^f = 0.5$, and $\hat{w}_2^f = 1$. If x_i does not appear in f, $\hat{w}_i^f = 0$.

Corollary 12.2. *Let $\mathcal{C}$ be a class of PBTNs each consisting of a pair of threshold functions. $\mathcal{C}$ is FIM-identifiable if for any $\{f_1, f_2\} \in \mathcal{C}$, $\hat{w}_i^{f_1} \geq \hat{w}_i^{f_2}$ holds for all i.*

Proof. If the condition is satisfied for $\{f_1, f_2\}, \{g_1, g_2\} \in \mathcal{C}$, the following hold for all $\mathbf{a}$: $\hat{f}_1(\mathbf{a}) \geq \hat{f}_2(\mathbf{a})$ and $\hat{g}_1(\mathbf{a}) \geq \hat{g}_2(\mathbf{a})$. Since it means that $f_1(\mathbf{a}) = g_2(\mathbf{a}) \neq f_2(\mathbf{a}) = g_1(\mathbf{a})$ does not hold for any $\mathbf{a}$, the corollary follows from Theorem 12.7. $\qquad\square$

As shown below, identifiability results are known for some simple but biologically relevant classes of PBNs containing general Boolean functions.

Proposition 12.2. *Let C be a class of Boolean function pairs of the form $\{f, f \wedge h\}$, where $|IN(f)| \geq 1$ and h does not include any variable appearing in f. Then, C is not PIM-identifiable but FIM-identifiable.*

Proof. Let $(f_1, f_2) = (x_1, x_1 \wedge x_2)$ and $(g_1, g_2) = (x_1, x_1 \wedge x_2 \wedge x_3)$. Then, $\{f_1(\mathbf{a}), f_2(\mathbf{a})\} \subseteq \{g_1(\mathbf{a}), g_2(\mathbf{a})\}$ holds for all $\mathbf{a}$. Therefore, it is seen from Theorem 12.2 that this class is not PIM-identifiable.

In order to prove FIM-identifiability, consider arbitrary two different pairs $(f_1, f_2) = (f_1, f_1 \wedge h_1)$ and $(g_1, g_2) = (g_1, g_1 \wedge h_2)$. If $f_1 \neq g_1$, there must exist $\mathbf{a}$ satisfying $f_1(\mathbf{a}) \neq g_1(\mathbf{a})$, for any of which $\{f_1(\mathbf{a}), f_2(\mathbf{a})\} \neq \{g_1(\mathbf{a}), g_2(\mathbf{a})\}$ holds and thus the condition of Theorem 12.2 is satisfied.

Otherwise, $f_1 = g_1$ holds. Recall that h_1 (resp., h_2) does not include any variable appearing in $f_1 = g_1$. Therefore, there must exist $\mathbf{a}$ satisfying $f_1(\mathbf{a}) = g_1(\mathbf{a}) = 1$ and $h_1(\mathbf{a}) \neq h_2(\mathbf{a})$, and thus the condition of Theorem 12.2 is satisfied. $\qquad \square$

Proposition 12.3. *Let C be a class of Boolean function pairs of the form $\{x_i, f\}$ where f is any Boolean function not including x_i or $\overline{x_i}$. Then, C is PIM-identifiable.*

Proof. Let $F = \{x_i, f\}$ and $G = \{x_j, g\}$. We consider two cases: $i = j$ and $i \neq j$.

First, consider the case of $i = j$. Since $F \neq G$, there exists $\mathbf{a}$ such that $f(\mathbf{a}) \neq g(\mathbf{a})$. We assume w.l.o.g. that $f(\mathbf{a}) = 1$ and $g(\mathbf{a}) = 0$. Let $\mathbf{a}_i^0$ (resp., $\mathbf{a}_i^1$) be a bit vector obtained by assigning 0 (resp., 1) to the ith bit in $\mathbf{a}$. Since x_i does not appear in f or g, $F(\mathbf{a}_i^1) = \{1\}$, $G(\mathbf{a}_i^1) = \{0, 1\}$, $F(\mathbf{a}_i^0) = \{0, 1\}$, and $G(\mathbf{a}_i^0) = \{0\}$ hold. Therefore, the proposition holds from Theorem 12.2.

Next, consider the case of $i \neq j$. We will show that $G(\mathbf{a}) \setminus F(\mathbf{a}) \neq \emptyset$ holds for some $\mathbf{a}$, where $F(\mathbf{a}) \setminus G(\mathbf{a}) \neq \emptyset$ can be shown in an analogous way. Suppose that f is a constant. We assume w.l.o.g. that $f = 0$. Then, $G(\mathbf{a}) \setminus F(\mathbf{a}) \neq \emptyset$ holds for $\mathbf{a}$ such that $\mathbf{a}[i] = 0$ and $\mathbf{a}[j] = 1$. Otherwise, f is not a constant. Then, for some $\mathbf{a}$, $\mathbf{a}[i] = 0$ and $f(\mathbf{a}) = 0$ hold. If $\mathbf{a}[j] = 0$ holds for each of such $\mathbf{a}$s, $f(\mathbf{a}) = 0$ implies $\mathbf{a}[j] = 0$, because x_i or $\overline{x_i}$ does not appear in f. For some $\mathbf{a}$, $\mathbf{a}[i] = 1$ and $f(\mathbf{a}) = 1$ also hold. If $\mathbf{a}[j] = 1$ holds for each of such $\mathbf{a}$s, $f(\mathbf{a}) = 1$ implies $\mathbf{a}[j] = 1$. Therefore, at least one of the following holds:

(i) $\mathbf{a}[i] = 0$, $f(\mathbf{a}) = 0$, and $\mathbf{a}[j] = 1$ hold for some $\mathbf{a}$,

(ii) $\mathbf{a}[i] = 1$, $f(\mathbf{a}) = 1$, and $\mathbf{a}[j] = 0$ hold for some $\mathbf{a}$,

(iii) $f = x_j$ holds.

If (i) or (ii) holds, $G(\mathbf{a}) \setminus F(\mathbf{a}) \neq \emptyset$ holds. Case (iii) corresponds to the case of $x_i = x_j$, which has already been analyzed in the former part of the proof.

Hence, $\mathcal{C}$ satisfies the condition of PIM-identifiability of Theorem 12.2 and the proposition follows. $\square$

12.3.4 *Sample Complexity for Identification of a PBN*

Here, we analyze the sample complexity for identifying the structure of a PBN for identifiable classes. We use a similar argument as in Chapter 6. Although we have considered the case of only one output variable so far, we consider the original PBN here. Accordingly, each sample consists of an n-bit input vector and an n-bit output vector. As an identification algorithm, we employ the following procedure, which is a simple extension of **IdentBN** and examines all possible elements of $\mathcal{C}$.

Procedure IdentPBN(S)
 for all nodes x_i **do**
  let $\mathcal{F}_i \leftarrow \emptyset$;
  for all $F \in \mathcal{C}$ **do**
   if F is consistent with S with respect to ith output values
    then $\mathcal{F}_i \leftarrow \mathcal{F}_i \cup \{F\}$;
  if $|\mathcal{F}_i| \neq 1$ **then return** FALSE;
 return TRUE.

Note that we need to adjust F so that the output variable corresponds to x_i. Note also that the above procedure is for the PIM-model. For the FIM-model, it is enough to replace "F is consistent ..." with "F is strongly consistent ...". In both models. only relevant variables (i.e., not the whole $\mathbf{a}$ but a part of $\mathbf{a}$ corresponding to the variables appearing in F) are taken into account in checking the (strong) consistency.

The correctness of the algorithm is obvious because it examines the consistency. If each Boolean function can be evaluated in polynomial time with respect to n, it is straightforward to see that the total time complexity is $O(|\mathcal{C}|poly(m, n))$, where $|\mathcal{C}|$ might be exponentially large.

In the analysis of the sample complexity, we do not consider all $\mathcal{C}$ but consider PBNs in which each node x_i has an L-tuplet of Boolean functions, $F_i = \{f_1^{(i)}, \ldots, f_L^{(i)}\}$, and the probability $c_j^{(i)}$ associated with $f_j^{(i)}$ is lower bounded by $c > 0$. Since we are considering n output variables, a sample is of the form $(\mathbf{a}, \mathbf{b})$, where $\mathbf{a}$ and $\mathbf{b}$ are n-bit vectors, respectively. We assume that each input sample $\mathbf{a}$ is generated uniformly at random, and the ith bit of the corresponding output vector $\mathbf{b}$ is obtained by first choosing j according to the underlying probabilities $c_j^{(i)}$, independently of other nodes, and then computing $f_j^{(i)}(\mathbf{a})$.

Theorem 12.8. *Let $\mathcal{C}$ be a class of PBNs consisting of L-tuplets of functions, each of which has at most K inputs, that satisfies the condition of PIM (resp., FIM) of Theorem 12.2, where L and K are constants. If $O(\frac{1}{c} \cdot 2^{2KL} \cdot (2KL+1+\alpha) \cdot \log n)$ samples are generated uniformly at random, then the correct PBN can be uniquely identified at all nodes with probability no less than $1 - \frac{1}{n^\alpha}$ under PIM (resp., FIM).*

Proof. We prove the theorem for the case of PIM; the FIM case can be proven in an analogous manner.

First we focus on one output node x_i. Suppose that $F = \{f_1, f_2, \ldots, f_L\}$ is the underlying function tuple for the ith node in a PBN and that $G = \{g_1, \ldots, g_L\}$ is another possible function tuple for the same node. Let I be the set of variables appearing in $F \cup G$. Note that $|I| \leq 2LK$ holds. It is seen from the proof of Theorem 12.2 that if all possible 0-1 assignments I and all possible corresponding values output by $f_1, \ldots, f_L$ are given, the inconsistency of G can be detected. This condition is referred to as Condition C1.

In order to analyze the probability that Condition C1 does not hold, we consider all possible I with $|I| = 2KL$ because we do not know I in advance. For a fixed I, the probability that $\mathbf{a}[i] = 1$ does not hold for some $x_i \in I$, or f_j is not selected for a fixed $j \in \{1, \ldots, L\}$ in a given sample $(\mathbf{a}, \mathbf{b})$ is at most $1 - c \cdot \frac{1}{2^{2KL}}$, and thus the probability that the same condition does not hold in any m samples is at most $(1 - c \cdot \frac{1}{2^{2KL}})^m$. Since the number of combinations of $2KL$ variables is less than n^{2KL}, the number of functions assigned per node is L, and the number of 0-1 assignments on $2KL$ bits is 2^{2KL}, the probability that Condition C1 does not hold is bounded above by

$$L \cdot 2^{2KL} \cdot n^{2KL} \cdot \left(1 - c \cdot \frac{1}{2^{2KL}}\right)^m.$$

Next we consider all n output nodes. Since output values for node x_i in samples are generated independently of those of the other nods, the probability that Condition C1 does not hold for one or more nodes is bounded above by

$$p_{K,L,n,m} = L \cdot 2^{2KL} \cdot n^{2KL+1} \cdot \left(1 - c \cdot \frac{1}{2^{2KL}}\right)^m.$$

By taking $\log(\cdots)$ of both sides and using $\ln(1-x) \leq -x$, it is seen that $p_{K,L,n,m} \leq p$ holds if

$$m > \frac{1}{c} \cdot \ln 2 \cdot 2^{2KL} \cdot [\log L + 2KL + (2KL+1)\log n - \log p].$$

Letting $p = \frac{1}{n^\alpha}$, the theorem holds. □

12.4 Additional Remarks and Bibliographical Notes

The COD measures described in Section 12.1 were given in [Shmulevich *et al.* (2002)], after which some heuristic inference methods were proposed [Li *et al.* (2007); Marshalla *et al.* (2007)]. The noisy Boolean network and its identification algorithm described in Section 12.2 were given in [Akutsu *et al.* (2000a)]. Section 12.3 is based on [Cheng *et al.* (2016); Melkman *et al.* (2017)]. The proofs of Theorems 12.4, 12.5, and 12.6 can be found in [Melkman *et al.* (2017)].

Chapter 13

Control of Probabilistic Boolean Networks

In Chapter 7, control of BNs was discussed. Historically, studies on control of PBNs precede those on BNs [Datta *et al.* (2003)]. In this chapter, we describe a basic version of the control problem on the PBN, a dynamic programming algorithm for the problem, and a result showing computational hardness of the problem.

13.1 Problem Definition

In BN Control, external nodes were introduced into the standard BN. In order to extend the framework for PBNs, we generalize the concept of external nodes. We assume that the transition matrix depends on the states of m bit control inputs $\mathbf{u} \in \{0,1\}^m$. Accordingly, the transition matrix is represented as $A(\mathbf{u})$.

It is assumed in BN Control that the initial and desired states are given. For controlling a PBN, we also assume that the initial state $\mathbf{x}(0)$ is given, where $\mathbf{x}(t)$ denotes the state of a PBN (i.e., the global state of internal nodes of a PBN) at time step t. However, it is almost impossible to always drive a PBN to the target state at the target time step $t = M$ because transitions in a PBN occur probabilistically. Therefore, instead of considering only one desired state, we consider the cost of states at $t = M$. In addition, we consider the cost of application of control $\mathbf{u}$ to $\mathbf{x}(t)$. We use $C_t(\mathbf{x})$ and $C_t(\mathbf{x}, \mathbf{u})$ to denote the cost of $\mathbf{x}$ at time t and the cost of application of $\mathbf{u}$ to $\mathbf{x}$ at time t, respectively. The total cost for a control sequence $U = \langle \mathbf{u}(0), \mathbf{u}(1), \cdots, \mathbf{u}(M-1) \rangle$ is defined by

$$J_U(\mathbf{x}(0)) = E \left[\sum_{t=0}^{M-1} C_t(\mathbf{x}(t), \mathbf{u}(t)) + C_M(\mathbf{x}(M)) \right].$$

In the above, $E[\cdots]$ means the expected cost when a PBN transits according to the transition probabilities given by $A(\mathbf{u})$. In the above, it is assumed that U is fixed. However, the total expected cost can be reduced if the control action $\mathbf{u}(t)$ is selected according to the current state $\mathbf{x}(t)$. We use $\mu_t(\mathbf{x})$ to denote the control action $\mathbf{u}(t)$ at time t when the state of the PBN is $\mathbf{x}$ at time t, where μ_t is a function from $\{0,1\}^n$ to $\{0,1\}^m$ and μ_t may also depend on t. Then, PBN Control is defined as follows.

Definition 13.1.   [PBN Control]
Instance: a PBN with control input, an initial state $\mathbf{x}^0$ of the PBN, a cost function $C_M(\mathbf{x})$ for $\mathbf{x}$ at time M, and a cost function $C_t(\mathbf{x}, \mathbf{u})$ for application of $\mathbf{u}$ to $\mathbf{x}$ at time t,
Problem: find a control law $\pi = \langle \mu_0, \mu_1, \ldots, \mu_{M-1} \rangle$ that minimizes the expected cost

$$
J_\pi(\mathbf{x}(0)) = E\left[\sum_{t=0}^{M-1} C_t(\mathbf{x}(t), \mu_t(\mathbf{x}(t))) + C_M(\mathbf{x}(M)) \right].
$$

Example 13.1. Consider PBNs given in Example 11.3 (ii) and (iii). Let $A^{(1)}$ and $A^{(2)}$ denote the transition matrices for (ii) and (iii), respectively:

$$
A^{(1)} = \begin{pmatrix} 1 & \frac{1}{2} & 0 & 0 \\ 0 & \frac{1}{2} & 0 & 0 \\ 0 & 0 & \frac{1}{2} & 0 \\ 0 & 0 & \frac{1}{2} & 1 \end{pmatrix},
$$

$$
A^{(2)} = \begin{pmatrix} 0 & 0 & \frac{1}{2} & \frac{1}{2} \\ 0 & 0 & \frac{1}{2} & \frac{1}{2} \\ \frac{1}{2} & \frac{1}{2} & 0 & 0 \\ \frac{1}{2} & \frac{1}{2} & 0 & 0 \end{pmatrix}.
$$

Suppose that $\mathbf{u}(t)$ is a one-dimensional vector (i.e., $\mathbf{u}(t) = [0]$ or $\mathbf{u}(t) = [1]$), $A([0]) = A^{(1)}$, and $A([1]) = A^{(2)}$. It means that in the resulting PBN with control input, $A^{(1)}$ is used if control of $\mathbf{u}(t) = [0]$ is applied, otherwise $A^{(2)}$ is used. Suppose also that $\mathbf{x}(0) = [0,0]$ and $M = 1$.

The probability distributions of the PBN at time $t = 1$ after applying

$A([0]) = A^{(1)}$ and $A([1]) = A^{(2)}$ to $\mathbf{x}(0) = [0, 0]$ are given respectively by

$$
\begin{pmatrix} 1 & \frac{1}{2} & 0 & 0 \\ 0 & \frac{1}{2} & 0 & 0 \\ 0 & 0 & \frac{1}{2} & 0 \\ 0 & 0 & \frac{1}{2} & 1 \end{pmatrix} \begin{pmatrix} 1 \\ 0 \\ 0 \\ 0 \end{pmatrix} = \begin{pmatrix} 1 \\ 0 \\ 0 \\ 0 \end{pmatrix},
$$

$$
\begin{pmatrix} 0 & 0 & \frac{1}{2} & \frac{1}{2} \\ 0 & 0 & \frac{1}{2} & \frac{1}{2} \\ \frac{1}{2} & \frac{1}{2} & 0 & 0 \\ \frac{1}{2} & \frac{1}{2} & 0 & 0 \end{pmatrix} \begin{pmatrix} 1 \\ 0 \\ 0 \\ 0 \end{pmatrix} = \begin{pmatrix} 0 \\ 0 \\ \frac{1}{2} \\ \frac{1}{2} \end{pmatrix}.
$$

Suppose that the cost functions are given as

$C_1([0, 0]) = 1, \quad C_1([0, 1]) = 1, \quad C_1([1, 0]) = 2, \quad C_1([1, 1]) = 1,$
$C_0([0, 0], [0]) = 2, C_0([0, 0], [1]) = 1, C_0([0, 1], [0]) = 1, C_0([0, 1], [1]) = 1, \cdots$

In this case, there are two possibilities for $\mu_0([0, 0])$, $\mu_0^{(1)}([0, 0]) = [0]$ and $\mu_0^{(2)}([0, 0]) = [1]$, where we ignore irrelevant parts of μ_0. Then, the expected costs are determined as

$$
\begin{aligned}
J_{\langle \mu_0^{(1)} \rangle}([0, 0]) &= C_0([0, 0], [0]) + 1 \cdot C_1([0, 0]) + 0 \cdot C_1([0, 1]) + 0 \cdot C_1([1, 0]) \\
&\quad + 0 \cdot C_1([1, 1]) \\
&= 3, \\
J_{\langle \mu_0^{(2)} \rangle}([0, 0]) &= C_0([0, 0], [1]) + 0 \cdot C_1([0, 0]) + 0 \cdot C_1([0, 1]) + \frac{1}{2} \cdot C_1([1, 0]) \\
&\quad + \frac{1}{2} \cdot C_1([1, 1]) \\
&= \frac{5}{2}.
\end{aligned}
$$

Therefore, $\langle \mu_0^{(2)} \rangle$ is the solution of PBN Control for this instance.

Next suppose that $\mathbf{x}(0) = [0, 1]$, $M = 1$, and the cost functions are the same as above. In this case, there are also two possibilities for $\mu_0([0, 1])$, $\mu_0^{(1)}([0, 1]) = [0]$ and $\mu_0^{(2)}([0, 1]) = [1]$, ignoring irrelevant parts of μ_0. Then, the expected costs are determined as

$$
J_{\langle \mu_0^{(1)} \rangle}([0, 1]) = 1 + \frac{1}{2} \cdot 1 + \frac{1}{2} \cdot 1 = 2,
$$

$$
J_{\langle \mu_0^{(2)} \rangle}([0, 1]) = 1 + \frac{1}{2} \cdot 2 + \frac{1}{2} \cdot 1 = \frac{5}{2}.
$$

Therefore, $\langle \mu_0^{(1)} \rangle$ is the solution for this instance.

13.2   Dynamic Programming Algorithm for PBN Control

PBN Control can be solved by using dynamic programming as in the case of BN Control. Indeed, the dynamic programming algorithm for BN Control shown in Chapter 7 is a simplified version of that for PBN Control [Datta *et al.* (2003)].

In dynamic programming algorithms, tables play a key role. In PBN Control, we use a table $J_t(\mathbf{x})$. $J_t(\mathbf{x})$ denotes the minimum expected cost when optimal controls are applied to the PBN from time step t to $M - 1$. The desired minimum expected cost is given by $J_0(\mathbf{x}(0))$. This table is computed backwards (from $t = M$ to $t = 0$). As the initial step, $J_M(\mathbf{x})$ is determined by

$$J_M(\mathbf{x}) = C_M(\mathbf{x}), \text{ for } \mathbf{x} \in \{0,1\}^n.$$

Suppose that $J_{t+1}(\mathbf{x})$ has been determined for all $\mathbf{x} \in \{0,1\}^n$. Then, $J_t(\mathbf{x})$ is determined by

$$J_t(\mathbf{x}) = \min_{\mathbf{u}} E\left[C_t(\mathbf{x}, \mathbf{u}) + J_{t+1}(\mathbf{w})\right]$$

$$= \min_{\mathbf{u}} \left[C_t(\mathbf{x}, \mathbf{u}) + \sum_{j=1}^{2^n} A_{ij}(\mathbf{u}(t)) \cdot J_{t+1}(\mathbf{w})\right],$$

where $i = id(\mathbf{x})$, $j = id(\mathbf{w})$, and the minimum is taken over $\mathbf{u} \in \{0,1\}^m$. $\mu_t(\mathbf{x})$ can be obtained as $\mathbf{u}$ that gives this minimum value (i.e., $\mu_t(\mathbf{x}) = \text{argmin}_{\mathbf{u}}[\cdots]$).

Theorem 13.1. *Suppose that a PBN is given in the matrix form $A_{ij}(\mathbf{u})$ of size $(2^n \times 2^n) \times 2^m$, each element of $A_{ij}(\mathbf{u})$ and $J_t(\cdots)$ can be accessed in $O(poly(n, m))$ time, and $C_t(\cdots)$ and $C_M(\cdots)$ can be computed in $O(poly(n, m))$ time per element. Then, PBN Control can be solved in $O(M \cdot 2^{2n+m} \cdot poly(n, m))$ time.*

Proof. Since the correctness is straightforward from the dynamic programming algorithm (see Fig. 13.1), we analyze the time complexity. The size of table $J_t(\mathbf{x})$ is clearly $O(M \cdot 2^n)$. In order to fill the table at each t, we need to examine all pairs $(\mathbf{x}, \mathbf{u})$ whose number is $O(2^n \cdot 2^m)$. Furthermore, for each of such pairs, we need to compute the sum of 2^n products. Therefore, the total computation time is $O(M \cdot 2^{2n+m} \cdot poly(n, m))$. $\qquad\square$

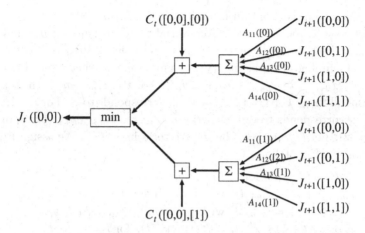

Fig. 13.1 Illustration for the dynamic programming algorithm for PBN Control, where $n = 2$ and $m = 1$.

13.3 Hardness of PBN Control

We have presented in Chapter 7 an ILP-based practical algorithm for BN Control. Therefore, it is reasonable to try to develop a similar ILP-based algorithm for PBN Control. However, it is not plausible that such an algorithm exists. In this section, we will provide a strong evidence for it.

We assume here that a PBN is not given in the matrix form A but in the form of pairs of Boolean functions and their probabilities because A's size is exponential to n and thus it is almost meaningless to discuss the time complexity using A as a part of input. Indeed, Theorem 13.1 gives an algorithm whose time complexity is polynomial with respect to $A(\mathbf{u})$, but the algorithm is far from practical even for $n = 20$ (e.g., 20 genes). We also assume that control signal $\mathbf{u}$ is given as an m bit vector on m nodes in a PBN. In addition, we assume that it is only required to output $\mu_0(\mathbf{x}(0))$ for a given $\mathbf{x}(0)$ and a PBN, otherwise we should output $\mu_t(\mathbf{x})$s for an exponential number of $\mathbf{x}$s. This assumption is reasonable because the number of possible $\mathbf{x}$ is 2^n but it is usually required to give a control action only for the current state at each time step t. Accordingly, we can keep both the sizes of input and output polynomial of n and m and thus can discuss the time complexity with respect to the number of nodes.

Theorem 13.2. *PBN Control is $\sum_2^P$-hard.*

Proof. As in the proof of Theorem 7.5, we use a polynomial-time reduction from the quantified Boolean formula problem for 3-DNF.

Let $\psi(\mathbf{y}, \mathbf{z})$ be a 3-DNF over variables $\mathbf{y} = [y_1, \ldots, y_m]$ and $\mathbf{z} = [z_1, \ldots, z_n]$. From a given $\psi(\mathbf{y}, \mathbf{z})$, we construct a PBN as follows. Let h be the number of terms in $\psi(\mathbf{y}, \mathbf{z})$. Then we construct a set of nodes by $V = \{x_1, x_2, \ldots, x_{m+n+h+1}, u_1, \ldots, u_m\}$. For $i = 1, \ldots, m$, both u_i and x_i correspond to y_i. For $i = 1, \ldots, n$, x_{m+i} corresponds to z_i. For $i = 1, \ldots, h$, x_{m+n+i} corresponds to the ith term of $\psi(\mathbf{y}, \mathbf{z})$. $x_{m+n+h+1}$ corresponds to $\forall \mathbf{z} \psi(\mathbf{y}, \mathbf{z})$. Let $\ell_{i_1} \wedge \ell_{i_2} \wedge \ell_{i_3}$ be the ith term in 3-DNF. We assign Boolean functions to V as follows:

$$x_i(t+1) = u_i(t) \text{ for } i = 1, \ldots, m,$$
$$x_{m+i}(t+1) = x_{m+i}(t) \text{ with probability } 0.5, \text{ for } i = 1, \ldots, n,$$
$$x_{m+i}(t+1) = \overline{x_{m+i}(t)} \text{ with probability } 0.5, \text{ for } i = 1, \ldots, n,$$
$$x_{m+n+i}(t+1) = \ell'_{i_1}(t) \wedge \ell'_{i_2}(t) \wedge \ell'_{i_3}(t), \text{ for } i = 1, \ldots, h,$$
$$x_{m+n+h+1}(t+1) = \bigvee_{i \in \{1, \ldots, h\}} x_{m+n+i}(t),$$

where ℓ'_{i_j} denotes the literal on $\{x_1, \ldots, x_{m+n}\}$ corresponding to ℓ_{i_j}. We let $\mathbf{x}(0) = [0, 0, \ldots, 0]$ and $M = 3$, where $\mathbf{x}(t)$ is an $(m+n+h+1)$-dimensional 0-1 vector. The cost functions are defined by: $C_t(\mathbf{x}, \mathbf{u}) = 0$ for all $\mathbf{x}$ and $\mathbf{u}$, $C_M(\mathbf{x}) = 0$ if $x_{m+n+h+1}(M) = 1$, otherwise $C_M(\mathbf{x}) = 1$.

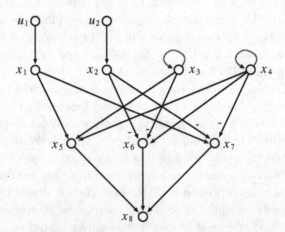

Fig. 13.2   Reduction from $(\exists \mathbf{y})(\forall \mathbf{z})((y_1 \wedge z_1 \wedge z_2) \vee (\overline{y}_2 \wedge \overline{z}_1 \wedge z_2) \vee (y_1 \wedge \overline{y}_2 \wedge \overline{z}_2))$ to PBN Control. In this instance, both u_1 and x_1 correspond to y_1, both u_2 and x_2 correspond to y_2, x_3 and x_4 correspond to z_1 and z_2, respectively, and x_5, x_6, and x_7 correspond to the first, second, third terms, respectively. Arrows with '-' correspond to negative inputs. Dotted arrows denote that positive and negative regulations occur with probability 0.5, respectively. In this case, PBN Control has a solution $\mathbf{u}(0) = \mu_0(\mathbf{x}(0)) = [1, 0]$, which corresponds to $[y_1, y_2] = [1, 0]$.

We prove that $J_0(\mathbf{x}(0)) = 0$ if and only if $(\exists\mathbf{y})(\forall\mathbf{z})\psi(\mathbf{y},\mathbf{z})$ is true. Suppose that $(\forall\mathbf{z})\psi(\mathbf{y},\mathbf{z})$ is true for an assignment of $\mathbf{y} = [b_1, b_2, \ldots, b_m]$. Then, it is straightforward to see that by letting $\mathbf{u}(0) = \mu_0(\mathbf{x}(0)) = [b_1, b_2, \ldots, b_m]$, $x_{m+n+h+1}(M) = 1$ holds for any choice of probabilistic rules and thus $J_0(\mathbf{x}(0)) = 0$ holds.

Conversely, suppose that $J_0(\mathbf{x}(0)) = 0$ holds for some $\mathbf{u}(0) = \mu_0(\mathbf{x}(0))$. Then, from the definition of the cost functions, $x_{m+n+h+1}(M) = 1$ must hold for any assignment on $[x_{m+1}(1), \ldots, x_{m+n}(1)]$. Therefore, $(\exists\mathbf{y})(\forall\mathbf{z})\psi(\mathbf{y},\mathbf{z})$ is true.

Since the reduction can be done in time polynomial in n, m, and h, the theorem holds. $\square$

13.4 Additional Remarks and Bibliographical Notes

PBN Control was introduced in [Datta *et al.* (2003)] along with the corresponding dynamic programming algorithm explained in Section 13.2. Although we have considered finite-horizon control in this chapter, infinite-horizon control (i.e., control for infinite processes) is also important [Pal *et al.* (2006)]. Furthermore, various extensions and modifications of PBN Control have been studied [Kobayashi and Hiraishi (2017); Shmulevich and Dougherty (2010)]. Semi-tensor product-based methods have also been studied for control of PBNs [Zhao and Cheng (2014)].

The $\sum_{2}^{P}$-hardness result in Section 13.3 is based on [Chen *et al.* (2013)], where it is still unclear which complexity class PBN Control belongs to.

Bibliography

Abdallah, E. B., Ribeiro, T., Magnin, M., Roux, O., and Inoue, K. (2017). Modeling delayed dynamics in biological regulatory networks from time series data. *Algorithms* **10**, 1, 8.

Acuña, V., Chierichetti, F., Lacroix, V., Marchetti-Spaccamela, A., Sagot, M-F., and Stougi, L. (2009). Modes and cuts in metabolic networks: Complexity and algorithms. *Biosystems* **95**, 1, pp. 51–60.

Akutsu, T., Kuhara, S., Maruyama, O., and Miyano, S. (1998). A system for identifying genetic networks from gene expression patterns produced by gene disruptions and overexpressions, *Genome Informatics* **9**, pp. 151–160.

Akutsu, T., Miyano, S., and Kuhara, S. (1999). Identification of genetic networks from a small number of gene expression patterns under the Boolean network model. *Proc. Pacific Symposium on Biocomputing 1999*, pp. 17–28.

Akutsu, T., Miyano, S., and Kuhara, S. (2000). Inferring qualitative relations in genetic networks and metabolic pathways. *Bioinformatics* **16**, 8, pp. 727–734.

Akutsu, T., Miyano, S., and Kuhara, S. (2000). Algorithms for identifying Boolean networks and related biological networks based on matrix multiplication and fingerprint function. *Journal of Computational Biology* **7**, 3-4, pp. 331–343.

Akutsu, T., Miyano, S., and Kuhara, S. (2003). A simple greedy algorithm for finding functional relations: efficient implementation and average case analysis. *Theoretical Computer Science* **292**, pp. 481–495.

Akutsu, T., Kuhara, S., Maruyama, O., and Miyano, S. (2003). Identification of genetic networks by strategic gene disruptions and gene overexpressions under a boolean model. *Theoretical Computer Science* **298**, pp. 235–251.

Akutsu, T., Hayashida, M., Ching, W-K., and Ng, M. K. (2007). Control of Boolean networks: Hardness results and algorithms for tree-structured networks. *Journal of Theoretical Biology* **244**, 4, pp. 670–679.

Akutsu, T., Hayashida, M., Zhang, S-Q., Ching, W-K., and Ng, M. K. (2008). Analyses and algorithms for predecessor and control problems for Boolean networks of bounded indegree. *IPSJ Transactions on Bioinformatics* **1**, pp. 23–34.

Akutsu, T. and Tamura, T. (2009). On finding a fixed point in a Boolean network with maximum indegree 2. *IEICE Transactions on Fundamentals of Electronics, Communications and Computer Sciences* **92-A**, 8, pp. 1771–1778.

Akutsu, T., Tamura, T., and Horimoto, K. (2009). Completing networks using observed data. *Proceedings of the 20th International Conference on Algorithmic Learning Theory* (Lecture Notes in Computer Science 5809), pp. 126–140.

Akutsu, T., Kosub, S., Melkman, A. A. and Tamura, T. (2012a). Finding a periodic attractor of a Boolean network. *IEEE/ACM Transactions on Computational Biology and Bioinformatics* **9**, 5, pp. 1410–1421.

Akutsu, T., Melkman, A. A., and Tamura, T. (2012b). Singleton and 2-periodic attractors of sign-definite Boolean networks. *Information Processing Letters* **112**, 1-2, pp. 35–38.

Akutsu, T., Zhao, Y., Hayashida, M. and Tamura, T. (2012). Integer programming-based approach to attractor detection and control of Boolean networks. *IEICE Transactions on Information and Systems* **E95-D**, 12, pp. 2960–2970.

Albert, R. and Thakar, J. (2014). Boolean modeling: a logic-based dynamic approach for understanding signaling and regulatory networks and for making useful predictions. *Wiley Interdisciplinary Reviews: Systems Biology and Medicine* **6**, 5, pp. 353–369.

Aldana, M., Coppersmith, S., and Kadanoff, L. P. (2003). Boolean dynamics with random couplings. In: *Perspectives and Problems in Nonlinear Science* (Eds. Kaplan, E., Marsden, J. E., Sreenivasan, K. R.), Springer, pp. 23–89.

Anthony, M. (2001). *Discrete Mathematics of Neural Networks, Selected Topics.* Philadelphia, PA: SIAM.

Aracena, J., Demongeot, J., and Goles, E. (2004a). Positive and negative circuits in discrete neural networks. *IEEE Trans. Neural Networks* **15**, 1, pp. 77–83.

Aracena, J., Demongeot, J., and Goles, E. (2004b). Fixed points and maximal independent sets in AND-OR networks. *Discrete Applied Mathematics* **138**, 3, pp. 277–288.

Aracena, J., Richard, A., and Salinas, L. (2014). Maximum number of fixed points in AND-OR-NOT networks. *Journal of Computer and System Sciences* **80**, 7, pp. 1175–1190.

Aracena, J., Richard, A., and Salinas, L. (2017). Fixed points in conjunctive networks and maximal independent sets in graph contractions. *Journal of Computer and System Sciences* **88**, pp. 145–163.

Arpe, J. and Reischuk, R. (2003). Robust inference of relevant attributes, *Proceedings of the 14th International Conference on Algorithmic Learning Theory* (Lecture Notes in Computer Science 2842), pp. 99–113.

Atias, N., Gershenzon, M., Labazin, K., and Sharan, R. (2014). Experimental design schemes for learning Boolean network models. *Bioinformatics* **30**, 17, pp. i445–i452.

Ballerstein, K., von Kamp, A., Klamt, S., and Haus, U. U. (2012). Minimal cut sets in a metabolic network are elementary modes in a dual network. *Bioinformatics* **28**, 3, pp. 381–387.

Balyo, T., Heule, M. J. G., and Järvisalo, M. (2017). SAT competition 2016: recent developments. *Proceedings of the 31st AAAI Conference on Artificial Intelligence*, pp. 5061–5063.

Barman, S. and Kwon, Y-K. (2017). A novel mutual information-based Boolean network inference method from time-series gene expression data. *PLoS ONE* **12**, 2, e0171097.

Barrett, C., Hunt III, H. B., Marathe, M. V., Ravi, S. S., Rosenkrantz, D. J., and Stearns,. E. (2006). Complexity of reachability problems for finite discrete dynamical systems. *Journal of Computer and System Sciences* **72**, 8, pp. 13170–1345,

Barrett, C., Hunt III, H. B., Marathe, M. V., Ravi, S. S., Rosenkrantz, D. J., Stearns,. E., and Thakur, M. (2007). Predecessor existence problems for finite discrete dynamical systems. *Theoretical Computer Science* **386**, 1-2, pp. 3–37.

Berestovsky, N. and Nakhleh, L. (2013). An evaluation of methods for inferring Boolean networks from time-series data. *PLoS ONE* **8**, 6, e66031.

Bordbar, A., Monk, J. N., King, Z. A., and Palsson, P. Ø. (2014). Constraint-based models predict metabolic and associated cellular functions. *Nature Reviews Genetics* **15**, pp. 107–120.

Bornholdt, S. (2008). Boolean network models of cellular regulation: prospects and limitations. *Journal of the Royal Society Interface* **5**, Suppl 1, pp. S85–S94.

Burgard, A. P., Pharkya, P., and Maranas, C. D. (2003). Optknock: a bilevel programming framework for identifying gene knockout strategies for microbial strain optimization. *Biotechnology and Bioengineering* **84**, 6, pp. 647–657.

Chang, C-J., Tamura, T., Chao, K-M., and Akutsu, T. (2015). A fixed-parameter algorithm for detecting a singleton attractor in an AND/OR Boolean network with bounded treewidth. *IEICE Transactions on Fundamentals of Electronics, Communications and Computer Sciences* **98-A**, 1, pp. 384–390.

Chen, X., Akutsu, T., Tamura, T., and Ching, W-K. (2013). Finding optimal control policy in probabilistic Boolean networks with hard constraints by using integer programming and dynamic programming. *International Journal of Data Mining and Bioinformatics* **7**, 3, pp. 321–343.

Cheng, D. (2009). Input-state approach to Boolean networks. *IEEE Transactions on Neural Networks* **20**, 3, pp. 512–521.

Cheng, D., and Qi, H. (2009). Controllability and observability of Boolean control networks. *Automatica* **45**, 7, pp. 1659–1667.

Cheng, D., Qi, H., and Li, Z. (2011). *Analysis and control of Boolean networks: A semitensor product approach.* London: Springer Verlag.

Cheng, D., Qi, H., and Zhao, Y. (2012). Analysis and control of general logical networks - An algebraic approach. *Annual Reviews in Control* **36**, pp. 11–25.

Cheng, X., Mori, T., Qiu, Y., Ching, W-K., and Akutsu, T. (2016). Exact identification of the structure of a probabilistic Boolean network from samples. *IEEE/ACM Transactions on Computational Biology and Bioinformatics* **13**, 6, pp. 1107–1116.

Cheng, X., Qiu, Y., Hou, W., and Ching, W-K. (2017). Integer programming-based method for observability of singleton attractors in Boolean networks. *IET Systems Biology* **11**, 1, pp. 30–35.

Cheng, X., Tamura, T., Ching, W-K., and Akutsu, T. (2017). Discrimination of singleton and periodic attractors in Boolean networks. *Automatica*, **84**, pp. 205–213.

Ching, W-K., Zhang, S., Ng, M. K., and Akutsu, T. (2007). An approximation method for solving the steady-state probability distribution of probabilistic Boolean networks. *Bioinformatics* **23**, 12, pp. 1511–1518.

Choo, S-M. and Cho, K-H. (2016). An efficient algorithm for identifying primary phenotype attractors of a large-scale Boolean network. *BMC Systems Biology* **10**, 95.

Coppersmith, S. N. (2007). Complexity of the predecessor problem in Kauffman networks. *Physical Review E* **75**, 5, 051108.

Crama, Y. and Hammer, P. L. (2011). *Boolean Functions: Theory, Algorithms, and Applications.* Encyclopedia of Mathematics and its Applications, Cambridge, UK: Cambridge University Press.

DasGupta, B. and Liang, J. (2011). *Models and Algorithms for Biomoleculaes and Molecular Networks.* Hoboken, New Jersey: Wiley-Interscience.

Datta, A., Choudhary, A., Bittner, M. L, and Dougherty, E. R. (2003). External Control in Markovian genetic regulatory networks. *Machine Learning* **52**, 1-2, pp. 169–191.

Datta, A., Pal, R., Choudhary, A., and Dougherty, E. R. (2007). Control approaches for probabilistic gene regulatory networks - what approaches have been developed for addreassinig the issue of intervention?. *IEEE Signal Processing Magazine* **24**, 1, pp. 54–63.

David, L. and Bockmayr, A. (2014). Computing elementary flux modes involving a set of target reactions. *IEEE/ACM Trans. Computational Biology and Bioinformatics* **11**, 6, pp. 1099–1107.

de Jong, H. and Page, M. (2008), Search for steady states of piecewise-linear differential equation models of genetic regulatory networks. *IEEE/ACM Trans. Computational Biology and Bioinformatics* **5**, 2, pp. 208–222.

Derrida, B. and Pomeau. Y. (1986). Random networks of automata: a simple annealed approximation. *Europhysics Letters* **1**, 2, pp. 45–49.

Devloo, V., Hansen, P., and Labbè, M. (2003). Identification of all steady states in large networks by logical analysis. *Bulletin of Mathematical Biology* **65**, 6, pp. 1025–1051.

Drossel, B. (2009). Random Boolean networks. *Reviews of Nonlinear Dynamics and Complexity.* (Ed. Schuster, H. G.), Wiley-VCH Verlag GmbH & Co. KGa, pp. 69–110.

Drossel, B., Mihaljev, T., and Greil, F. (2005). Number and length of attractors in a critical Kauffman model with connectivity one. *Physical Review Letters* **94**, 8, 088701.

Dubrova, E., Teslenko, M., and Martinelli, A. (2005). Kauffman networks: analysis and applications. *Proceedings of IEEE/ACM International Conference on Computer-Aided Design*, pp. 479–484.

Dubrova, E. and Teslenko, M. (2011). A SAT-based algorithm for finding attractors in synchronous Boolean networks. *IEEE/ACM Trans. Computational Biology and Bioinformatics* **8**, 5, pp. 1393–1399.

Flum, J. and Grohe. M. (2006). *Parameterized Complexity Theory.* Berlin: Springer.

Flöttmann, M., Krause, F., Klipp, E., and Krantz, M. (2013). Reaction-contingency based bipartite Boolean modelling. *BMC Systems Biology* **7**, 58.

Fomin, F. V. and Kratsch, D. (2010). *Exact Exponential Algorithms.* Berlin: Springer.

Freuder, E. C. (1990). Complexity of k-tree structured constraint satisfaction problems, *Proceedings of the 8th AAAI Conferende on Artificial Intelligence*, pp. 4–9.

Fukagawa, D, and Akutsu, T. (2005). Performance analysis of a greedy algorithm for inferring Boolean functions. *Information Processing Letters*, **93**, 1, pp. 7–12.

Garey, M. R. and Johnson, D. S. (1979). *Computers and Intractability: A Guide to the Theory of NP-Completeness.* W. H. Freeman and Company, New York.

Garg, A., Di Cara, A., Xenarios, I., Mendoza, L., and De Micheli, G. (2008). Synchronous versus asynchronous modeling of gene regulatory networks. *Bioinformatics* **24**, 17, pp. 1917–1925.

Goles, E. and Salinas, L. (2010). Sequential operator for filtering cycles in Boolean networks, *Advances in Applied Mathematics* **45**, 3, pp. 346–358.

Haider, S. and Pal, R. (2012). Boolean network inference from time series data incorporating prior biological knowledge. *BMC Genomics* **13**, Suppl 6, S9.

Handorf, T., Christian, N,, Ebenhöh, O., and Kahn, D. (2008). An environmental perspective on metabolism. *Journal of Theoretical Biology* **252**, 3, pp. 530–537.

Harris, S. E., Sawhill, B. K, Wuensche, A., and Kauffman, S. (2002). A model of transcriptional regulatory networks based on biases in the observed regulation rules. *Complexity* **7**, 4, pp. 23–40.

Harvey, T. and Bossomaier, T. (2007). Time out of joint: Attractors in asynchronous random boolean networks, *Proceedings of 4th European Conference on Artificial Life*, pp. 67–75.

Haus, U-U., Klamt, S., and Stephen, T. (2008). Computing knock-out strategies in metabolic networks. *Journal of Computational Biology* **15**, 3, pp. 259–268.

Hertli, T. (2014). 3-SAT faster and simpler - unique-SAT bounds for PPSZ hold in general. *SIAM Journal on Computing* **43**, 2, pp. 718–729.

Hickman, H. J. and Hodgman, C, (2009). Inference of gene regulatory networks using Boolean-network inference methods. *Journal of Bioinformatics and Computational Biology* **7**, 6, pp. 1013–1029.

Hou, W., Tamura, T., Ching, W-K., and Akutsu, T. (2016). Finding and analyzing the minimum set of driver nodes in control of Boolean networks. *Advances in Complex Systems* **19**, 3, pp. 1–32.

Inoue, K. (2011). Logic programming for Boolean networks. *Proceedings of the 22nd International Joint Conference on Artificial Intelligence*, pp. 924–930.

Irons, D. J. (2006). Improving the efficiency of attractor cycle identification in Boolean networks. *Physica D* **217**, 1, pp. 7–21.

Jarrah, A. S., Raposa, B., and Laubenbacher, R. (2007). Nested canalyzing, unate cascade, and polynomial functions. *Physica D* **233**, 2, pp. 167–174.

Jarrah, A. S., Laubenbacher, R., and Veliz-Cuba, A. (2010). The dynamics of conjunctive and disjunctive Boolean network models. *Bulletin of Mathematical Biology* **72**, 6, pp. 1425–1447.

Jiang, D., Zhou, S., and Chen, Y-P, P. (2009). Compensatory ability to null mutation in metabolic networks. *Biotechnology and Bioengineering* **103**, 2, pp. 361–369.

Jiang, H., Tamura, T., Ching, W-K., and Akutsu, T. (2013). On the complexity of inference and completion of Boolean networks from given singleton attractors, *IEICE Transactions on Fundamentals of Electronics, Communications and Computer Sciences* **E96-A**, 11, pp. 2265–2274.

Just, W. (2006). The steady state system problem is NP-hard even for monotone quadratic Boolean dynamical systems. Preprint available at http://www.ohio.edu/people/just/publ.html.

Kauffman, S. A. (1969a). Metabolic stability and epigenesis in randomly constructed genetic nets. *Journal of Theoretical Biology* **22**, 3, pp. 437–467.

Kauffman, S. A. (1969b). Homeostasis and differentiation in random genetic control networks. *Nature* **224**, 5215, pp. 177–178.

Kauffman, S. A. (1983) *The Origins of Order: Self-Organization and Selection in Evolution.* Oxford, UK: Oxford University Press,

Kauffman, S. A., Peterson, C., Samuelsson, B., and Troein, C. (2004). Genetic networks with canalyzing Boolean rules are always stable. *Proceedings of National Academy of Sciences U.S.A.* **101**, 49, pp. 17102–17107.

Kinoshita, S., Iguchi, K., and Yamada, H. S. (2009). Intrinsic properties of Boolean dynamics in complex networks. *Journal of Theoretical Biology* **256**, 3, pp. 351–369.

Kitano, H. (2002). Computational systems biology. *Nature* **420**, pp. 206–210.

Kitano, H. (2004). Cancer as a robust system: implications for anticancer therapy. *Nature Reviews Cancer* **4**, pp. 227–235.

Klamt, S. and Gilles, E. D. (2004). Minimal cut sets in biochemical reaction networks. *Bioinformatics* **20**, 2, pp. 226–234.

Kobayashi, K. and Hiraishi, K. (2013). Optimal control of Boolean biological networks modeled by Petri nets. *IEICE Transactions on Fundamentals of Electronics, Communications and Computer Sciences* **E96-A**, 2, pp. 532–539.

Kobayashi, K. and Hiraishi, K. (2017). Optimization-based approaches to control of probabilistic Boolean networks. *Algorithms* **10**, 31.

Kunz, W. and Stoffel, D. (1997). *Reasoning in Boolean Networks. Logic Synthesis and Verification using Testing Techniques.* Berlin: Springer.

Lähdesmäki, H., Hautaniemi, S., Shmulevich, I., and Yli-Harja, O. (2006). Relationships between probabilistic Boolean networks and dynamic Bayesian networks as models of gene regulatory networks. *Signal Processing* **86**, 4. pp. 814–834.

Langmead, C. J. and Jha, S. K. (2009). Symbolic approaches for finding control strategies in Boolean networks. *Journal of Bioinformatics and Computational Biology* **7**, 2, pp. 323–338.

Laschov, D., Margaliot, M., and Even, G. (2013). Observability of Boolean networks: A graph-theoretic approach. *Automatica* **49**, 8, pp. 2351–2362.

Layne, L., Dimitrova, E., and Macauley, M. (2012). Nested canalyzing depth and network stability. *Bulletin of Mathematical Biology* **74**, 2, pp. 422–433.

Lemke, N., Herédia, F., Barcellos, C. K., Dos Reis, A. N., and Mombach, J. C. (2004). Essentiality and damage in metabolic networks. *Bioinformatics* **20**, 1, pp. 115–119.

Leone, M., Pagnani, A., Parisi, G. and Zagordi, O. (2006). Finite size corrections to random Boolean networks. *Journal of Statistical Mechanics* **2006**, P12012.

Levy, H., and Low, D. W. (1988). A contraction algorithm for finding small cycle cutsets. *Journal of Algorithms* **9**, 4, pp. 470–493.

Li, P., Zhang, C., Perkins, E. J., Gong, P., and Deng, Y. (2007). Comparison of probabilistic Boolean network and dynamic Bayesian network approaches for inferring gene regulatory networks. *BMC Bioinformatics* **8**, Suppl 7, S13.

Li, R., Yang, M., and Ch, T. (2015). Controllability and observability of Boolean networks arising from biology. *Chaos* **25**, 023104.

Li, Y., John O. Adeyeye, J. O., Murrugarra, D., Aguilar, B., and Laubenbacher, R. (2013). Boolean nested canalizing functions: A comprehensive analysis. *Theoretical Computer Science* **481**, pp. 24–36.

Li, Z., Wang, R-S., Zhang, X-S., and Chen, L. (2009). Detecting drug targets with minimum side effects in metabolic networks. *IET Systems Biology* **3**, 6, pp. 523–522.

Liang, S., Fuhrman, S., and Somogyi, R. (1998). REVEAL, a general reverse engineering algorithm for inference of genetic network architectures. *Proc. Pacific Symposium on Biocomputing 1998*, pp. 18–29.

Liu, Y-Y., Slotine, J-J., and Barabási, A. L. (2011). Controllability of complex networks. *Nature* **473**, 7346, pp. 168–173.

Liu, Y-Y. and Barabási, A. L. (2016). Control principles of complex systems. *Reviews of Modern Physics* **88**, 3, 035006.

Makino, K., Tamaki, S., and Yamamoto, M. (2013). Derandomizing the HSSW algorithm for 3-SAT. *Algorithmica* **67**, 2, pp. 112–124.

Marshall, S., Yu, L., Xiao,, Y., and Dougherty, E. R. (2007). Inference of a probabilistic Boolean network from a single observed temporal sequence. *EURASIP Journal on Bioinformatics and Systems Biology* **2007**, 32454.

Melkman, A. A., Tamura, T., and Akutsu, T. (2013). Determining a singleton attractor of an AND/OR Boolean network in $O(1.587^n)$ time. *Information Processing Letters* **110**, pp. 565–569.

Melkman, A. A. and Akutsu, T. (2013). An improved satisfiability algorithm for nested canalyzing functions and its application to determining a singleton attractor of a Boolean network. *Journal of Computational Biology* **20**, 12, pp. 958–969.

Melkman, A. A., Cheng, X., Ching, W-K. and Akutsu, T. (2017). Identifying a probabilistic Boolean threshold network from samples, *IEEE Transactions on Neural Networks and Learning Systems*, in press.

Mochizuki, A. (2005). An analytical study of the number of steady states in gene regulatory networks. *Journal of Theoretical Biology* **236**, pp. 291–310.

Mochizuki, A., Fiedler, B., Kurosawa, G., and Saito, D. (2013). Dynamics and control at feedback vertex sets. II: A faithful monitor to determine the diversity of molecular activities in regulatory networks. *Journal of Theoretical Biology* **335**, pp. 130–146.

Mori, F. and Mochizuki, A. (2017). Expected number of fixed points in Boolean networks with arbitrary topology. *Physical Review Letters* **119**, 028301.

Mori, T., Flöttmann, M., Krantz, M., Akutsu, T., and Klipp, E. (2015). Stochastic simulation of Boolean *rxncon* models: towards quantitative analysis of large signaling networks. *BMC Systems Biology* **9**, 45.

Mossel, E., O'Donnell, R., and Servedio, R. A. (2004). Learning functions of k relevant variables. *Journal of Computer and System Sciences* **69**, 3, pp. 421–434.

Nacher, J. C. and Akutsu, T. (2016). Minimum dominating set-based methods for analyzing biological networks. *Methods* **102**, pp. 57–63.

Newman, A. M. and Weiss, M. (2013). A survey of linear and mixed-integer optimization tutorials. *INFORMS Transactions on Education.* **14**, 1, pp. 26–38.

O'Donnell, R. (2014) *Analysis of Boolean Functions.* New York: Cambridge University Press,

Orth, J. D,, Thiele, I., and Palsson, B. Ø. (2010). What is flux balance analysis? *Nature Biotechnology* **28**, 3, pp. 245–248.

Pal, R., Ivanov, I., Datta, A., Bittner, M. L., and Dougherty, E. R. (2005). Generating Boolean networks with a prescribed attractor structure. *Bioinformatics* **21**, 21, pp. 4021–4025.

Pal, R., Datta, A., and Dougherty, E. R. (2006). Optimal infinite-horizon control for probabilistic Boolean networks. *IEEE Transactions on Signal Processing* **54**, 6, pp. 2375–2387.

Palma, E., Salinas, L., and Aracena, J. (2016). Enumeration and extension of non-equivalent deterministic update schedules in Boolean networks. *Bioinformatics* **32**, 5, pp. 722–729.

Perkins, T. J. and Hallett, M. T. (2010). A trade-off between sample complexity and computational complexity in learning Boolean networks from time-series data. *IEEE/ACM Transactions on Computational Biology and Bioinformatics.* **7**, 1, pp. 118–125.

Qiu, Y., Tamura, T., Ching, W-K., and Akutsu, T. (2014). On control of singleton attractors in multiple Boolean networks: integer programming-based method, *BMC Systems Biology* **8**, Suppl 1, S7.

Rother, M., Münzner, U., Thieme, S., and Krantz, M. (2013). Information content and scalability in signal transduction network reconstruction formats, *Molecular Biosystems* **9**, 8, pp. 1993–2004.

Saadatpour, A., Albert, I., and Albert, R. (2010). Attractor analysis of asynchronous Boolean models of signal transduction networks. *Journal of Theoretical Biology* **266**, pp. 641–656.

Samuelsson, B. and Troein, C. (2003). Superpolynomial growth in the number of attractors in Kauffman networks. *Physics Review Letters*, **90**, 9, 098701.

Schuster, S. and Hilgetag, C. (1994). On elementary flux modes in biochemical reaction systems at steady state. *Journal of Biological Systems* **2**, 2, pp. 165–182.

Seshadhri, C., Vorobeychik, Y., Mayo, J. R., Armstrong, R. C., and Ruthruff, J. R. (2011). Influence and dynamic behavior in random Boolean networks. *Physical Review Letters* **107**, 108701.

Sharan, R. and Karp, R, M, (2013). Reconstructing Boolean models of signaling. *Journal of Computational Biology* **20**, 3, pp. 249–257.

Shmulevich, I., Dougherty, E. R., Kim, S., and Zhang, W. (2002). Probabilistic Boolean Networks: a rule-based uncertainty model for gene regulatory networks. *Bioinformatics* **18**, 2, pp. 261–274.

Shmulevich, I., Gluhovsky, I., Hashimoto, R. F., Dougherty, E. R., and Zhang, W. (2003). Steady-state analysis of genetic regulatory networks modeled by Probabilistic Boolean networks. *Comparative and Functional Genomics* **4**, 6, pp. 601–608.

Shmulevich, I. and Kauffman, E. R. (2004). Activities and Sensitivities in Boolean Network Models. *Physical Review Letters* **93**, 4, 048701.

Shmulevich, I. and Dougherty, E. R. (2010). *Probabilistic Boolean Networks: The Modeling and Control of Gene Regulatory Networks*. Philadelphia, PA: SIAM.

Sipser, M. (2012). *Introduction to the Theory of Computation. Third Edition.* Boston MA: Cengage Learning.

Smart, A. G., Amaral, L. A. N., and Ottino, J. M. (2008). Cascading failure and robustness in metabolic networks. *Proceedings of the National Academy of Sciences of the USA* **105**, 36, pp. 13223–13228.

Sridhar, P., Song, B., Kahveci, T., and Ranka, S. (2008). Mining metabolic networks for optimal drug targets. *Proceedings of Pacific Symposium on Biocomputing* **2008**, pp. 291–302.

Stockmeyer, L. J. (1976). The polynomial-time hierarchy. *Theoretical Computer Science* **3**, pp. 1–22.

Takahashi, K., Tanabe, K., Ohnuki, M., Narita, M., Ichisaka, T., Tomoda, K., and Yamanaka, S. (2007). Induction of pluripotent stem cells from adult human fibroblasts by defined factors. *Cell* **131**, pp. 1–12.

Takemoto, K,, Tamura, T., Cong, Y., Ching, W-K., Vert, J-P., and Akutsu, T. (2012). Analysis of the impact degree distribution in metabolic networks using branching process approximation, *Physica A* **391**, pp. 379–397.

Takemoto, K,, Tamura, T., and Akutsu, T. (2013). Theoretical estimation of metabolic network robustness against multiple reaction knockouts using branching process approximation, *Physica A*, **392**, pp. 5525–5535.

Tamaki, H. (2010). A directed path-decomposition approach to exactly identifying attractors of Boolean networks, *Proceedings of 10th International Symposium on Communication and Information Technologies*, pp. 844–849.

Tamura, T. and Akutsu, T. (2009). Detecting a singleton attractor in a Boolean network utilizing SAT algorithms. *IEICE Transactions on Fundamentals of Electronics, Communications and Computer Sciences* **E92-A**, 2, pp. 493–501.

Tamura, T. and Akutsu, T. (2010). Exact algorithms for finding a minimum reaction cut under a Boolean model of metabolic networks. *IEICE Transactions on Fundamentals of Electronics, Communications and Computer Sciences* **E93-A**, 8, pp. 1497–1507.

Tamura, T., Takemoto, K., and Akutsu, T. (2010). Finding minimum reaction cuts of metabolic networks under a Boolean model using integer programming and feedback vertex sets. *International Journal of Knowledge Discovery in Bioinformatics* **1**, pp. 14–31.

Tamura, T., Cong, Y., Akutsu, T., and Ching, W-K. (2011). An efficient method of computing impact degrees for multiple reactions in metabolic networks with cycles, *IEICE Transactions on Information and Systems* **E94-D**, 12, pp. 2393–2399.

Tamura, T., Lu, W., and Akutsu, T. (2015). Computational methods for modification of metabolic networks. *Computational and Structural Biotechnology Journal* **13**, pp. 376–381.

Thomas, R. (1973). Boolean formalization of genetic control circuits. *Journal of Theoretical Biology* **42**, 3, pp. 563–585.

Thomas, R., Thieffry, D., and Kaufman, M. (1995). Dynamical behaviour of biological regulatory networks I. Biological role of feedback loops and practical use of the concept of the loop-characteristic state. *Bulletin of Mathematical Biology* **57**, 2, pp. 247–276.

Trairatphisan, P., Mizera, A., Pang, J., Tantar, A. A., Schneider, J., Thomas Sauter, T. (2013). Recent development and biomedical applications of probabilistic Boolean networks. *Cell Communication and Signaling* **11**, 46.

Valiant, L. (1979). The complexity of computing the permanent. *Theoretical Computer Science* **8**, 2, pp. 189–201.

Veliz-Cuba, A. and Laubenbacher, R. (2012). On the computation of fixed points in Boolean networks. *Journal of Applied Mathematics and Computing* **39**, 1-2, pp. 145–153.

Veliz-Cuba, A., Aguilar, B., Hinkelmann, F., and Laubenbacher, R. (2014).

Steady state analysis of Boolean molecular network models via model reduction and computational algebra. *BMC Bioinformatics* **15**, 221.

Vielma, J. P. (2015). Mixed integer linear programming formulation techniques. *SIAM Review* **57**, 1, pp. 3–57.

Vizel, Y., Weissenbacher, G., and Malik, S. (2015). Boolean satisfiability solvers and their applications in model checking. *Proceedings of the IEEE.* **103**, 11, pp. 2021–2035.

von Kamp, A. and Klamt, S. (2014). Enumeration of smallest intervention strategies in genome-scale metabolic networks. *PLoS Computational Biology* **10**, 1, e1003378.

Wu, Y., Xu, J., Sun, X-M., and Wang, W. (2017). Observability of Boolean multiplex control networks. *Scientific Reports* **7**, 46495.

Wuensche, A. (2000). Basins of attraction in cellular automata. *Complexity* **5**, 6, pp. 19–25.

Yamamoto, M. (2005). An improved $\tilde{O}(1.234^m)$-time deterministic algorithm for SAT. *Proceedings of 16th International Symposium on Algorithms and Computation* (Lecture Notes in Computer Science 3827), pp. 644–653.

Zañudo, J. G. T. and Albert, R. (2013). An effective network reduction approach to find the dynamical repertoire of discrete dynamic networks. *Chaos* **23**, 025111.

Zhang, S-Q., Hayashida, M., Akutsu, T., Ching, W-K. and Ng, M. K. (2007a). Algorithms for finding small attractors in Boolean networks. *EURASIP Journal on Bioinformatics and Systems Biology* **2007**, 20180.

Zhang, S-Q., Ching, W-K., Ng, M. K., and Akutsu, T. (2007b). Simulation study in Probabilistic Boolean Network models for genetic regulatory networks. *International Journal of Data Mining and Bioinformatics* **1**, pp. 217–240.

Zhang, L. and Zhang, K. (2013). Controllability and observability of Boolean control networks with time-variant delays in states. *IEEE Transactions on Neural Networks and Learning Systems* **24**, 9, pp. 1478–1484.

Zhao, Y., Tamura, T, Akutsu T, and Vert, J-P. (2013). Flux balance impact degree: a new definition of impact degree to properly treat reversible reactions in metabolic networks. *Bioinformatics* **29**, 17, pp. 2178–2185.

Zhao, Y. and Cheng, D. (2014). On controllability and stabilizability of probabilistic Boolean control networks. *SCIENCE CHINA Information Sciences* **57**, 12202.

Zou, Y. M. (2010). Modeling and analyzing complex biological networks incooperating experimental information on both network topology and stable states. *Bioinformatics* **26**, 16, pp. 2037–2041.

Index

Printed in the United States
By Bookmasters